The Structure and

History of The Cockroach

(Periplaneta Orientalis)

An Introduction to the Study of Insects

L. C. Miall,

A. R. Hammond

Alpha Editions

This edition published in 2020

ISBN : 9789354018541

Design and Setting By
Alpha Editions
email - alphaedis@gmail.com

STUDIES IN COMPARATIVE ANATOMY—III

THE STRUCTURE AND LIFE-HISTORY

OF

THE COCKROACH

(PERIPLANETA ORIENTALIS)

An Introduction to the Study of Insects

BY

L. C. MIALL

PROFESSOR OF BIOLOGY IN THE YORKSHIRE COLLEGE, LEEDS

AND

ALFRED DENNY

LECTURER ON BIOLOGY IN THE FIRTH COLLEGE, SHEFFIELD

LONDON : LOVELL REEVE & CO.

LEEDS : RICHARD JACKSON

1886

4

STUDIES IN COMPARATIVE ANATOMY.

I.—THE SKULL OF THE CROCODILE. A Manual for
Students. By Professor L. C. MIALL. 8vo, 2s. 6d.

II.—THE ANATOMY OF THE INDIAN ELEPHANT. By
Professor L. C. MIALL and F. GREENWOOD. 8vo, 5s.

III.—THE COCKROACH: An Introduction to the Study of
Insects. By Professor L. C. MIALL and A. DENNY. 8vo, 7s. 6d.

IV.—MEGALICHTHYS; A Ganoid Fish of the Coal Measures.
By Professor L. C. MIALL (*In preparation*).

MAY BE HAD OF

LOVELL REEVE & CO., LONDON;

RICHARD JACKSON, LEEDS.

PREFACE.

THAT the thorough study of concrete animal types is a necessary preliminary to good work in Zoology or Comparative Anatomy will now be granted by all competent judges. At a time when these subjects, though much lectured upon, were rarely taught, Döllinger, of Würzburg, found out the right way. He took young students, often singly, and made them master such animal types as came to hand, thereby teaching them how to work for themselves, and fixing in their minds a nucleus of real knowledge, around which more might crystallise. "What do you want lectures for? Bring any animal and dissect it here," said he to Baer, then a young doctor longing to work at Comparative Anatomy.* It was Döllinger who trained Purkinje, Pander, Baer, and Agassiz, and such fame cannot be heightened by words of praise. In our own time and country Döllinger's methods have been practised by Professor Huxley, whose descriptive guides, such as the Elementary Biology and the delightful little book on the Crayfish, now make it easy for every teacher to work on the same lines. From the description of the Cockroach in Huxley's Anatomy of Invertebrated Animals came the impulse which has encouraged us to treat that type at length. It may easily turn out that in adding some facts and a great many words to his account, we have diluted what was valuable for its concentration. But there are students—those, namely, who intend to give serious attention to Entomology—who will find our explanations deficient rather than excessive in detail. It is our belief and hope that naturalists will some day recoil from their extravagant love of words and names, and turn to

* Baer's account of Döllinger is to be found in the Leben und Schriften von K. E. von Baer, § 8.

structure, development, life-history, and other aspects of the animal world which have points of contact with the life of man. We have written for such as desire to study Insects on this side.

Whoever attempts to tell all that is important about a very common animal will feel his dependence upon other workers. Much of what is here printed has been told before. The large number of new figures is, however, some proof that we have worked for ourselves.

It is a pleasant duty to offer our thanks for friendly help received. Professor Félix Plateau, of Ghent; Mr. Joseph Nusbaum, of Warsaw; and Mr. S. H. Scudder, of Cambridge, Massachusetts, have very kindly consented to treat here of those parts of the subject which they have specially illustrated by their own labours.* Mr. E. T. Newton, of the Jermyn Street Museum, has lent us the wood blocks used to illustrate one of his papers on the Brain of the Cockroach. A number of the figures have been very carefully and faithfully drawn for us by Miss Beatrice Boyle, a student in the Yorkshire College. We are much indebted to Dr. Murie, the Librarian of the Linnean Society, for procuring us access to the extensive literature of Insect Anatomy, and for answering not a few troublesome questions.

Five articles on the Cockroach were contributed by us to Science Gossip in 1884, and some of the figures were then engraved and published.

In issuing a book which has been long in hand, but which can never hope to be complete, we venture to adopt the words already used by Leydig concerning his Lehrbuch der Histologie:—" Die eigentlich nie fertig wird, die man aber für fertig erklären muss, wenn man nach Zeit und Umständen das Möglichste gethan hat."

* Prof. Plateau's chief communications will be found on pp. 131 and 159; Mr. Nusbaum has furnished the account of the Development of the Cockroach, pp. 180 to 195; and Mr. Scudder the Geological History of the Cockroach, chap. xi.

CONTENTS.

₊ Where the species is not named, it is to be understood that the figures are drawn from the Cockroach.

LEEDS:

McCorquodale & Co. Limited,

Basinghall Street.

THE COCKROACH.

CHAPTER I.

WRITINGS ON INSECT ANATOMY.

MARCELLO MALPIGHI. 1628–1694.
JAN SWAMMERDAM. 1637–1680.
PIERRE LYONNET. 1707–1789.
HERCULE STRAUS-DÜRCKHEIM. 1790–1865.

THE lovers of minute anatomy have always been specially attracted to Insects; and it is not hard to tell why. No other animals, perhaps, exhibit so complex an organisation condensed into so small a body. We possess, accordingly, a remarkable succession of memoirs on the structure of single Insects, beginning with the revival of Anatomy in the 17th century and extending to our own times. The most memorable of these Insect-monographs bear the names of Malpighi, Swammerdam, Lyonnet, and Straus-Dürckheim.

Malpighi on the Silkworm.

Malpighi's treatise on the Silkworm (1669) is an almost faultless essay in a new field. No Insect—hardly, indeed, any animal—had then been carefully described, and all the methods of work had to be discovered. "This research," says Malpighi, "was extremely laborious and tedious" (it occupied about a year) "on account of its novelty, as well as the minuteness, fragility, and intricacy of the parts, which required a special manipulation; so that when I had toiled for many months at this incessant and fatiguing task, I was plagued next autumn with fevers and inflammation of the eyes. Nevertheless, such

B

was my delight in the work, so many unsuspected wonders of nature revealing themselves to me, that I cannot tell it in words." We must recall the complete ignorance of Insect-anatomy which then prevailed, and remember that now for the first time the dorsal vessel, the tracheal system, the tubular appendages of the stomach, the reproductive organs, and the structural changes which accompany transformation were observed, to give any adequate credit to the writer of this masterly study. Treading a new path, he walks steadily forward, trusting to his own sure eyes and cautious judgment. The descriptions are brief and simple, the figures clear, but not rich in detail. There would now be much to add to Malpighi's account, but hardly anything to correct. The only positive mistakes which meet the eye relate to the number of spiracles and nervous ganglia—mistakes promptly corrected by Swammerdam. Had the tract De Bombycibus been the one work of its author, this would have kept his memory bright, but it hardly adds to the fame of the anatomist who discovered the cellular structure of the lung, the glandular structure of the liver and kidney, and the sensory papillæ of the skin, who first saw the blood-corpuscles stream along a vessel, who studied very early and very completely the minute structure of plants and the development of the chick, and whose name is rightfully associated with the mucous layer of the epidermis, the vascular tufts of the kidney, and the follicles of the spleen, as well as with the urinary tubules of Insects.

All that we know of Malpighi commands our respect. Precise and rapid in his work, keen to discover points of real interest, never losing himself in details, but knowing when he had done enough, he stands pre-eminent in the crowd of minute anatomists, who are generally faithful in a few things, but very unfit to be made rulers over many things. The last distinct glimpse which we get of him is interesting. Dr. Tancred Robinson, writing to John Ray, from Geneva, April 18th, 1684, tells how he met Malpighi at Bologna. They talked of the origin of fossils, and Malpighi could not contain himself about Martin Lister's foolish hypothesis that fossils were sports of nature. "Just as I left Bononia," he continues, "I had a lamentable spectacle of Malpighi's house all in flames, occasioned by the negligence of his old wife. All his pictures, furniture, books, and manuscripts were burnt. I saw him in the very heat of the calamity, and methought I never beheld so much Christian patience and philosophy in any man before ; for he comforted his wife, and condoled nothing but the loss of his papers, which are more lamented than the Alexandrian Library, or Bartholine's Bibliothece, at Copenhagen." *

Swammerdam on the Honey Bee.

Swammerdam's great posthumous work, the Biblia Naturæ, contains about a dozen life-histories of Insects worked out in more or less detail. Of these the May-fly (published during the author's life-time, in 1675) is the most famous ; that on the Honey Bee the most elaborate. Swammerdam was ten years younger than Malpighi, and knew Malpighi's treatise on the Silkworm—a not inconsiderable advantage. His working-life as a naturalist comes within the ten years between 1663 and 1673 ; and this short space of time was darkened by anxiety about money, as well as by the religious fanaticism, which in the end completely extinguished his activity. The vast amount of highly-finished work which he accomplished in these ten years justifies Boerhaave's rather rhetorical account of his industry. Unfortunately, Boerhaave, whom we have to thank not only for a useful sketch of Swammerdam's life, but also for the preservation of most of his writings, was only twelve years old when the great naturalist died, and his account cannot be taken as personal testimony. Swammerdam, he tells us, worked with a simple microscope and several powers. His great skill lay in his dexterous use of scissors. Sometimes he employed tools so fine as to require whetting under the microscope. He was famous for inflated and injected preparations. As to his patience, it is enough to say that he would spend whole days in clearing a single caterpillar. Boerhaave gives us a picture of Swammerdam at work which the reader does not soon forget. " His labours were superhuman. Through the day he observed incessantly, and at night he described and drew what he had seen. By six o'clock in the morning in summer he began to

* Correspondence of John Ray, p. 142.

find enough light to enable him to trace the minutiæ of natural objects. He was hard at work till noon, in full sunlight, and bareheaded, so as not to obstruct the light; and his head streamed with profuse sweat. His eyes, by reason of the blaze of light and microscopic toil, became so weakened that he could not observe minute objects in the afternoon, though the light was not less bright than in the morning, for his eyes were weary, and could no longer perceive readily."

Comparing Swammerdam's account of the Bee with the useful and amply illustrated memoir of Girdwoyn (Paris, 1876), it is plain that two centuries have added little to our knowledge of the structure of this type. Much has been made out since 1675 concerning the life-history of Bees, but of what was to be discovered by lens and scalpel, Swammerdam left little indeed to others. It is needless to dwell upon the omissions of so early an explorer. Swammerdam proved by dissection that the queen is the mother of the colony, that the drones are males, and the working-bees neuters; but he did not find out that the neuters are only imperfect females. In this instance, as in some others, Swammerdam's authority served, long after his death, to delay acceptance of the truth. It is far from a reproach to him that in the Honey Bee he lit upon an almost inexhaustible subject. In the 17th century no one suspected that the sexual economy of any animal could be so complicated as that which has been demonstrated, step by step, in the Honey Bee.

Lyonnet on the Goat Moth.

In Lyonnet's memoir on the larva of the Goat Moth (Traité Anatomique de la Chenille qui ronge le bois de Saule, 1760*) we must not look for the originality of Malpighi, nor for the wide range of Swammerdam. One small thing is attempted, and this is accomplished with unerring fidelity and skill. There is something of display in the delineation of the four thousand and forty-one muscles of the Caterpillar, and the author's skill as a dissector is far beyond his knowledge of animals, whether live or dead. The dissections of the head are perhaps the most

---

* Copies dated 1762 have a plate representing the microscope and dissecting instruments used by the author.

extraordinary feat, and will never be surpassed. Modern treatises on Comparative Anatomy continue to reproduce some of these figures, such as the general view of the viscera, the structure of the leg, and the digestive tract. Nearly the whole interest of the volume lies in the plates, for the text is little more than a voluminous explanation of the figures.

It is not without surprise that we find that Lyonnet was an amateur, who had received no regular training either in anatomy or engraving, and that he had many pursuits besides the delineation of natural objects. He was brought up for the Protestant ministry, turned to the bar, and finally became cipher-secretary and confidential translator to the United Provinces of Holland. He is said to have been skilled in eight languages. His first published work in Natural History consisted of remarks and drawings contributed to Lesser's Insect Theology (1742). About the same time, Trembley was prosecuting at the Hague his studies on the freshwater Polyp, and Lyonnet gave him some friendly help in the work. Those who care to turn to the preface of Trembley's famous treatise (Mémoires pour servir à l'histoire des Polypes d'eau douce, 1744) will see how warmly Lyonnet's services are acknowledged. He made all the drawings, and engraved eight of them himself, while Trembley is careful to note that he was not only a skilful draughtsman, but an acute and experienced observer. When the work was begun, Lyonnet had never even seen the operation of engraving a plate. Wandelaar, struck by the beauty of his drawings, persuaded him to try what he could do with a burin. His first essay was made upon the figure of a Dragon-fly, next he engraved three Butterflies, and then, without longer apprenticeship, he proceeded to engrave the plates still required to complete the memoir on Hydra.

Lyonnet tells us that the larva of the Goat Moth was not quite his earliest attempt in Insect Anatomy. He began with the Sheep Tick, but suspecting that the subject would not be popular, he made a fresh choice for his first memoir. Enough interest was excited by the Traité Anatomique to call for the fulfilment of a promise made in the preface that the description of the pupa and imago should follow. But though Lyonnet continued for some time to fill his portfolio with drawings and

notes, he never published again. Failing eyesight was one
ground of his retirement from work. What he had been able
to finish, together with a considerable mass of miscellaneous
notes, illustrated by fifty-four plates from his own hand, was
published, long after his death, in the Mémoires du Muséum
(XVIII.-XX.).

Straus-Dürckheim on the Cockchafer.

In beauty and exact fidelity Straus-Dürckheim's memoir on the
Cockchafer (Considérations Générales sur l'Anatomie Comparée
des Animaux Articulés, auxquelles on a joint l'Anatomie Descriptive du Melolontha vulgaris, 1828) rivals the work of Lyonnet.
Insect Anatomy was no longer a novel subject in 1828, but
Straus-Dürckheim was able to treat it in a new way. Writing
under the immediate influence of Cuvier, he sought to apply
that comparative method, which had proved so fertile in the
hands of the master, to the Articulate sub-kingdom. This
conception was realised as fully as the state of zoology at that
time allowed, and the Considérations Générales count as an
important step towards a complete comparative anatomy of
Arthropoda. Straus-Dürckheim had at command a great mass
of anatomical facts, much of which had been accumulated by his
own observations. He systematically compares Insects with
other Articulata, Coleoptera with other Insects, and the Cockchafer with other Coleoptera. Perhaps no one before him had
been perfectly clear as to the morphological equivalence of the
appendages in all parts of the body of Arthropods, and here he
was able to extend the teaching of Savigny. His limitations are
those of his time. If in certain sections we find his collection
of facts to be meagre, and his generalisations nugatory, we
must allow for the progress of the last sixty years—a progress
in which Straus-Dürckheim has his share. It is the work of
science continually to remake its syntheses, and no work
becomes antiquated sooner than morphological generalisation.

It is therefore no reproach to Straus-Dürckheim that his
treatise should now be chiefly valuable, not as " Considérations
Générales," but as the anatomy of the Cockchafer. Long after
his theories and explanations have ceased to be instructive, when

the morphology and physiology of 1828 have become as obsolete
as the Ptolemaic astronomy, the naturalist will study these
exquisite delineations of Insect-structure with something of the
pleasure to be found in examining for the hundredth time a
delicate organism familiar to many generations of microscopic
observers.

The fidelity and love of anatomical detail which characterise
the description of the Cockchafer are not less conspicuous in
Straus-Dürckheim's Anatomie Descriptive du Chat (1846). Both
treatises have become classical.

We have seen how, in Straus-Dürckheim's hands, Insect
anatomy became comparative. New studies—histology, embryonic development, and palæontology—have since arisen to com-
plicate the task of the descriptive anatomist, and it appears to
be no longer possible for one man to complete the history
of any animal of elaborate structure and ancient pedigree.
As a method of research the monograph has had its day. The
path of biological discovery now follows an organ or a function
across all zoological boundaries, and it is in the humbler
office of biological teaching that the monograph finds its proper
use.

Later Insect Anatomists.

It is impossible even to glance at the many anatomists who
have illustrated the structure of Insects by studies, less simple
in plan, but not less profitable to science, than those of the
monographers. If we attempt to select two or three names for
express mention, it is with a conviction that others are left
whom the student is bound to hold in equal honour.

Dufour* laboured, not unsuccessfully, to construct a General
Anatomy of Insects, which should combine into one view a
crowd of particular facts. The modern reader will gratefully
acknowledge his industry and the beauty of his drawings, but
will now and then complain that his sagacity does not do
justice to his diligence.

* Dufour. Rech. anat. et phys. sur les Hémiptères (1833) les Orthoptères, les
Hymenoptères et les Neuroptères (1841), et les Diptères (1851). Mém. de l'Institut,
Tom. IV., VII., XI. Also many memoirs in Ann. des Sci. Nat.

Newport,* a naturalist of greater weight and interest, is
memorable for his skill in minute dissection, for his many
curious observations upon the life-history of Insects (see, for
example, his memoir on the Oil-beetle), and especially for his
early appreciation of the value of embryological study.

Leydig† was the first to occupy fully the new field of Insect
histology, and point out its resources to the physiologist. In
all his works the student finds beauty and exactness of delineation, suggestiveness in explanation. Leydig's contributions to
Insect anatomy and physiology, valuable as they are to the
specialist, are not isolated researches, but form part of a new
comparative anatomy, based upon histology. Incomplete so
vast a work must necessarily remain, but it already extends
over considerable sections of the animal kingdom.

---

* Newport. Art. "Insecta," in Cycl. of Anat. and Phys. (1839), besides many
special memoirs in the Phil. and Linn. Trans.

† Leydig. Vom Bau des Thierischen Körpers (1864), Tafeln zur vergl. Anatomie
(1864), Untersuchungen zur Anat. und Histologie der Thiere (1883), &c., besides
many special memoirs in Müller's Archiv., Zeits. f. wiss. Zool., Nova Acta, &c.

CHAPTER II.

THE ZOOLOGICAL POSITION OF THE COCKROACH.

Sub-kingdom ARTHROPODA.
Class I. Crustacea.
,, II. Arachnida.
,, III. Myriopoda.
,, IV. INSECTA.
Order 1. Thysanura.
,, 2. *Orthoptera.*
,, 3. Neuroptera.
,, 4. Hemiptera.
,, 5. Coleoptera.
,, 6. Diptera.
,, 7. Lepidoptera.
,, 8. Hymenoptera.

THE place of the Cockroach in the Animal Kingdom is illustrated by the above table. It belongs to the sub-kingdom Arthropoda, to the class Insecta, and to the order Orthoptera.

Characters of Arthropoda.

Arthropoda are in general readily distinguished from other animals by their jointed body and limbs. In many Annelids the body is ringed, and each segment bears a pair of appendages, but these appendages are soft, and never articulated. The integument of an Arthropod is stiffened by a deposit of the tough, elastic substance known as Chitin, which resembles horn in appearance, though very different in its chemical composition. In marine Arthropoda, as well as in many Myriopoda and Insects, additional firmness may be gained by the incorporation of carbonate and phosphate of lime with the chitin. However rigid the integument may be, it is rendered compatible with energetic movements by its unequal thickening. Along defined, usually transverse lines it remains thin, the chitinous layer, though perfectly continuous, becoming extremely flexible, and allowing a certain amount of deflection or retraction (fig. 1).

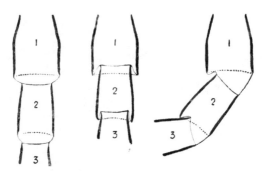

Fig. 1.—Diagram of Arthropod limb extended, retracted, and flexed.
Graber has given a similar figure (Insekten, fig. 8*).

The joints of the trunk and limbs may thus resemble stiff tubes. Muscles are attached to their inner surface, and are therefore enclosed by the system of levers upon which they act (fig. 2B). In Vertebrate animals, on the contrary, which possess a true internal skeleton, the muscles clothe the levers (bones) to which

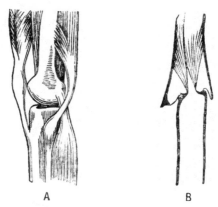

A   B

Fig. 2.—Vertebrate and Arthropod joints. A, Vertebrate joint, the skeleton clothed with muscles. B, Arthropod joint, the skeleton enclosing the muscles.

they are attached (fig. 2A). The whole outer surface of an Arthropod, including the eyes, auditory membrane (if there is one), and surface-hairs, is chitinised. Chitin may also stiffen the larger tendons, internal ridges and partitions, and the lining membrane of extensive internal cavities, such as the alimentary canal, and the air-tubes of Insects.

In most Arthropoda the body is provided with many appendages. In Crustacea there are often twenty pairs, but some Myriopoda have not far from two hundred pairs. Some of these may be converted to very peculiar functions; in particular, several pairs adjacent to the mouth are usually appropriated to mastication. One or more pairs of appendages are often transformed into antennæ.

The relative position of the chief organs of the body, viz.:—heart, nerve-cord, and alimentary canal, is constant in Arthropoda. The heart is dorsal, the nerve-cord ventral, the alimentary canal intermediate. (See fig. 3.) The œsophagus passes between the connectives of the nerve-cord. Not a few other animals, such as Annelids and Mollusca, exhibit the same arrangement.

Arthropoda are not known to be ciliated in any part of the body, or in any stage of growth. Another histological peculiarity, not quite so universal, is the striation of the muscular fibres throughout the body. In many Invertebrates there are no striated muscles at all, while in Vertebrates only voluntary muscles, as a rule, are striated.

The circulatory organs of Arthropoda vary greatly in plan and degree of complication, but there is never a completely closed circulation.

The development of Arthropoda may be accompanied by striking metamorphosis, e.g., in many marine Crustacea, but, as in other animals, the terrestrial and fluviatile forms usually develop directly. Even in Insects, which appear to contradict this rule flatly, the exception is more apparent than real. The Insect emerges from the egg as a fully formed larva, and so far its development is direct. It is the full-grown larva, however, which corresponds most nearly to the adult Myriopod, while the pupa and imago are stages peculiar to the Insect. It is not by any process of embryonic development, but by a secondary metamorphosis of the adult that the Insect acquires the power of flight necessary for the deposit of eggs in a new site.

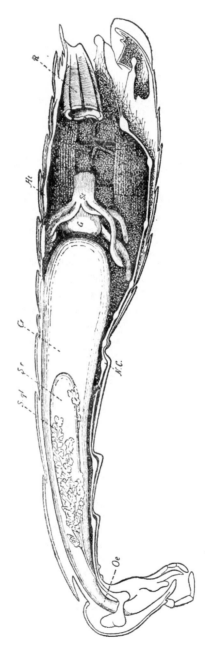

Fig. 3.—Longitudinal section of Female Cockroach, to show the position of the principal organs. *Oe*, oesophagus ; *S.gl*, salivary gland ; *S.r*, salivary reservoir ; *Cr*, crop ; *G*, gizzard ; *St*, chylific stomach ; *R*, rectum ; *Ht*, heart ; *N.C*, nerve-cord. × 7.

Characters of Insects.

Insects are distinguished from other Arthropoda by the arrangement of the segments of the body into three plainly marked regions—head, thorax, and abdomen ; by the three pairs of ambulatory legs carried upon the thorax ; by the single pair of antennæ ; and by the tracheal respiration. Myriopods and Arachnida have no distinct thorax. Most Crustacea have two pairs of antennæ, while in Arachnida antennæ are wanting altogether. Crustacea, if they possess special respiratory organs at all, have branchiæ (gills) in place of tracheæ (air-tubes). In Arachnida, Myriopoda, and Crustacea there are usually more than three pairs of ambulatory legs in the adult.

The appendages of an Insect's head (antennæ, mandibles, maxillæ) are appropriated to special senses, or to the operations of feeding, and have lost that obvious correspondence with walking legs which they still retain in some lower Arthropoda (*Peripatus, Limulus, Arachnida*). The thorax consists of three* segments, each of which carries a pair of ambulatory legs. No abdominal legs are found in any adult insect. The middle thoracic segment may carry a pair of wings or wing-covers, and the third segment a pair of wings.

The lower or less-specialised Insects, such as the Cockroach, have nearly as many nerve-ganglia as segments, and the longitudinal connectives of the nerve-cord are double. In the adult of certain higher Insects† (*e.g.*, many Coleoptera, and some Diptera) the nerve-ganglia are concentrated, reduced in number, and restricted to the head and thorax ; while all the connectives, except those of the œsophageal ring, may be outwardly single.

The heart, or dorsal vessel, is subdivided by constrictions into a series of chambers, from which an aorta passes forwards to the head.

Air is usually taken into the body by stigmata or breathing-pores,‡ which lie along the sides of the thorax and abdomen.

---

* In some Insects there are traces of a fourth thoracic segment.

† So also in some larvæ (*Calandra, Œstrus,* &c.).

‡ In some aquatic Insects the exchange of gases is effected by "pseudobranchiæ," and the tracheal system is closed.

It circulates through repeatedly-branching tracheal tubes, whose lining is strengthened by a spiral coil. Air-sacs (dilated portions of the air-tubes) occur in Insects of powerful flight.

The generative organs are placed near the hinder end of the body.* Most Insects are oviparous.† The sexes are always distinct ; but imperfect females ("neuters") occur in some kinds of social Insects. Agamogenesis (reproduction by unfertilised eggs) is not uncommon.

Orders of Insects.

The orders of Insects are usually defined with reference to the degree of metamorphosis and the structure of the parts of the mouth. Five of the orders (3, 5–8) in the table on page 9 undergo complete metamorphosis, and during the time of most rapid change the insect is motionless. In the remaining orders (1, 2, 4) there is either no metamorphosis (*Thysanura*), or it is incomplete—*i.e.*, the insect is active in all stages of growth. Among these three orders we readily distinguish the minute and wingless Thysanura. Two orders remain, in which the adult is commonly provided with wings ; of these, the Orthoptera have biting jaws, the Hemiptera, jaws adapted for piercing and sucking.

The name of Black Beetle, often given to the Cockroach, is therefore technically wrong. True Beetles have a resting or chrysalis stage, and may further be recognised in the adult state by the dense wing-covers, meeting along a straight line down the middle of the back, and by the transversely folded wings. Cockroaches have no resting stage, the wing-covers overlap, and the wings fold up fan-wise.

Further Definition of Cockroaches.

In the large order of Orthoptera, which includes Earwigs, Praying Insects, Walking Sticks, Grasshoppers, Locusts, Crickets, White Ants, Day-flies, and Dragon-flies, the family of Cockroaches is defined as follows :—

* Dragon-flies have the male copulatory apparatus, but not the genital aperture, in the fore part of the abdomen.

† Aphis and Cecidomyia are at times viviparous, and a viviparous Moth has been observed by Fritz Müller (Trans. Entom. Soc. Lond., 1883).

Family *Blattina*. Body usually depressed, oval. Pronotum shield-like. Legs adapted for running only. Wing-covers usually leathery, opaque, overlapping (if well developed) when at rest, anal area defined by a furrow (fig. 4). Head declivent, or sloped backwards, retractile beneath the pronotum. Eyes large, ocelli rudimentary, usually two, antennæ long and slender.

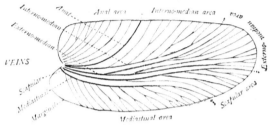

Fig. 4.—Generalised sketch of Cockroach wing-cover.

About eight hundred species of Cockroaches have been defined, and to facilitate their arrangement, three groups have been proposed, under which the different genera are ranked.*

Group 1. Both sexes wingless (*Polyzosteria*).

Group 2. Males winged, females wingless (*Perisphæria, Heterogamia*).

Group 3. Both sexes with more or less developed wings (about 7 genera).

* For descriptions of the species Fischer's Orthoptera Europæa (1853) or Brunner von Wattenwyl's Nouveau Système des Blattaires (1865) may be consulted. The classification adopted by the last-named author is here summarised.

BLATTARIÆ.

A.—Femora spinous (*Spinosæ*).

    Fam. 1.—*Ectobidæ*. Seventh abdominal sternum undivided in female. Sub-anal styles absent in male. Wings with triangular apical area. *Ectobia*, including *E. lapponica* (*Blatta*) and other genera.

    Fam. 2.—*Phyllodromidæ*. Seventh abdominal sternum undivided in female. Sub-anal styles usual in male (0 or rudimentary in *Phyllodromia*). Wings without triangular apical area. *Phyllodromia*, including *P. germanica* (*Blatta*) and other genera.

    Fam. 3.—*Epilampridæ*.

    Fam. 4.—*Periplanetidæ*. Seventh abdominal sternum divided in female. Sub-anal styles conspicuous in male. *Polyzosteria, Periplaneta*, &c.

B.—Femora not spinous (*Muticæ*).

    Families.—*Chorisoneuridæ, Panchloridæ, Perisphæridæ, Corydidæ, Heterogamidæ, Blaberidæ, Panesthidæ*.

Many useful references will be found in Scudder's Catalogue of N. American Orthoptera, Smiths. Misc. Coll., viii. (1868).

In Group 3 occur the only two genera which we shall find it necessary to describe—viz., *Blatta*, which includes the European Cockroaches, and *Periplaneta*, to which belong the Cockroaches of tropical Asia and America.

> Genus *Blatta*. A pulvillus between the claws of the feet. The seventh sternum of the abdomen entire in both sexes; sub-anal styles rudimentary in the male.

> Genus *Periplaneta*. Readily distinguished from Blatta by the divided seventh abdominal sternum of the female, and the sub-anal styles of the male.

Two species of Periplaneta have been introduced into Europe. These are—

1. *P. orientalis* (Common Cockroach, Black Beetle). Wing-covers and wings not reaching the end of the abdomen in the male; rudimentary in the female.

2. *P. americana* (American Cockroach). Wing-covers and wings longer than the body in both sexes.

CHAPTER III.

THE NATURAL HISTORY OF THE COCKROACH.

SPECIAL REFERENCES.

HUMMEL. Essais Entomologiques. No. 1 (1821).

CORNELIUS. Beiträge zur nähern Kenntniss von Periplaneta orientalis (1853.)

GIRARD. La domestication des Blattes. Bull. Soc. d'Acclimatisation, 3ᵉ Sér., Tom. IV., p. 296 (1877).

Range.

THE common Cockroach is native to tropical Asia,* and long ago made its way by the old trade-routes to the Mediterranean countries. At the end of the sixteenth century it appears to have got access to England and Holland, and has gradually spread thence to every part of the world.

Perhaps the first mention of this insect in zoological literature occurs in Moufet's Insectorum Theatrum (1634), where he speaks of the Blattæ as occurring in wine cellars, flour mills, &c., in England. It is hard to determine in all cases of what insects he is speaking, since one of his rude woodcuts of a " Blatta " is plainly *Blaps mortisaga;* another is, however, recognisable as the female of *P. orientalis;* a third, more doubtfully, as the male of the same species. He tells how Sir Francis Drake took the ship " Philip,"† laden with spices, and found a great multitude of winged Blattæ on board, " which were a little larger, softer, and darker than ours." Perhaps these belonged to the American species, but the description is obscure. Swammerdam also was acquainted with our Cockroach as an inhabitant of Holland early in the seventeenth century. He speaks of it as "insectum

---

* Linnæus was certainly mistaken in his remark (Syst. Nat., 12th ed.) that this species is native to America, and introduced to the East—"Habitat in America : hospitatur in Oriente." He adds, "Hodie in Russiæ adjacentibus regionibus frequens ; incepit nuperis temporibus Holmiæ, 1739, uti dudum in Finlandia."

† This must have been the "San Felipe," a Spanish East Indiaman, taken in 1587. See Motley, United Netherlands, Vol. II., p. 283.

illud Indicum, sub nomine Kakkerlak satis notum," and very properly distinguishes from it "the species of Scarabæus" (*Blaps*), which Moufet had taken for a Blatta.*

The American Cockroach is native to tropical America, but has now become widely spread by commerce. An Australian species also (*P. australasiæ*) has begun to extend its native limits, having been observed in Sweden,† Belgium, Madeira, the East and West Indies,‡ Florida,§ &c. In Florida it is said to be the torment of housekeepers.

To the genus *Blatta* belong a number of small European species, which mostly lurk in woods and thickets. Some of these are found in the south of England. *B. lapponica* is one of the commonest and most widely distributed. It is smaller than the common Cockroach, and both sexes have long wings and wing-cases. The males are black and the females yellow. It is found on the mountains of Norway and Switzerland as high as shrubs extend, and when sheltered by human dwellings, can endure the extreme cold of the most northern parts of Europe. This is the insect of which Linnæus tells, that in company with *Silpha lapponica* it has been known to devour in one day the whole stock of dried but unsalted fish of a Lapland village. *B. germanica* also has the wings and wing-cases well developed in both sexes. Two longitudinal stripes on the pronotum, or first dorsal plate of the thorax, are the readiest mark of this species, which is smaller and lighter in colour than the common Cockroach. It is plentiful in most German towns, and has been introduced from Germany into many other countries;|| but it appears to be native, not to Germany alone, but to Asia and all parts of central and southern Europe. Where and how it first became domesticated we do not know.

---

* Biblia Naturæ, Vol. I., p. 216.

† De Borck. Skandinaviens rätvingade Insekters Nat. Hist., I., i., 35.

‡ Brunner. N. Syst. d. Blattaires, p. 234.

§ Scudder. Proc. Boston Soc. N.H., Vol. XIX., p. 94.

|| For example, the Russians often call it *Proussaki*, the Prussian Cockroach, and believe that their troops brought it home with them after the Seven Years' War. The native Russian name is *Tarakan*. In Finland and Sweden the same species is called *Torraka*, which appears to be a corruption of the Russian word, and confirms the account of Linnæus quoted above.

B. germanica is found in the United States from the Atlantic to the Pacific. It is generally known as the Croton Bug, because in New York it is often met with about the water pipes, which are supplied from the Croton River (Dr. Scudder).

The other species of Cockroaches which have been met with in Europe are *Panchlora maderæ*, said by Stephens to be occasionally seen in London, and *Blabera gigantea*, the Drummer of the West Indies, which has often been found alive in ships in the London Docks.

Blatta germanica, *Periplaneta orientalis*, and *P. americana*, are so similar in habits and mode of life as to be interchangeable, and each is known to maintain itself in particular houses or towns within the territory of another species, though usually without spreading.

Orientalis is, for example, the common Cockroach of England, but *germanica* frequently gets a settlement and remains long in the same quarters. H. C. R., in Science-Gossip for 1868, p. 15, speaks of it as swarming in an hotel near Covent Garden, where it can be traced back as far as 1857. In Leeds, one baker's shop is infested by this species; it is believed to have been brought by soldiers to the barracks, after the Crimean war, and to have been carried to the baker's in bread-baskets. We have met with no instance in which it has continued to gain ground at the expense of *orientalis*. *Americana* also seems well established in particular houses or districts in England. H. C. R. (loc. cit.) mentions warehouses near the Thames, Red Lion and Bloomsbury Squares, and the Zoological Gardens, Regent's Park. It frequents one single warehouse in Bradford, and is similarly local in other towns with foreign trade.

Many cases are recorded in which *germanica* has been replaced by *orientalis*, as in parts of Russia and Western Germany, but detailed and authenticated accounts are still desired. On the whole *orientalis* seems to be dominant over both *germanica* and *americana*.

The slow spread of the Cockroaches in Europe is noteworthy, not as exceptional among invading species, but as one more illustration of the length of time requisite for changes of the equilibrium of nature. It took two centuries from the first introduction of *orientalis* into England for it to spread far from London. Gilbert White, writing, as it would appear, at some date before 1790, speaks of the appearance of "an unusual insect," which proved to be the Cockroach, at Selborne, and says: "How long they have abounded in England I cannot say;

but have never observed them in my house till lately."*   It is
probable that many English villages are still clear of the pest.
The House Cricket, which the Cockroaches seem destined to
supplant, still dwells in our houses, often side by side with its
rival, sharing the same warm crannies, and the same food. The
other imported species, though there is reason to suppose that
they cannot permanently withstand *orientalis*, are by no means
beaten out of the field; they retreat slowly where they retreat
at all, and display inferiority chiefly in this, that in countries
where both are found, they do not spread, while their competitor
does. It may yet require some centuries to settle the petty wars
of the Cockroaches.

It is also worth notice that in this, as in most other cases, the
causes of such dominance over the rest as one species enjoys are
very hard to discover.   We cannot explain what peculiarities
enable Cockroaches to invade ground thoroughly occupied by
the House Cricket, an insect of quite similar mode of life :
and it is equally hard to account for the superiority of *orientalis*
over the other species. It is neither the largest nor the smallest;
it is not perceptibly more prolific, or more voracious, or fonder
of warmth, or swifter than its rivals, nor is it easy to see how
the one conspicuous structural difference—viz., the rudimentary
state of the wings of the female, can greatly favour *orientalis*.
Some slight advantage seems to lie in characteristics too subtle
for our detection or comprehension.

Food and Habits.

As to the food of Cockroaches, we can hardly except any
animal or vegetable substance from the long list of their depre-
dations.   Bark, leaves, the pith of living cycads, paper, woollen
clothes, sugar, cheese, bread, blacking, oil, lemons, ink, flesh,
fish, leather, the dead bodies of other Cockroaches, their own
cast skins and empty egg-capsules, all are greedily consumed.
Cucumber, too, they will eat, though it disagrees with them
horribly.

In the matter of temperature they are less easy to please.
They are extremely fond of warmth, lurking in nooks near the

* Bell's Edition, Vol. I., p. 454.

oven, and abounding in bakehouses, distilleries, and all kinds of factories which provide a steady heat together with a supply of something eatable. Cold is the only check, and an unwarmed room during an English winter is more than they can endure. They are strictly nocturnal, and shun the light, although when long unmolested they become bolder. The flattened body enables the Cockroach to creep into very narrow crevices, and during cold weather it takes refuge beneath the flags of a kitchen floor, or in other very confined spaces. .

The Cockroach belongs to a miscellaneous group of animals, which may be described as in various degrees parasitic upon men. These are all in a vague sense domestic species, but have not, like the ox, sheep, goat, or pig, been forcibly reduced to servitude; they have rather attached themselves to man in various degrees of intimacy. The dog has slowly won his place as our companion; the cat is tolerated and even caressed, but her attachment is to the dwelling and not to us; the jackal and rat are scavengers and thieves; the weasel, jackdaw, and magpie are wild species which show a slight preference for the neighbourhood of man. All of these, except the cat, which holds a very peculiar place, possess in a considerable degree qualities which bring success in the great competitive examination. They are not eminently specialised, their diet is mixed, their range as natural species is wide. Apart from man, they would have become numerous and strong, but those qualities which fit them so well to shift for themselves, have had full play in the dwellings of a wealthy and careless host. Of these domestic parasites at least two are insects, the House-fly and the Cockroach; and the Cockroach in particular is eminent in its peculiar sphere of activity. The successful competition of Cockroaches with other insects under natural conditions is sufficiently proved by the fact that about nine hundred species have already been described,* while their rapid multiplication and almost worldwide dissemination in the dwellings of man is an equally striking proof of their versatility and readiness to adapt themselves to artificial circumstances. In numerical frequency they

---

* British Museum Catalogue of Blattariæ (1868) and Supplement (1869). It is probable that the number is over-estimated in this catalogue, the same species being occasionally renamed.

probably exceed all domestic animals of larger size, while in
geographical range the five species, *lapponica*, *germanica*,
orientalis, *americana*, and *australasiæ*, are together comparable to
the dog or pig, which have been multiplied and transported by
man for his own purposes, and which cover the habitable globe.

The Cockroach a persistent type.

The Cockroach is historically one of the most ancient, and
structurally one of the most primitive, of our surviving insects.
Its immense antiquity is shown by the fact that so many Cockroaches have been found in the Coal Measures, where about
eighty species have been met with. The absence of well-defined
stages of growth, such as the soft-bodied larva or inactive pupa,
the little specialised wings and jaws, the simple structure of the
thorax, the jointed appendages carried on the end of the
abdomen, and the unconcentrated nervous system, are marks of
the most primitive insect-types. The order Orthoptera is un-
deniably the least specialised among winged insects at least, and
within this order none are more simple in structure, or reach
farther back in the geological record than the Cockroaches.
The wingless Thysanura are even more generalised, but their
geological history is illegible.*

Life-History.

The eggs of the Cockroach are laid sixteen together in a
large horny capsule. This capsule is oval, with roundish ends,
and has a longitudinal serrated ridge, which is uppermost while
in position within the body of the female. The capsule is
formed by the secretion of a "colleterial" gland, poured out
upon the inner surface of a chamber (vulva) into which the
oviducts lead. The secretion is at first fluid and white, but
hardens and turns brown on exposure to the air. In this way a
sort of mould of the vulva is formed, which is hollow, and opens
forwards towards the outlet of the common oviduct. Eggs are

---

* Brongniart has just described a Carboniferous Insect which he considers a
Thysanuran (*Dasyleptus Lucasi*), though it has but one anal appendage. See C. R.
Soc. Ent., France, 1885.

now passed one by one into the capsule ; and as it becomes full, its length is gradually increased by fresh additions, while the first-formed portion begins to protrude from the body of the female. When sixteen eggs have descended, the capsule is closed in front, and after an interval of seven or eight days, is dropped in a warm and sheltered crevice. In *Periplaneta orientalis* it measures about ·45 in. by ·25 in. (fig. 5). The ova

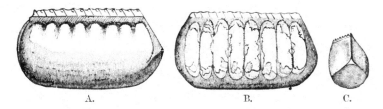

A.   B.   C.

Fig. 5.—Egg-capsule of *P. orientalis* (magnified). A, external view ;
B, opened ; C, end view.

develop within the capsule, and when ready to escape are of elongate-oval shape, resembling mummies in their wrappings. Eight embryos in one row face eight others on the opposite side, being alternated for close packing. Their ventral surfaces, which are afterwards turned towards the ground, are opposed, and their rounded dorsal surfaces are turned towards the wall of capsule ; their heads are all directed towards the serrated edge. The ripe embryos are said by Westwood to discharge a fluid (saliva ?) which softens the cement along the dorsal edge, and enables them to escape from their prison. In *Blatta germanica* the female is believed to help in the process of extrication.* The larvæ are at first white, with black eyes, but soon darken. They run about with great activity, feeding upon any starchy food which they can find.

The larvæ of the Cockroach hardly differ outwardly from the adult, except in the absence of wings. The tenth tergum is notched in both sexes, as in the adult female. The sub-anal styles of the male are developed in the larva.

Cornelius, in his Beiträge zur nähern Kenntniss von Peri-planeta orientalis (1853), gives the following account of the moults

* Hummel, loc. cit.

of the Cockroach.   The first change of skin occurs immediately
after escape from the egg-capsule, the second four weeks later,
the third at the end of the first year, and each succeeding moult
after a year's interval.   At the sixth moult the insect becomes
a pupa,* and at the seventh (being now four years old) it
assumes the form of the perfect Insect.   The changes of skin

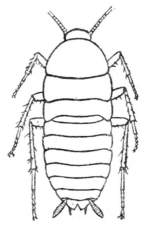

Fig. 6.—Young nymph (male).   × 6.

are annual, and like fertilisation and oviposition, take place in
the summer months only.   He tells us further that the ova
require about a year for their development.   These statements
are partly based upon observation of captive Cockroaches, and
are the only ones accessible; but they require confirmation by
independent observers, especially as they altogether differ from
Hummel's account of the life-history of *Blatta germanica*, and
are at variance with the popular belief that new generations of
the Cockroach are produced with great rapidity.

The antennæ of the male nymph resemble those of the adult
female.   Wings and wing-covers appear first in the later larval

* The use of the term *pupa* to denote the last stage before the complete assumption of wings in the Cockroach, is liable to mislead.   There is no resting-stage at all;
wings are developed gradually, and are nearly as conspicuous in the last larval state
as in the so-called pupa.   There seems no reason for speaking of pupæ in this case.

It is preferable to designate as "nymphs" young and active Insects, immature
sexually, but with mouth-parts like those of the adult.   See Lubbock, Linn. Trans.,
1863, and Eaton, Linn. Trans., 1883.

stages, but are then rudimentary, and constitute a mere prolongation of the margins of the thoracic rings. Cornelius says that the round white spot internal to the antenna first appears plainly in the pupa, but we have readily found it in a very young larva. The Insect is active in all its stages, and is

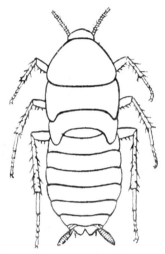

Fig. 7.— Older nymph (male) with rudiments of wings. × 2¼.

therefore, with other Orthoptera, described as undergoing "incomplete metamorphosis." After each moult it is for a few hours nearly pure white. Of the duration of life in this species we have no certain information, and there is great difficulty in procuring any.

Sexual Differences.

Male Cockroaches are readily distinguished from the females by the well-developed wings and wing-covers. They are also slighter and weaker than the females; their terga and sterna are not so much thickened; their alimentary canal is more slender, and they feed less greedily (the crop of the male is usually only half-full of food). They stand higher on their legs than the females, whose abdomen trails on the ground. The external anatomical differences of the sexes may be tabulated thus :—

Female.	*Male.*
Antenna shorter than the body, the third joint longer than the second.	Antenna rather longer than the body, the third joint about as long as the second.
Wings and wing-covers rudimentary.	Wings and wing-covers well developed.
Mesosternum divided.	Mesosternum entire.
Abdomen broader.	Abdomen narrower.
Terga 8 and 9 not externally visible.	Terga 8 and 9 externally visible.
The 10th tergum notched.	The 10th tergum hardly notched.
The 7th sternum divided behind.	The 7th sternum undivided.
The external outlet of the rectum and vulva between the 10th tergum and the 7th sternum.	The outlet between the 10th tergum and the 9th sternum.
No sub-anal styles.	Sub-anal styles.

Parasites.

We have before us a long list of parasites* which infest the Cockroach. There is a conferva, an amœba, several infusoria, nematoid worms (one of which migrates to and fro between the rat and the Cockroach), a mite, as well as hymenopterous and coleopterous Insects. The Cockroach has a still longer array of foes, which includes monkeys, hedgehogs, pole-cats, cats, rats, birds, chamæleons, frogs, and wasps, but no single friend, unless those are reckoned as friends which are the foes of its foes.

Names in common use.

A few lines must be added upon the popular and scientific names of this insect. Etymologists have found it hard to explain the common English name, which seems to be related to

* See Appendix.

cock and *roach*, but has really nothing to do with either. The lexicographers usually hold their peace about it, or give derivations which are absurd. Mr. James M. Miall informs us that *"Cockroach* can be traced to the Spanish *cucarácha*, a diminutive form of *cuco* or *coco* (Lat. *coccum*, a berry). *Cucarácha* is used also of the woodlouse, which, when rolled up, resembles a berry. The termination -*ácha* (Ital. -*accio*, -*accia*) signifies *mean* or *contemptible*. The Spanish word has also taken a French form; at least *coqueraches* has some currency (see, for example, Tylor's Anahuac, p. 325)." In provincial English *Black Clock* is a common name. The German word *Schabe*, often turned into *Schwabe*, means perhaps *Suabian*, as Moufet, quoting Cordus, seems to explain.* *Franzose* and *Däne* are other German words for the insect, applied specially to *Blatta germanica;* and all seem to imply some popular theory as to the native country of the Cockroach.† This etymology of *Schabe* is not free from suspicion, particularly as the same term is commonly applied to the clothes-moth. *Kakerlac*, much used in France and French-speaking colonies, is a Dutch word of unknown signification. *P. Americana* is usually named *Kakerlac* or *Cancrelat* by the French; while *orientalis* has many names, such as *Cafard, Ravet*, and *Bête noire.*‡ The name *Blatta* was applied by the ancients to quite different insects, of which Virgil and Pliny make mention; *Periplaneta* is a modern generic term, coined by Burmeister.

Uses.

Of the uses to which Cockroaches have been put we have little to say. They constitute a popular remedy for dropsy in Russia, and both cockroach-tea and cockroach-pills are known in the medical practice of Philadelphia. Salted Cockroaches are said to have an agreeable flavour which is apparent in certain popular sauces.

---

* Insectorum Theatrum, p. 138. The name *Schwabe* is frequent in Franconia, where it is believed to have taken origin. Suabia adjoins Franconia, to the south.

† Compare the Swedish name (*supra*, p. 18).

‡ A fuller list of vernacular names is given by Rolland, Faune Populaire de la France, Vol. III., p. 285. See also Nennich, Polyglotten Lexicon, Vol. I., p. 620.

CHAPTER IV.

THE OUTER SKELETON.

SPECIAL REFERENCES.

KRUKENBERG. Vergleichend-Physiologische Vorträge. IV.—Vergl. Physiologie der Thierischen Gerüstsubstanzen. (1885.) [Chemical Relations of Chitin.]

GRABER. Ueber eine Art fibrilloiden Bindegewebes der Insectenhaut. Arch. f. mikr. Anat. Bd. X. (1874.) [Minute Structure of Integument.] Also,

VIALLANES. Recherches sur l'Histologie des Insectes. Ann. Sci. Nat., Zool. VIe Série, Tom. XIV. (1882).

AUDOUIN. Recherches anatomiques sur le thorax des Insectes, &c. Ann. Sci. Nat. Tom. I. (1824.) [Theoretical Composition of Insect Segments.] Also,

MILNE-EDWARDS. Leçons sur la Physiologie et l'Anatomie Comparée. Tom. X. (1874.)

SAVIGNY. Mémoires sur les animaux sans vertèbres. Partie I^e. Théorie des organes de la bouche des Crustacées et des Insectes. (1816.) [Comparative Anatomy of the Mouth-parts.]

MUHR. Ueber die Mundtheile der Orthopteren. Prag. 1877. [Mouth-parts of Orthoptera.]

Chitin.

WHEN the skin of an Insect is boiled successively in acids, alkalies, alcohol, and ether, an insoluble residue known as Chitin ($C_{15} H_{26} N_2 O_{10}$) is obtained. It may be recognised and sufficiently separated by its resistance to boiling liquor potassæ. Chitin forms less than one-half by weight of the integument, but it is so coherent and uniformly distributed that when isolated by chemical reagents, and even when cautiously calcined, it retains its original organised form. The colour which it frequently exhibits is not due to any essential ingredient; it may be diminished or even destroyed by various bleaching processes. The colouring-matter of the chitin of the Cockroach, which is amber-yellow in thin sheets and blackish-brown in dense masses, is particularly stable and difficult of removal. Its composition does not appear to have been ascertained; it is white when first secreted, but darkens on exposure to air. Fresh-

moulted Cockroaches are white, but gradually darken in three
or four hours. Lowne* observes that in the Blow-fly the pigment is "first to be met with in the fat-bodies of the larvæ.
These are perfectly white, but when cut from the larva, and
exposed to the air, they rapidly assume an inky blackness.
. . . . When the perfect insect emerges from the pupa, and
respiration again commences, the integument is nearly white,
or a faint ashy colour prevails. This soon gives place to the
characteristic blue or violet tint, first immediately around those
portions most largely supplied with air vessels." Professor
Moseley† tells us that, thinking it just within the limits of
possibility that the brown coloration of the Cockroach might be
due to the presence of silver, he analysed one pound weight of
Blatta. He found no silver, but plenty of iron, and a remarkable quantity of manganese. That light has some action upon
the colouring matter seems to be indicated by the fact that in a
newly-moulted Cockroach the dorsal surface darkens first.

Chitin is not peculiar to Insects, nor even to Arthropoda.
The pen of cuttle-fishes and the shell of Lingula contain the
same substance,‡ which is also proved, or suspected, to occur in
many other animals.

The chemical stability of chitin is so remarkable that we
might well expect it to accumulate like the inorganic constituents of animal skeletons, and form permanent deposits.
Schlossberger§ has, however, shown that it changes slowly
under the action of water. Chitin kept for a year under water
partially dissolved, turned into a slimy mass, and gave off a
peculiar smell. This looks as if it were liable to putrefaction.
The minute proportion of nitrogen in its composition may
explain the complete disappearance of chitin in nature.

The Chitinous Cuticle.

The chitinous exoskeleton is rather an exudation than a true
tissue. It is not made up of cells, but of many superposed

---

* Anatomy of the Blow-fly. p. 11.

† Q. J. Micr. Sci., 1871, p. 394.

‡ Krukenberg. Vergl. Physiologische Vorträge, p. 200. Halliburton, Q. J. Micr.
Sci., 1885, p. 173.

§ Ann. d. Chem. u. Pharm., Bd. 98.

laminæ, secreted by an underlying epithelium, or "chitino-genous layer." This consists of a single layer of flattened cells, resting upon a basement membrane. A cross-section of the chitinous layer, or "cuticle," examined with a high power

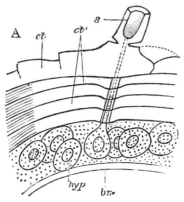

Fig. 8.—Diagram of Insect integument, in section. *bm*, basement membrane ; *hyp*, hypodermis, or chitinogenous layer ; *ct*, *ct′*, chitinous cuticle ; *s*, a seta.

shows extremely close and fine lines perpendicular to the laminæ. The cells commonly form a mosaic pattern, as if altered in shape by mutual pressure. The free surface of the integument of the Cockroach is divided into polygonal, raised spaces. Here and there an unusually long, flask-shaped, epithelial cell projects through the cuticle, and forms for itself an elongate chitinous sheath, commonly articulated at the base ; such hollow sheaths form the hairs or setæ of Insects—structures quite different histologically from the hairs of Vertebrates.

The polygonal areas of the cuticle correspond each to a chitinogenous cell. Larger areas, around which the surrounding ones are radiately grouped, are discerned at intervals, and these carry hairs, or give attachment to muscular fibres.

Viallanes (loc. cit.) has added some interesting details to what was previously known of Insect-hairs. There are, he points out, two kinds of hairs, distinguished by their size and struc-ture. The smaller spring from the boundary between contiguous polygonal areas, and have no sensory character. The larger ones occupy unusually large areas, surmount chitinogenous cells of corresponding size, and receive a special nervous supply.

The nerve* expands at the base of the hair into a spindle-shaped, nucleated mass (bipolar ganglion-cell), from which issues a filament which traverses the axis of the hair, piercing the chitinogenous cell, whose protoplasm surrounds it with a sheath which is continued to the tip of the hair. Such sensory hairs are abundant in parts which are endowed with special sensibility.

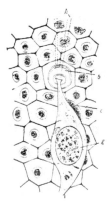

Fig. 9.—Nerve-ending in skin of Stratiomys larva. *h*, hairs; *b*, their chitinous base; *c*, nucleus of generating cell; *g*, ganglion cell. × 250. Copied from Viallanes.

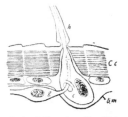

Fig. 10.—Diagram of sensory hair of Insect. *Cc*, chitinous cuticle; *h*, hair; *c*, its generating cell; *g*, ganglion cell; *bm*, basement-membrane.

The chitinous cuticle is often folded in so as to form a deep pit, which, looked at from the inside of the body, resembles a lever, or a hook. Such inward-directed processes serve chiefly for the attachment of muscles, and are termed *apodemes* (*apodemata*). A simple example is afforded by the two glove-tips which lie in the middle line of the under-surface of the thorax (p. 58, and fig. 27). In other cases the pit is closed from the

* Previously observed by Leydig in *Corethra*.

first, and the apodeme is formed in the midst of a group of chitinogenous cells distant from the superficial layer, though continuous therewith. Many tendons of insertion are formed in this way. The two forked processes in the floor of the thorax (p. 58, and fig. 27) are unusually large and complex structures of the same kind. In the tentorium of the head (p. 39, and fig. 17) a pair of apodemes are supposed to unite and form an extensive platform which supports the brain and gullet.

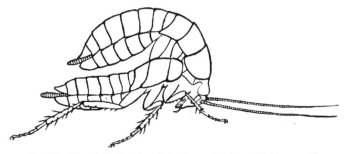

Fig. 11.—Nymph (in last larval stage) escaping from old skin.   × 2½.

Like other Arthropoda, Insects shed their chitinous cuticle from time to time. A new cuticle, at first soft and colourless, is previously secreted, and from it the old one gradually becomes detached. The setæ probably serve the same purpose as the "casting-hairs" described by Braun in the crayfish, and by Cartier in certain reptiles,* that is, they mechanically loosen the old skin by pushing beneath it. In many soft-bodied nymphs the new skin can be gathered up into a multitude of fine wrinkles, which facilitate separation, but we have not found such wrinkles in the Cockroach, except in the wings. The integument about to be shed splits along the back of the Cockroach, from the head to the end of the thorax,† and the animal draws its limbs out of their discarded sheaths with much effort. It is remarkable that the long, tapering, and many-jointed antennæ are drawn out from an entire sheath. At the

---

* A condensed and popular account of these researches will be found in Semper's Animal Life, p. 20.

† Prof. Huxley (Anat. Invert. Animals, p. 419) states that the integument splits along the abdomen also, but this is a mistake.

same time the chitinous lining of the tracheal tubes is cast, while that of the alimentary canal is broken up and passed through the body.

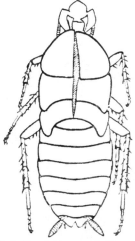

Fig. 12.—Cast skin of older nymph ("pupa"). × 2½.

Prolonged boiling in caustic potash, though it dissolves the viscera, does not disintegrate the exoskeleton. This shows that the segments of the integument are not separate chitinous rings, but thickenings of a continuous chitinous investment. Nevertheless, their constancy in position and their conformity in structure often enable us to trace homologies between different segments and different species as certainly as between corresponding elements of the osseous vertebrate skeleton.

Parts of a Somite.

Audouin's laborious researches into the exoskeleton of Insects* resulted in a nomenclature which has been generally adopted. He divides each somite (segment) into eight pieces, grouped in pairs—viz., *terga* (dorsal plates), *sterna* (ventral plates), *epimera* (adjacent to the terga), and *episterna* (adjacent to the sterna).

While admitting the usefulness of these terms, we must warn the reader not to suppose that this subdivision is either normal or primitive. The eight-parted segment exists in no single

* Audouin. Rech. anat. sur le thorax des Insectes, &c. (Ann. Sci. Nat., Tom I., p. 97. 1824.)

larval or adult Arthropod. Lower forms and younger stages take us further from such a type, instead of nearer to it ; and Audouin's theoretical conception is most fully realised in the thorax of an adult Insect with well-developed legs and wings.

The morphologist would derive all the varieties of Arthropod segments from the very simple and uniform chitinous cuticle found in Annelids and many Insect-larvæ. This becomes differentiated by unequal thickening and folding in, and a series of rings connected by flexible membranes is produced. Locomotive and respiratory activity commonly lead to the definition of terga and sterna, which are similarly attached to each other by flexible membranes. A pair of limbs may next be inserted between the terga and sterna, and the simple segment thus composed occurs so extensively in the less modified regions and in early stages that it may well be considered the typical Arthropod somite.

Special needs may lead to the division of the sterna into lateral halves, but this is purely an adaptive change. The third thoracic sternum of the male Cockroach, and the second and third of the female are thus divided, as is also the hinder part of the seventh abdominal sternum of the female.

In an early stage every somite has its tergal region divided into lateral halves, owing to the late completion of the body on this side. Traces of this division may survive even in the imago. There is often a conspicuous dorsal groove in the thoracic terga, and at the time of moult the terga split along an accurately median line (see fig. 12).

Additional pieces may be developed between the terga and sterna, and these have long been termed *pleural.** There may be, for example, single stigmatic plates, as in the abdomen of the Cockroach, pieces to support the thoracic legs, and pieces to support the wings ; but the number and position of these plates depends upon their immediate use, and their homologies become very uncertain when Insects of different orders are compared. In general, the pleural elements of the segment are late in development, variable, and highly adaptive.

---

* This application of the word to denote parts intermediate between terga and sterna has become general since its adoption by Audouin. It appears also in the older and deservedly obsolete nomenclature of Kirby and Spence. Professor Huxley has unfortunately disturbed the consistent use of this term by giving the name *pleura* to the free edges of the terga in Crustacea.

Somites of the Cockroach.

The exoskeleton of the Cockroach is divisible into about seventeen segments, which are grouped into three regions, as follows :—

Head { Procephalic lobes			
{ Post-oral segments		...	3
Thorax	... ...	...	3*
Abdomen ...	... ...	...	11
			17

It is a strong argument in favour of this estimate that many Insects, at the time when segmentation first appears, possess seventeen segments.† The procephalic lobes, from which a great part of the head, including the antennæ, is developed, are often counted as an additional segment.‡

The limbs, which in less specialised Arthropoda are carried with great regularity on every segment of the body, are greatly reduced in Insects. Those borne by the head are converted into sensory and masticatory organs; those on the abdomen are either totally suppressed, or extremely modified, and only the thoracic limbs remain capable of aiding in locomotion.

The primitive structure of the Arthropod limb is adapted to locomotion in water, and persists, with little modification, in most Crustacea. Here we find in most of the appendages§ a basal stalk (protopodite), often two-jointed, an inner terminal branch (endopodite), and an outer terminal branch (exopodite), each of the latter commonly consisting of several joints. It does not appear that the appendages of Insects conform to the biramous Crustacean type, though the ends of the maxillæ are often divided into an outer and an inner portion.

We shall now proceed to describe, in some detail, the regions of the body of the adult Cockroach.

---

* Where the thorax apparently consists of four somites, as in some Hymenoptera, Hemiptera, Coleoptera, and Lepidotera, the first abdominal segment has become blended with it.

† Balfour. Embryology, Vol. I., p. 337.

‡ E.g., by Graber. Insekten, Vol. II., p. 423.

§ See, for example, Huxley on the Crayfish.

Head ; Central Parts.

The head of the Cockroach, as seen from the front, is pear-shaped, having a semi-circular outline above, and narrowing downwards. A side-view shows that the front and back are flattish, while the top and sides are regularly rounded. In the

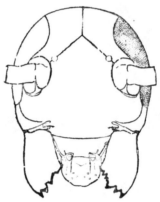

Fig. 13.—Front of Head.   × 10.

living animal the face is usually inclined downwards, but it can be tilted till the lower end projects considerably forward. The mouth, surrounded by gnathites or jaws, opens below. On the hinder surface is the occipital foramen, by which the head communicates with the thorax. A rather long neck allows the head to be retracted beneath the pronotum (first dorsal shield of the thorax) or protruded beyond it.

On the front of the head we observe the clypeus, which occupies a large central tract, extending almost completely across the widest part of the face. It is divided above by a sharply bent suture from the two epicranial plates, which form the top of the head as well as a great part of its back and sides. The labrum hangs like a flap from its lower edge. A little above the articulation of the labrum the width of the clypeus is suddenly reduced, as if a squarish piece had been cut out of each lower corner. In the re-entrant angle so formed, the ginglymus, or anterior articulation of the mandible, is situated.

The labrum is narrower than the clypeus, and of squarish shape, the lower angles being rounded. It hangs downwards, with a slight inclination backwards towards the mouth, whose front wall it forms. On each side, about halfway between the lateral margin and the middle line, the posterior surface of the labrum is strengthened by a vertical chitinous slip set with large setæ. Each of these plates passes above into a ring, from the upper and outer part of which a short lever passes upwards, and gives attachment to a muscle (*levator menti*).

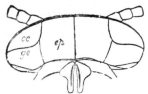

Fig. 14.—Top of Head. *ep*, epicranial plate ; *oc*, eye ; *ge*. gena. × 10.

The top and back of the head are defended by the two epicranial plates, which meet along the middle line, but diverge widely as they descend upon the posterior surface, thus enclosing a large opening, the occipital foramen. Beyond the foramen, they pass still further downwards, their inner edges receding in a sharp curve from the vertical line, and end below in cavities for the articulation of the mandibular condyles.*

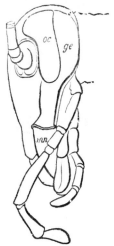

Fig. 15.—Side of Head. *oc*, eye ; *ge*, gena ; *mn*, mandible. × 10.

* One of the few points in which we have to differ from the admirable description of the Cockroach given in Huxley's Comparative Anatomy of Invertebrated Animals, relates to the articulation of the mandible, which is there said to be carried by the gena.

The sides of the head are completed by the eyes and the genæ. The large compound eye is bounded above by the epicranium; in front by a narrow band which connects the epicranium with the clypeus ; behind, by the gena. The gena passes downwards between the eye and the epicranial plate, then curves forwards beneath the eye, and just appears upon the front of the face, being loosely connected at this point with the clypeus. Its lower edge overlaps the base of the mandible, and encloses the extensor mandibulæ.

The occipital foramen has the form of an heraldic shield. Its lateral margin is strengthened by a rim continuous with the tentorium, or internal skeleton of the head. Below, the foramen is completed by the upper edge of the tentorial plate,

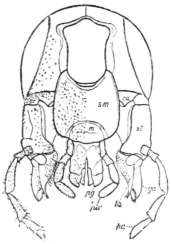

Fig. 16.—Back of Head. *ca*, cardo ; *st*, stipes ; *ga*, galea ; *la*, lacinia ; *pa*, palp ; *sm*, submentum ; *m*, mentum ; *pg*, paraglossa. × 10.

which nearly coincides with the upper edge of the submentum (basal piece of the second pair of maxillæ) ; a cleft, however, divides the two, through which nerve-commissures pass from the sub-œsophageal to the first thoracic ganglion. Through the occipital foramen pass the œsophagus, the salivary ducts, the aorta, and the tracheal tubes for the supply of air to the head.

The internal skeleton of the head consists of a nearly transparent chitinous septum, named *tentorium* by Burmeister, which extends downwards and forwards from the lower border of the occipital foramen. In front it gives off two long crura, or props, which pass to the ginglymus, and are reflected thence upon the inner surface of the clypeus, ascending as high as the antennary socket, round which they form a kind of rim. Each crus is twisted, so that the front surface becomes first internal and then posterior as it passes towards the clypeus. The form of the tentorium is in other respects readily understood from

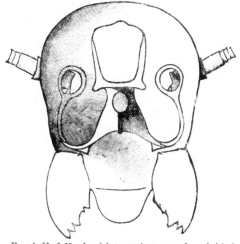

Fig. 17.—Fore-half of Head, with tentorium, seen from behind. × 12.

the figure (fig. 17). Its lower surface is strengthened by a median keel which gives attachment to muscles. The œsophagus passes upwards between its anterior crura, the long flexor of the mandible lies on each side of the central plate; the supra-œsophageal ganglion rests on the plate above, and the sub-œsophageal ganglion lies below it, the nerve-cords which unite the two passing through the circular aperture. A similar internal chitinous skeleton occurs in the heads of other Orthoptera, as well as in Neuroptera and Lepidoptera. Palmén* thinks that it represents a pair of stigmata or spiracles, which have thus become modified for muscular attachment, their respiratory function being wholly lost. In Ephemera he finds that the tentorium breaks across the middle when the skin is changed, and each half is drawn out from the head like the chitinous lining of a tracheal tube.

* Morphologie des Tracheen-systems, p. 103.

Antennæ; Eyes.

A pair of antennæ spring from the front of the head. In the male of the common Cockroach they are a little longer than the body; in the female rather shorter. From seventy-five to ninety joints are usually found, and the three basal joints are larger than the rest. Up to about the thirtieth, the joints are

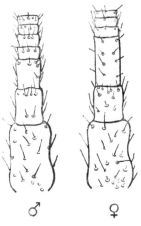

Fig. 18.—Base of Antenna of Male (to left) and Female (to right). × 24.

about twice as wide as long; from this point they become more elongate. The joints are connected by flexible membranes, and provided with stiff, forward-directed bristles. The ordinary position of the antennæ is forwards and outwards.

Each antenna is attached to a relatively large socket (fig. 15), which lies between the epicranium and clypeus, to the front and inner side of the compound eyes. A flexible membrane unites the antenna to the margin of the socket, from the lower part of which a chitinous pin projects upwards and supports the basal joint.

It is well known that in many Crustacea two pairs of antennæ are developed, the foremost pair (antennules) bearing two complete filaments. Some writers have suggested that both pairs may be present in Insects, though not simultaneously, the Crustacean antennule being found in the larva, and the Crustacean antenna in the adult. This view was supported by the familiar fact that in many larvæ the antennæ are placed further forward than in the adult. The three large joints at the base of Orthopterous antennæ have been taken to correspond with those of Crustacean antennules, and it has been inferred that in Insects with incomplete metamorphosis, only antennules or larval antennæ are developed.* This reasoning was never very cogent, and it has been impaired by further inquiry. Weismann has shown that in *Corethra plumicornis*, the adult antenna, though inserted much further back than that of the larva, is developed within it,† and Graber has described a still more striking case of the same thing in a White Butterfly.‡ There is, therefore, no reason to suppose that Insects possess more than one pair of antennæ, which is probably preoral, not corresponding with either of the Crustacean pairs.

We have already noticed (p. 26) the superficial points in which the antenna of the male Cockroach differs from that of the female.

The eyes of some Crustacea are carried upon jointed appendages, but this is never the case in Insects, though the eye-bearing surface may project from the head, as in *Diopsis* and *Stylops*. Professor Huxley§ supposes that the head of an Insect may contain six somites, the eyes representing one pair of appendages. The various positions in which the eyes of Arthropoda may be developed weakens the argument drawn from the stalk-eyed Crustacea. Claus and Fritz Müller go so far on the other side as to deny the existence of an eye-segment even in Crustacea.

Mouth-parts of the Cockroach.

Before entering upon a full description of the mouth-parts of the Cockroach, which present some technical difficulties, the beginner in Insect anatomy will find it useful to get a few points of nomenclature fixed in his memory. Unfortunately, the terms employed by entomologists are at times neither convenient nor philosophical.

* Zaddach, Entw. des Phryganiden Eies, p. 86; Rolleston, Forms of Animal Life, p. 75, &c.

† Zeits. f. wiss. Zool., Bd. XVI., pl. vii., fig. 33.

‡ Insekten, Vol. II., p. 508.

§ Anat. Invert. Animals, p. 398.

There are three pairs of jaws, disposed behind the labrum, as in the diagram :—

LABRUM.

1st pair of Jaws (MANDIBLES).
2nd   ,,   (MAXILLÆ).
3rd   ,,   (LABIUM, or 2nd pair of Maxillæ).

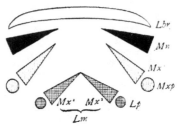

Fig. 19.—Diagram of Cockroach Jaws, in horizontal section.

The mandible is undivided in all, or nearly all, Insects.   Each maxilla may consist of

A *palp* on the outer side,
A *galea* (hood),
A *lacinia* (blade), on the inner side.

The galea (hood) of the 3rd pair of jaws is sometimes called the *paraglossa*.

A tongue-like process may be developed from the front wall of the mouth (*epipharynx*), or from the back wall (*hypopharynx* or *lingua*).* Both epipharynx and hypopharynx project into the mouth, and, in some Diptera, far beyond it.

The tip of the labium is sometimes produced into a long tongue, called the *ligula* (strap).

The mouths of Insects may be classed as :—

BITING.—Orthoptera, Neuroptera, Coleoptera (in some Coleoptera a licking tongue is developed), most Hymenoptera.

LICKING AND SUCKING.—Some Hymenoptera—*e.g.*, Honey Bee.

SUCKING.—(*a*) With lancets—Diptera, Hemiptera.
       (*b*) Without lancets—Lepidoptera.

---

* Professor Huxley has proposed to call the attached base *hypopharynx*, and the free tip *lingua*.

The reference of these to a common plan, and the determination of the constituent parts, is mainly the work of Savigny. Mouth-parts were made the basis of the classification of Insects by Fabricius (1745–1808).

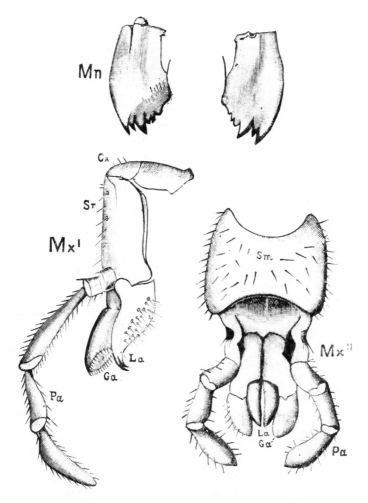

Fig. 20.—The Jaws, separated. *Mn*, mandible, seen from behind (to left) and front (to right); *Mx¹* maxilla (first pair); *Mx¹¹* labium, or second pair of maxillæ. The other letters as before. × 20.

The mandibles of the Cockroach are powerful, single-jointed*
jaws, each of which is articulated by a convex "condyle" to the
lower end of the epicranial plate, and again by a concave
"ginglymus" to the clypeus. The opposable inner edges are
armed with strong tooth-like processes of dense chitin, which
interlock when the mandibles close; those towards the tip of
the mandible are sharp, while others are blunt, as if for crushing. Each mandible can be moved through an angle of about
30°. A flexible chitinous flap extends from its inner border to
the labrum. The powerful flexor of the mandible arises within
the epicranial vault; its fibres converge to a chitinous tendon,
which passes outside the central plate of the tentorium, and at
a lower level through a fold on the lower border of the clypeus,
being finally inserted near the ginglymus. A short flexor arises
from the crus of the tentorium. The extensor muscle arises
from the side of the head, passes through the fold formed by
the lower end of the gena, and is inserted close to the outer side
of the condyle of the mandible.

The anterior maxillæ lie behind the mandibles, and like them
are unconnected with each other. They retain much more of
the primitive structure of a gnathite than the mandibles, in
which parts quite distinct in the maxillæ are condensed or
suppressed. The constituent pieces are seen in fig. 20. There
is a two-jointed basal piece, consisting of the *cardo* (*ca*) and the
stipes (*st*). The cardo is a transverse plate bent upon itself, and
enclosing muscles; it is attached to the outward-directed pedicel
of the occipital frame, and carries the vertical stipes. To the
side and lower end of the stipes is attached the five-jointed
palp (*pa*), a five-jointed limb used in feeding and in exploration,
while the lacinia (*la*) and galea (*ga*) are articulated to its
extremity. The lacinia is internal and posterior to the galea ;
it is broad above, but narrows below to a bifid tooth of dense
chitin ; its inner surface is beset with a cluster of strong setæ.
The galea is more flexible, and forms an irregular three-cornered

---

* Professor J. Wood-Mason points out that in *Machilis* (one of the Thysanura) the
mandible shows signs of segmentation, while the apical portion is deeply divided into
an inner and an outer half. Ripe embryos of *Panesthia* (*Blatta*) *javanica* are said to
exhibit folds which indicate the consolidation of the mandible out of separate joints,
while the cutting and crushing portions of the edge are divided by a "sutural mark,"
which may correspond to the line of junction of the divisions of a biramous appendage (Trans. Ent. Soc., 1879, pt. 2, p. 145).

prism with an obliquely truncated end, upon which are many fine hairs. A flexible and nearly transparent flap connects the inner edges of the stipes and cardo, and joins both to the labium. The muscles which move the bases of the maxillæ spring from the crura, central plate, and keel of the tentorium. On the posterior surface of the head, below the occipital foramen, we find a long vertical flap, the labium, which extends downwards to the opening of the mouth. It represents a second pair of maxillæ, fused together in their basal half, but retaining elsewhere sufficient resemblance to the less modified anterior pair to permit of the identification of their component parts. The upper edge is applied to the occipital frame, but is neither continuous with that structure nor articulated thereto. By stripping off the labium upwards it may be seen that it is really continuous with the chitinous integument of the neck. The broad shield-like base is incompletely divided by a transverse hinge into an upper and larger piece, the *submentum*, and a distal piece, the *mentum*. To the mentum are appended representatives of the galeæ (here named *paraglossæ*) and laciniæ, while a three-jointed palp with an additional basal joint (distinguished as the *palpiger*) completes the resemblance to the maxillæ of the first pair.* In front of the labium, and lying in the cavity of the mouth is a chitinous fold of the oral integument, the *lingua*, which lies like a tongue in the floor of the mouth. The common duct of the salivary glands enters the lingua, and opens on its hinder surface. The lingua is supported by the chitinous skeleton represented in the figures of the salivary glands. (Chap. vii., *infra*.)

The epipharynx, which is a prominent part in Coleoptera and Diptera, is not recognisable in Orthoptera.

Functions of the Antennæ and Mouth-parts.

We must now shortly consider the functions of the parts just described. The antennæ have long been regarded as sense-organs, and even the casual observer can hardly fail to remark that they are habitually used by the Insect to gain information

---

* The homology of the labium with the first pair of maxillæ is in no other Insects so distinct as in the Orthoptera.

concerning its immediate surroundings. Long antennæ, such
as those of the Cockroach, are certainly organs of touch, but it
has been much disputed whether they may not also be the seat
of some special sense, and if so, what that sense may be.
Several authors have found reason to suppose that in the Insect-
antenna resides the sense of hearing, but no evidence worth the
name is forthcoming in favour of this view. Much better
support can be found for the belief that the antenna is an
olfactory organ,* and some experiments which seem conclusive
on this point will be cited in a later chapter.

In the Cockroach the mandibles and maxillæ are the only
important instruments of mastication. The labium is indirectly
concerned as completing the mouth behind and supporting the
lingua, which is possibly of importance in the ordinary operations of feeding. Plateau† has carefully described the mode of
mastication as observed in a Carabus, and his account seems to
hold good of biting Insects in general. The mandibles and
maxillæ act, as he tells us, alternately, one set closing as the
others part. The maxillæ actually push the morsel into the
buccal cavity. When the mandibles separate, the head is
slightly advanced, so that the whole action has some superficial
resemblance to that of a grazing quadruped.

The palps of the maxillæ and labium have been variously
regarded as sensory and masticatory instruments. Not a few
authors believe that they are useful in both ways. The question
has lately been investigated experimentally by Plateau,‡ who
finds that removal of both maxillary and labial palps does not
interfere either with mastication or the choice of food. He
observes that in the various Coleoptera and Orthoptera submitted to experiment the palps are passive while food is being
passed into the mouth.

Plateau's experiments are conclusive as to the subordinate
value of the palps in feeding. The observation of live Cock-

---

* Rosenthal, Ueb. d. Geruchsinn der Insekten. Arch. f. Phys. Reil u. Autenrieth,
Bd. X. (1811). Hauser, Zeits. f. wiss. Zool., Bd. XXXIV. (1880).

† Mém. Acad. Roy. de Belgique, Tom. XLI. (1874). Prof. Plateau's writings will
often be referred to in these pages. We owe to him the most important researches
into the physiology of Invertebrates which have appeared for many years.

‡ Exp. sur le Rôle des Palpes chez les Arthropodes Maxillés. Pt. I. Bull. Soc.
Zool. de France, Tom. X. (1885).

roaches has satisfied us that the palps are constantly used when the Insect is active, whether feeding or not, to explore the surface upon which it moves. We have seen no ground for attributing to the palps special powers of perceiving odours or flavours, nor have we observed that they aid directly in filling the mouth with food.

It is worthy of note that Leydig has described and figured in the larva of *Hydroporus* (?), and Hauser in *Dytiscus*, *Carabus*, &c., a peculiar organ, apparently sensory, which is lodged in the maxillary and labial palps. It consists of whitish spots, sometimes visible to the naked eye, characterised by unusual thinness of the chitinous cuticle and by the aggregation beneath it of a crowd of extremely minute sensory rods. Of this organ no satisfactory explanation has yet been given.[*]

Comparison of Mouth-parts in different Insects.

The jaws of the Cockroach form an excellent standard of comparison for those of other Insects, and we shall attempt to illustrate the chief variations by referring them to this type.[†] Mouth-parts are so extensively used in the classification of Insects that every entomologist ought to have a rational as well as a technical knowledge of their comparative structure. No part of Insect anatomy affords more striking examples of adaptive modification. In form, size, and mode of application the jaws vary extremely. It would be hard to find feeding-organs more unlike, at first sight, than the stylets of a Gnat and the proboscis of a Moth, yet the study of a few well-selected types will satisfy the observer that both are capable of derivation from a common plan. Nor is this common plan at all vague. It is accurately pictured in the jaws of the Cockroach and other Orthoptera. These correspond so entirely with the primitive arrangement, inferred by a process of abstraction from

---

[*] Leydig, Taf. z. vergl. Anat., pl. x., fig. 3. Hauser, Zeits. f. wiss. Zool., Bd. XXXIV., p. 386. Jobert has figured the sensory organs of the maxillary palps of the Mole-cricket (Ann. Sci. Nat., 1872), and Forel similar organs in Ants (Bull. Soc. Vaudoise, 1885).

[†] The reader who desires to follow this subject further is recommended to study chap. vi. of Graber's Insekten, which we have found very useful.

the most dissimilar Insects, as to furnish a strong argument for the descent of all higher Insects from forms not unlike Orthoptera in the structure of their mouth-parts.

Though the jaws of the Cockroach are eminently primitive with respect to those of most other Insects, they are themselves derived from a far simpler arrangement, which is demonstrable in all embryonic Insects. Fig. 21 shows an Aphis within the

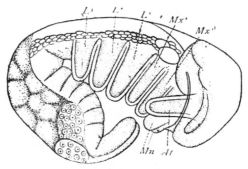

Fig. 21.—Embryo of Aphis.   Copied from Mecznikow, Zeits. f. wiss. Zool.,
Bd. XVI., taf. xxx., fig. 30.   References in text.   × 220.

egg. The rudiments of the antennæ (At), mandibles (Mn), and maxillæ (Mx^1, Mx^2) form simple blunt projections, similar to each other and to the future thoracic legs (L^1, L^2, L^3). We see, therefore, that all the appendages of an Insect are similar in an early stage of growth ; and we may add that a Centipede, a Scorpion, or a Spider would present very nearly the same appearance in the same stage. A Crustacean in the egg would not resemble an Insect or its own parent so closely.* Aquatic life favours metamorphosis, and most Crustacea do not begin life with their full quota of legs, but acquire them as they are wanted.

Paired appendages of perfectly simple form are therefore the first stage through which all Insect-jaws must pass. Our second stage is a little more complex, and not nearly so universal as the first. A caterpillar (fig. 22) has its own special wants, and these are met by the unequal development of its jaws. The mandibles are already as complete as those of the Cockroach, which they

* Freshwater Crustacea, however, are sometimes similar to their parents at the time of hatching.

closely resemble, but the maxillæ are stunted cylinders formed mainly of simple rings, and very like the antennæ. They show, however, the beginnings of three processes (palp, galea, and lacinia), which are usually conspicuous in well-developed maxillæ. The second pair of maxillæ (*Lm*) are coalesced, as usual, and

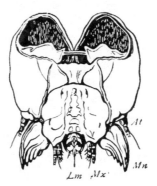

Fig. 22.—Head of larva of Goat Moth, seen from behind.
Copied from Lyonnet.

form the spinneret. The mouth-parts of the Caterpillar do not therefore in all respects represent a universal stage of development, but show important adaptive modifications. The mandibles are rapidly pushed forward, and attain their full development in the larva : the first pair of maxillæ are temporarily arrested in their growth, and persist for a long time in a condition which Orthopterous embryos quickly pass through ; the maxillæ of the second pair are not only arrested in their growth, but converted to a special use, which seems to stop all further progress. The labial palps, indeed, which are not at all developed in the caterpillar, survive, and become important parts in the moth ; but the greater part of the labium disappears when the time for spinning the coccoon is over.

We come next to the Orthopterous mouth, which is well illustrated by the Cockroach. This is retained with little modification in all the biting Insects (Coleoptera and Neuroptera). The mandibles may become long and pointed, as in *Staphylinus* and other predatory forms ; in some larvæ of strong carnivorous propensities (Ant-lion, *Dytiscus*,* *Chrysopa*) they are perforate at

* In *Dytiscus* the mandibles are perforate at the base, and not at the tip. See Burgess in Proc. Bost. Soc. Nat. Hist., Vol. XXI., p. 223.

E

the tip, and through them the juices of the prey are sucked into
the mouth, which has no other opening. The labium undergoes
marked adaptive change, without great deviation from the common plan, in the "mask" of the larva of the Dragon-fly. This
well-known implement has a rough likeness, in the arrangement
and use of its parts, to a man's fore-limb. The submentum
forms the arm, the mentum the fore-arm. Both these are
simple, straight pieces, connected by an elbow-joint. The hand
is wider, and carries a pair of opposable claws, the paraglossæ.
In some Coleoptera the labium is reduced to a stiff spine, while
in the Stag-beetle it is flexible and hairy, and foreshadows the
licking tongue of the Bee. The maxillæ become long and hairy
in flower-haunting Beetles, and even the mandibles are flexible
and hairy in the Scarabæus-beetles. Fritz Müller has found a
singular resemblance to the proboscis of a Moth in a species of
Nemognatha, where the maxillæ are transformed into two sharp
grooved bristles 12 mm. long, which, when opposed, form a
tube, but are incapable of rolling up.*

In the Honey Bee (fig. 23) nearly all the mouth-parts of the
Cockroach are to be made out, though some are small and others
extremely produced in length. The mandibles (*Mn*) are not
much altered, and are still used for biting, as well as for knead-
ing wax and other domestic work. The mandibular teeth have
proved inconvenient, and are gone. The lacinia of the maxilla
(*Mx¹*) forms a broad and flexible blade, used for piercing succu-
lent tissues, but the galea has disappeared, and there is only a
vestige of the maxillary palp (*Mxp*). In the second pair of
maxillæ the palp (*Lp*) is prominent; its base forms a blade,
while the tip is still useful as an organ of touch. The paraglossæ (*Pa*) can be made out, but the laciniæ are fused to form
the long, hairy tongue. This ends in a spoon-shaped lobe (not
unlike the "finger" of an elephant's trunk), which is used both
for licking and for sucking honey.

The proboscis of the Bee is therefore more like a case of
instruments than a single organ. The mandibles form a strong
pair of blunt scissors. The maxillæ are used for piercing, for
stiffening and protecting the base of the tongue, and when

* Ein Käfer mit Schmetterlingsrüssel, Kosmos, Bd. VI. We take this reference
from Hermann Müller's Fertilisation of Flowers.

closed they form an imperfect tube outside the tongue, which, according to Hermann Müller, is probably suctorial. The labial palps are protective and sensory. Lastly, the central part, or tongue, is a split tube used for suction ; it is very long, so as to

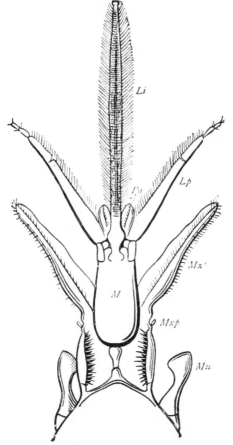

Fig. 23.—Mouth-parts of Honey Bee.

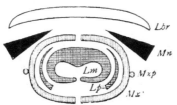

Fig. 23A.—Diagram of Mouth-parts of Honey Bee.

penetrate deep flower-cups, and hairy, so that pollen may stick
to it. When the proboscis is not in use it can be slid into the
mentum (*M*), while it and the mentum together can be drawn
out of the way downwards and backwards.*

In the singular suctorial mouth of Moths and Butterflies we
observe, first of all, the great development of the maxillæ.

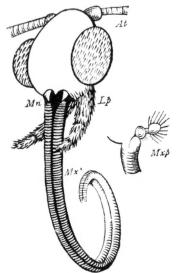

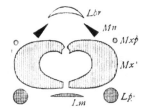

Fig. 24.—Mouth-parts of Burnet Moth.   Fig. 24A.—Diagram of Mouth-parts
                                                         of Moth.

Each forms a half-tube, which can be accurately applied to its
fellow, so as to form an efficient siphon. In many species the
two halves can be held together by a multitude of minute
hooks.† At the base of each maxilla is a rudimentary palp
(*Mxp*). The mandibles (*Mn*) are also rudimentary and perfectly
useless. The labium, which was so important to the larva as a
spinneret, has disappeared almost completely, but the labial
palps (*Lp*) are large and evidently important.

* An interesting account of the structure and mode of action of the Bee's tongue
is to be found in Hermann Müller's Fertilisation of Flowers, where also the evolu-
tion of the parts is traced through a series of graduated types.

† See Newport's figure of Vanessa atalanta (Todd's Cyc., Art. Insecta), or Burgess
on the Anatomy of the Milk-weed Butterfly, in Anniversary Mem. of Boston Soc.
Nat. Hist., pl. ii., figs. 8–10 (1880).

ITS OUTER SKELETON. 53

In Diptera both piercing and sucking parts are usually present. The mouth-parts of a Gad-fly (fig. 25) are typically developed. Here we recognise the labrum (*Lbr*)-mandibles (*Mn*), typical maxilla (*Mx*), of the Cockroach transformed into stylets. The maxillary palp (*Mxp*) is still well-developed from the back of the labrum. This is the

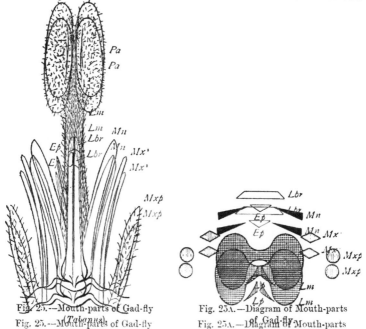

Fig. 25.—Mouth-parts of Gad-fly (*Tabanus*).

Fig. 25A.—Diagram of Mouth-parts of Gad-fly.

epipharynx (*Ep*), a process undeveloped in the Cockroach, though conspicuous in some Coleoptera. All these parts are thread-like spicules suited to piercing (*Lm*), which are parts to do so by expansion at the oral labium. In the more specialised Diptera this becomes a kind of cupping-glass. The Gad-fly is one of this less obscure kind of Gnat; and like the Gad-fly parts are numerous, piercing organs which ordinarily lengthen and sharpness, and spiders, as the House-fly did. But in length there sharpness and such firmness though House-fly most elaborate kind, the piercing organs undergoing a marked reduction rate. Except that the teeth in labium is sharper is double and triple-hinged, so that it can be readily tucked away under the chin.

In Hemiptera the long four-jointed labium (*Lm*) forms a
sheath for the stylets. When not in use the whole apparatus
is drawn up beneath the head and prothorax. The mandibles
(*Mn*) are sharp at the tip, and close like a pair of forceps, enclosing the maxillæ (*Mx*). These are of unequal length, only
one reaching the end of the mandibular case. Both have saw
teeth on the free edge. Palps are entirely wanting.

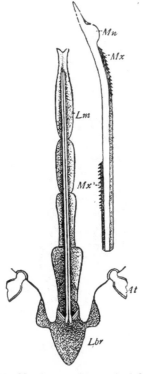

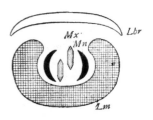

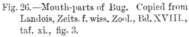

Fig. 26.—Mouth-parts of Bug. Copied from
    Landois, Zeits. f. wiss. Zool., Bd. XVIII.,
    taf. xi., fig. 3.

Fig. 26A.—Diagram of Mouth-parts
    of Bug.

Comparing the four kinds of suctorial mouths, of which the
Bee, the Moth, the Fly, and the Bug furnish examples, we
observe that the sucking-tube is formed in the Moth out of the
two maxillæ, in the other three out of the labium. Of these
last the Bee has the edges of the labium turned *down*, so that
the siphon becomes *ventral* ; in the Bug and Fly the edges

are turned *up*, and the siphon becomes *dorsal*. The more specialised flies have the simple arrangement of the Bug complicated by a system of branching tubes, which are probably a special modification of the salivary duct. Similar as the mouth-parts of the four types may be in regard to their mode of working, they cannot be reduced to any common plan which differs materially from that presented by the jaws of the Cockroach.

Composition of Head.

In all Insects fusion of the primitive elements of the head begins so early and is carried so far, that it is extremely difficult to discover the precise way in which they are fitted together. The following facts have been ascertained respecting the development of the parts in question. At a very early stage of embryonic life the body of the Insect becomes divided into a series of segments, which are at fewest fourteen (in some Diptera), while they are not known to exceed seventeen.* Each segment is normally provided with a pair of appendages. The foremost segment soon enlarges beyond the rest, and becomes divided by a median groove into two "procephalic lobes."† Of the appendages the first eight pairs are usually more prominent than the rest, and of different form; those of the eighth segment, which may be altogether inconspicuous, never attain any functional importance. The first four pairs of appendages are budded off from the future head, while the next three pairs form the walking legs, and are carried upon the thoracic segments. All the existing appendages of the fore part of the body are thus accounted for, but the exact mode of formation of the head has not yet been made out. The chief part of its walls, including the clypeus, the compound eyes, and the epicranial plates, arise from the procephalic lobes, and represent the much altered segment of which the antennæ are the appendages. The labrum is a secondary outgrowth from this segment, and, in some cases at least, it originates as a pair of processes which resemble true

---

* Balfour, Embryology, Vol. I., p. 337.

† Huxley, Med. Times and Gazette, 1856-7 ; Linn. Trans., Vol. XXII., p. 221, and pl. 38 (1858).

appendages, though it is unlikely that such is their real
character. No means at present exist for identifying the terga
and sterna of the head, nor have the gena, the occipital frame,
and the cervical sclerites (described below) been assigned to
their segments.* It is worthy of notice that in the stalk-eyed
Crustacea, the head, or what corresponds to the head of Insecta,
consists of either five or six somites, taking into account a
diversity of opinion with respect to the eyestalks, while only
four pairs of appendages can be certainly traced in the head of
the Insect. The mandibles and maxillæ exist to the same
number in both groups, and are homologous organs, so far as is
known; the numerical difference relates therefore to the antennæ,
of which the Crustacean possesses two pairs, the Insect only
one. Whether the pair deficient in the Insect is altogether
undeveloped, or represented by the pair of prominences which
give rise to the labrum,† is a question of much theoretical
interest and of not a little difficulty.

The following table shows the appendages of the head and
thorax in the two classes. The homologies indicated are, however, by no means established.‡

CRAYFISH.	COCKROACH.
	Antennæ.
Eyestalks.	
Antennules.	
Antennæ.	
Mandibles.	Mandibles.
Maxillæ (1).	Maxillæ (1).
Maxillæ (2).	Maxillæ (2).
Maxillipeds (1).	Thoracic Legs (1).
Maxillipeds (2).	Thoracic Legs (2).
Maxillipeds (3).	Thoracic Legs (3).

* " I think it is probable that these cervical sclerites represent the hindermost of
the cephalic somites, while the band with which the maxillæ are united, and the
genæ, are all that is left of the sides and roof of the first maxillary and the mandibular somites."—Huxley, Anat. Invert. Animals, p. 403.

† Balfour, Embryology, Vol. I., note to p. 337.

‡ J. S. Kingsley in Q. J. Micr. Sci. (1885), has reviewed the homology of Insect,
Arachnid, and Crustacean appendages, and comes to conclusions very different from

Neck.

The neck is a narrow cylindrical tube, with a flexible wall strengthened by eight plates, the cervical sclerites, two of which are dorsal, two ventral, and four lateral. The dorsal sclerites lie immediately behind the head (fig. 14) ; they are triangular, and closely approximated to the middle line. The inferior plates (fig. 27) resemble segments of chitinous hoops set transversely, one behind the other, rather behind the dorsal sclerites, and close behind the submentum. There are two lateral sclerites on each side of the neck (fig. 27), a lower squarish one, which is set diagonally, nearly meeting its fellow across the ventral surface, and an oblong piece, closely adherent to the other, which extends forwards and upwards towards the dorsal side.

Thorax.

The elements of the thoracic exoskeleton are simpler in the Cockroach than in Insects of powerful flight, where adaptive changes greatly obscure the primitive arrangement. There are three segments, each defended by a dorsal plate (*tergum*) and a ventral plate (*sternum*). The sterna are often divided into lateral halves. Of the three terga the first (*pronotum*) is the largest ; it has a wide free edge on each side, projects forwards over the neck, and when the head is retracted, covers this also, its semi-circular fore-edge then forming the apparent head-end of the animal. The two succeeding terga are of nearly equal size, and each is much shorter than the pronotum, contrary to the rule in winged Insects.*

those hitherto accepted. He classifies the appendages as pre-oral (Insect-antennæ) and post-oral, and makes the following comparisons :—

HEXAPODA.	ACERATA.	CRUSTACEA.
(= Insecta + Myriopoda?)	(= Arachnida + Limulus.)	
(1) Antennæ.	Absent.	Absent.
(2) Mandibles.	Cheliceræ.	Antennules.
(3) Maxillæ.	Pedipalpi.	Antennæ.
(4) Labium.	1st pair legs.	Mandibles.
(5) 1st pair legs.	2nd pair legs.	1st Maxillæ.
(6) 2nd pair legs.	3rd pair legs.	2nd Maxillæ.
(7) 3rd pair legs.	4th pair legs.	1st Maxillipeds.

Pelseneer (Q. J. Micr. Sci., 1885), concludes that both pairs of antennæ are post-oral in *Apus*, and probably in all other Crustacea.

* Many Orthoptera, which seize their prey with the fore legs, have a very long pronotum.

All the terga are dense and opaque in the female; in the
male the middle one (*mesonotum*) and the hindmost (*metanotum*) are thin and semi-transparent, being ordinarily overlaid
by the wing-covers. While the thoracic terga diminish backwards, the sterna increase in extent and firmness, proportionally
to the size of the attached legs. The prosternum is small and
coffin-shaped ; the mesosternum partly divided into lateral
halves in the male, and completely so in the female. The
metasternum is completely divided in both sexes, while a
median piece, carrying the post-furca, intervenes between its
lateral halves in the male. Behind the sterna, especially in the

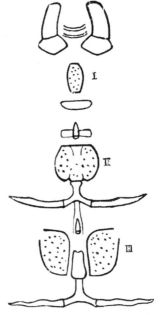

Fig. 27.—Ventral Plates of Neck and Thorax of Male Cockroach.
I, prosternum; II, mesosternum; III, metasternum.   × 6.

case of the second and third, the flexible under-surface of the
thorax is inclined, so as to form a nearly vertical step. In the
two hinder of these steps a chitinous prop is fixed ; each is
Y-shaped, with long, curved arms for muscular attachment, and
a central notch, which supports the nerve-cord. The hindmost of these, known as the *post-furca*, lies immediately behind

the metasternum, and its short basal piece is attached between the lateral halves of that plate. Behind the mesosternum is a somewhat slighter prop, the *medi-furca*. A third piece of similar nature (the *ante-furca*), which is well developed in some Insects— *e.g.*, in Ants—is apparently wanting in the Cockroach, though there is a transverse oval plate behind the prosternum, which may be a rudimentary furca.

Fig. 27 shows two conical processes which lie in the middle line of the ventral surface of the thorax, one in front of the metasternum, the other in front of the mesosternum. These are the thoracic pits, tubular apodemata, serving for the insertion of muscles. The occurrence of stink-glands in the thorax of Hemiptera,* and of so-called poison-glands in the thorax of *Solpuga*, led us to look for glands in connection with these processes, but we have found none.

Thoracic Appendages. Legs; Wings.

Three pairs of legs are attached to the thoracic segments; they regularly increase in size from the first to the third, but hardly differ except in size; the peculiar modifications which affect the fore pair in predatory and burrowing Orthoptera (*Mantis, Gryllotalpa*), and the third pair in leaping Orthoptera (Grasshoppers, &c.), being absent in the cursorial Blattina. Each leg is divided into the five segments usual in Insects (see fig. 28). The coxa is broad and flattened. The trochanter is a small piece obliquely and almost immovably attached to the proximal end of the femur, on its inner side. The femur is nearly straight and narrowed at both ends; along its inner border, in the position occupied by the stridulating apparatus of the hind leg of the Grasshoppers, is a shallow longitudinal groove, fringed by stiff bristles. The tibia is shorter than the femur in the fore leg, of nearly the same length in the middle leg, and longer in the hind leg; it is armed with numerous stiff spines directed towards the free end of the limb. There are usually reckoned five joints in the tarsus, which regularly diminish in length, except that the last joint is as long as the second. All the

* Also in *Phasmidæ* (see Scudder, Psyche, Vol. I., p. 137).

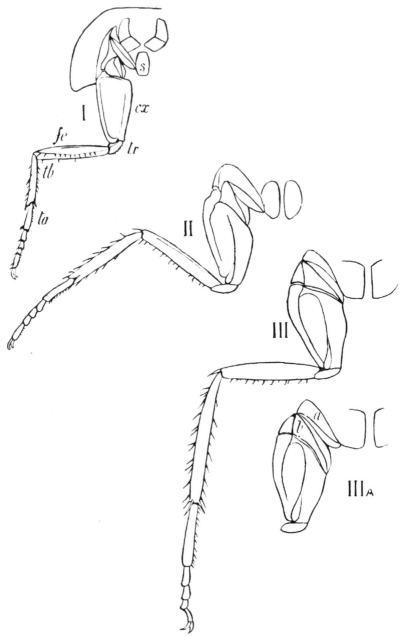

Fig. 28.—The three Thoracic Legs of a Female Cockroach. I, s, sternum ; cx, coxa ;
tr, trochanter ; fe, femur ; tb, tibia ; ta, tarsus.   In IIIA the coxa is
abducted, and the joints a (episternum) and b slightly separated.   × 4.

joints bear numerous fine but stiff hairs upon the walking surface. The extremity of the fifth joint is segmented off, and carries a pair of equal and strongly curved claws.*

At the base of each leg are several chitinous plates (fig. 28), upon which no small labour has been bestowed by different anatomists. They are arranged so as to form two joints intermediate between the coxa and the sternum, and these two joints admit of a hinge-like movement upon each other, while their other ends are firmly attached to the coxa and sternum respectively. (Compare III and IIIA, fig. 28.) These parts in the Cockroach may be taken for two basal leg-joints which have become adherent to the thorax. In other cases, however, they plainly belong to the thorax, and not to the leg. In the Molecricket, for instance, similar plates occur ; but here they are firmly united, and form the lateral wall of the thorax. In the Locust they become vertical, and lie one in front of the other. Most authors have looked upon them as regular elements of a typical somite. They regard such a segment as including two pleural elements—viz., a dorsal plate (*epimeron*), and a ventral plate (*episternum*). We have already (p. 34) given reasons for doubting the constancy of the pieces so named. It is not inconvenient, however, to denote by the term *episternum* the joint which abuts upon the sternum; for the joint which is applied to the coxa no convenient term exists, and its occurrence in Insects is so partial, that the want need not be supplied at present.† Both joints are incompletely subdivided. In the first thoracic segment of the Cockroach they are less firmly connected than in the other two.

Cockroaches of both sexes are provided with wings, which, however, are only functional in the male. The wing-covers (or anterior pair of wings) of the male are carried by the second thoracic segment. As in most *Orthoptera genuina*, they are denser than the hind wings, and protect them when at rest. They reach to the fifth segment of the abdomen, and one

---

* Professor Huxley (Anat. Invert. Animals, p. 404) points out that the so-called *pulvillus* ought to be counted as a sixth joint. The same is true of the foot of Diptera and Hymenoptera, where there are six tarsal joints, the last carrying the claws. (Tuffen West on the Foot of the Fly. Linn. Trans., Vol. XXIII.)

† The nomenclature adopted by Packard (Third Report of U.S. Entomological Commission) seems to us open to theoretical objections.

wing-cover overlaps the other. Branching veins or nervures
form a characteristic pattern upon the surface (figs. 4, 29), and
it is mainly by means of this pattern that many of the fossil
species are identified and distinguished. The true or posterior
wings are attached to the metathorax. They are membranous
and flexible, but the fore-edge is stiffened, like that of the wing-
covers, by additional chitinous deposit. When extended, each
wing forms an irregular quadrant of a circle ; when at rest, the
radiating furrows of the hinder part close up fan-wise, and the
inner half is folded beneath the outer.* The wing reaches back
as far as the hinder end of the fourth abdominal segment. The
wing-covers of the female are small, and though movable, seem
never to be voluntarily extended ; each covers about one-third
of the width of the mesonotum, and extends backwards to the

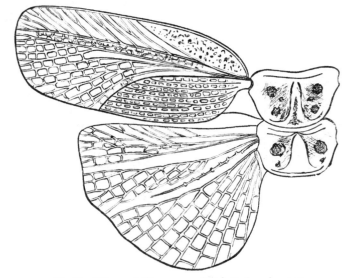

Fig. 29.—Wings and Wing-covers of Male Cockroach.   × 4.

middle of the metanotum. A reticulated pattern on the outer
fourth of the metanotum plainly represents the hind wing ; it
is clearly rather a degeneration or survival than an anticipation
of an organ tending towards useful completeness.

* On wing-plaiting and wing-folding in Blattariæ see Saussure, Etudes sur l'aile
des Orthoptères.   Ann. Sci. Nat., Sér. 5e (Zool.), Tom. X.

The rudimentary wing of the female Cockroach illustrates the homology of the wings of Insects with the free edges of thoracic terga, and this correspondence is enforced by the study of the development of the more complete wings and wing-covers of the male. The hinder edges of the terga become produced at the later moults preceding the completely winged stage, and may even assume something of the shape and pattern of true wings; it is not, however, true, though more than once stated, that winged nymphs are common. Adults with imperfectly developed wings have been mistaken for such.

Origin of Insect Wings.

The structure of the wing testifies to its origin as a fold of the chitinous integument. It is a double lamina, which often encloses a visible space at its base. The nervures, with their vessels and tracheal tubes, lie between the two layers, which, except at the base, are in close contact. Oken termed the wings of an Insect "aerial gills," and this rather fanciful designation is in some degree justified by their resemblance to the tracheal gills of such aquatic larvæ as those of Ephemeridæ, Perlidæ, Phryganidæ, &c. In the larva of *Chloeon (Ephemera) dipterum* (fig. 30), for example, the second thoracic segment carries a pair of large expansions, which ultimately are replaced by organs of aerial flight. The abdominal segments carry similarly placed respiratory leaflets, the tracheal gills, which by their vigorous flapping movements bring a rush of water against their membranous and tracheated surfaces.

Gegenbaur[*] has argued from the resemblance of these appendages to wings, that the wing and the tracheal leaflet are homologous parts, and this view has been accepted as probable by so competent an observer as Sir John Lubbock.[†]

The leaflets placed most advantageously for propulsion seem to have become exclusively adapted to that end, while the abdominal gills have retained their respiratory character. At the time of change from aquatic to terrestrial life, which takes place in many common Insects when the adult condition is

---

[*] Grundzüge der Vergl. Anat. (Arthropoden, Athmungsorgane.)

[†] Origin and Metamorphoses of Insects, p. 73.

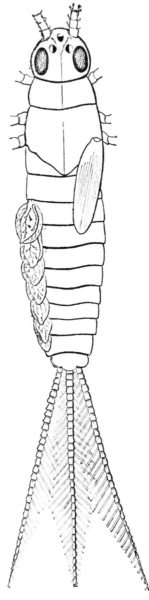

Fig. 30.   Chloeon (Chloeopsis) dipterum.   Larva in eighth stage, with wings
and respiratory leaflets.   × 14.   Copied from Vayssière (loc. cit.).

assumed, and which, according to Gegenbaur, was a normal event among primitive Insects, the tracheal gill is supposed to disappear, and in its place, at the next moult, an opening, the stigma, is formed by the rupture of an air-tube. Gegenbaur supposes that the primitive Insects were aquatic, and their tracheal system closed. The tracheal gill he takes to be the common structure which has yielded organs so unlike as the wing and the stigma.

The zoological rank of the Insects (Ephemeridæ, Perlidæ, and Libellulidæ), in which tracheal gills are most usual, is not unfavourable to such an explanation. Lubbock has given reasons for regarding *Campodea* and the Collembola (of the order Thysanura) as surviving and not very much altered representatives of the most primitive Insects, and he has shown that no great amount of modification would be required to convert the terrestrial *Campodea* into the aquatic *Chloëon*-nymph.[*] We must not forget, however, that tracheal gills are by no means restricted to these families of low grade. Trichoptera, a few Diptera, two Lepidoptera (*Nymphula* and *Acentropus*), and two Coleoptera (*Gyrinus* and *Elmis*),[†] have tracheal gills, and a closed tracheal system in the larval condition. We cannot suppose that these larvæ of higher orders represent an unbroken succession of aquatic forms, but if we refuse to adopt this alternative, we must admit that the closed tracheal system with tracheal gills may be an adaptive modification of the open system with stigmata.

It is well known[‡] that in certain Ephemeridæ (*e.g.*, *Tricorythus* and *Cænis*) a pair of anterior tracheal gills may become transformed into large plates, which partly protect the gills behind (fig. 31). A similar modification of the second and third thoracic gills in *Prosopistoma* and *Bætisca* brings all the functional respiratory organs under cover, and these enlarged plates resemble stiff and simple wings very closely.

---

[*] Palmén cites one striking proof of the low position of Ephemeridæ among Insects. Their reproductive outlets are paired and separate, as in Worms and Crustacea.

[†] These examples are cited by Palmén.

[‡] Eaton, Trans. Ent. Soc., 1868, p. 281 ; Vayssière, Ann. Sci. Nat., Zool., 1882, p. 91.

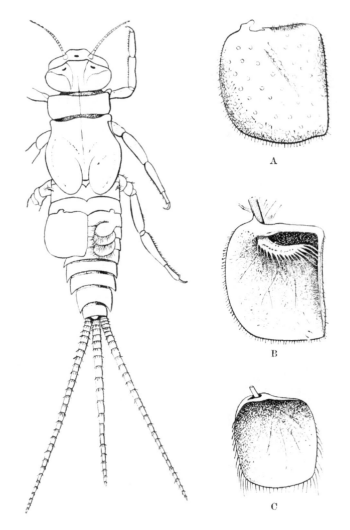

Fig. 31.—Tricorythus. Adult larva, with three functional leaflets. The next leaflet in front is converted into a protective plate. × 7.

A, protective plate of Tricorythus larva, seen from the outside. × 26. B, the same from within, showing the attached respiratory appendage. C, protective plate of Cœnis larva, without respiratory appendage.

All the figures are copied from Vayssière.

Palmén* has subjected Gegenbaur's hypothesis to a very searching examination. He observes that :—

1. In *Campodea*, and presumably in other primitive Insects, the tracheal system is not closed and adapted for aquatic respiration, but open. Tracheal gills are not by any means confined to the lowest Insects. (See above, p. 65.)

2. Tracheal gills are not always homodynamous or morphologically equivalent. In Ephemeridæ, some are dorsal in position, some ventral (first abdominal pair in *Oligoneuria* and *Rhithrogena*) ; they may be cephalic, springing from the base of the maxilla, as in *Oligoneuria* and *Jolia* ; *Jolia* has a branchial tuft at the insertion of each of the fore legs.† In Perlidæ the tracheal gills may have a tergal, pleural, sternal, or anal insertion. In some Libellulidæ also, anal leaflets occur.‡

3. Tracheal gills never perfectly agree in position and number with the stigmata throughout the body. Sometimes they occur on different rings, sometimes on different parts of the same ring. Gegenbaur's statements on this point are incorrect.

4. Tracheal gills may co-exist with stigmata. In Perlidæ the tracheal gills persist in the imago, and may be found, dry and functionless, beneath the stigmata. In Trichoptera they gradually abort at successive moults, and in some cases remain after the stigmata have opened.

5. Stigmata do not form by the breaking off of tracheal appendages, but by the enlargement of rudimentary tracheal

* Zur Morphologie des Tracheensystems (1877).

† We take these instances from Eaton, Monograph of Ephemeridæ, Linn. Trans., 1883, p. 15.

‡ Charles Brougniart has lately described a fossil Insect from the Coal Measures of Commentry, which he names *Corydaloides Scudderi*, and refers to the Pseudo-Neuroptera. In this Insect every ring of the abdomen carries laminæ, upon which the ramified tracheæ can still be made out by the naked eye. Stigmata co-existed with these tracheal gills. (Bull. Soc. Sci. Nat. de Rouen, 1885.)

Some Crustacea are furnished with respiratory leaflets, curiously like those of Tracheates, with which, however, they have no genetic connection. In Isopod Crustacea the exopodites of the anterior abdominal segments often form opercula, which protect the succeeding limbs. In the terrestrial Isopods, *Porcellio* and *Armadillo*, these opercula contain ramified air-tubes, which open externally, and much resemble tracheæ. The anterior abdominal appendages of *Tylus* are provided with air-chambers, each lodging brush-like bundles of air-tubes, which open to the outer air. Lamellæ, projecting inwards from the sides of the abdominal segments, incompletely cover in the hinder part of the ventral surface of the abdomen, and protect the modified appendages. (Milne Edwards, Hist. Nat. des Crustacés, Vol. III.)

branches, which open into the main longitudinal trunks. In larvæ with aquatic respiration these branches exist, though they are not functional.

Palmén's objections must be satisfactorily disposed of before Gegenbaur's explanation, interesting as it is, can be fully accepted. Palmén has proved, what is on other grounds clear enough, that stigmata are more ancient than tracheal gills, aerial tracheate respiration than aquatic. But there is nothing as yet to contradict the view that the first Insect-wings were adapted for propulsion in water, and that they were respiratory organs before they became motor. It is Gegenbaur's explanation of the origin of stigmata, and not his explanation of the origin of wings, which is refuted by Palmén.

Abdomen.

In the abdomen of the female Cockroach eight terga (1–7 ; 10) are externally visible. Two more (8, 9) are readily displayed by extending the abdomen ; they are ordinarily concealed beneath the seventh tergum. The tenth tergum is notched in the middle of its posterior margin. A pair of triangular "podical plates," which lie on either side of the anus, and towards the dorsal surface, have been provisionally regarded by Prof. Huxley as the terga of an eleventh segment. Seven abdominal sterna (1–7) are externally visible. The first is quite rudimentary, and consists of a transversely oval plate ; the second is irregular and imperfectly chitinised in front ; the seventh is large, and its hinder part, which is boat-shaped, is divided into lateral halves, for facilitating the discharge of the large egg-capsule.

In the male Cockroach ten abdominal terga are visible without dissection (fig. 33, p. 70), though the eighth and ninth are greatly overlapped by the seventh. The tenth tergum is hardly notched. Nine abdominal sterna are readily made out, the first being rudimentary, as in the female. The eighth is narrower than the seventh, the ninth still narrower, and largely concealed by the eighth ; its covered anterior part is thin and transparent, the exposed part denser. This forms the extreme end of the body, except that the small sub-anal styles project beyond it. The podical plates resemble those of the female.

Pleural elements are developed in the form of narrow stigmatic plates, with the free edge directed backwards. These lie between the terga and sterna, and defend the spiracle.*

The modifications of the hindmost abdominal segments will be more fully considered in connection with the reproductive organs.

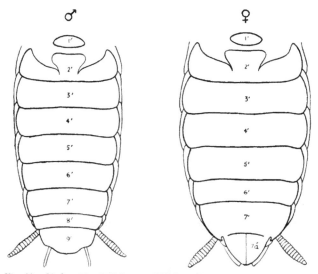

Fig. 32.—Under side of Abdomen of Male and Female Cockroach. × 4.

The high number of abdominal segments found in the Cockroach (ten or eleven) is characteristic of the lower orders of Insecta. It is never exceeded; though in the more specialised orders, such as Lepidoptera and Diptera, it may be reduced to nine, eight, or even seven. The sessile abdomen of the Cockroach is primitive with respect to the pedunculate abdomen found in such insects as Hymenoptera, where the constricted and flexible waist stands in obvious relation to the operations of stinging and boring, or to peculiar modes of oviposition. The first abdominal segment, which is especially liable to dislocation and alteration in Insects, occupies its theoretical position in the Cockroach, though both tergum and sternum

* Gerstaecker has found in the two first abdominal segments of *Corydia carunculigera* (*Blattariæ*) pleural appendages, which are hollow and capable of protrusion. They have no relation to the stigmata, which are present in the same segments, and their function is quite unknown. See Arch. f. Naturg., 1861, p. 107.

are reduced in size. The sternum is often altogether wanting, while the tergum may unite with the metathorax.

The externally visible appendages of the abdomen are the cerci and the styles of the male Cockroach. The cerci are found in both sexes; they are composed of sixteen rings each, and project beneath the edge of the tenth tergum. They are capable of erection by special muscles, and are supplied by large nerves.* The sub-anal styles are peculiar in their insertion, being carried upon the sternum of their segment (the ninth).

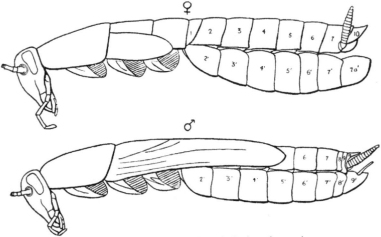

Fig. 33.—Profile of Male and Female Cockroach.   × 4.

The abdominal segments are never furnished with functional legs in adult Insects, but representatives of the lost appendages are often met with in larvæ. According to Bütschli,† all the abdominal segments are provided with appendages in the embryo of the Bee, though they disappear completely before hatching. Some Hymenopterous larvæ have as many as eight pairs of abdominal appendages, Lepidopterous larvæ at most five (3-6 ; 10).‡

* Jointed cerci are commonly found in Orthoptera (including Pseudo-Neuroptera); in the Earwig they become modified and form the forceps. The "caudal filaments" of *Apus* are curiously like cerci.

The cerci are concealed in the American *Cryptocercus*, Scudd. (Fam. *Panesthidæ*).

† Entw. der Biene. Zeits. f. wiss. Zool. Bd. XX. Or, see Balfour's Embryology, Vol. I., p. 338.

‡ From more recent observations it is probable that abdominal appendages are usually present in the embryos of Orthoptera, Coleoptera, Lepidoptera, and possibly Hymenoptera. The subject is rapidly advancing, and more will be known very shortly.

CHAPTER V.

The Muscles; the Fat-Body and Cœlom.

SPECIAL REFERENCES.

Viallanes. Histologie et Développement des Insectes. Ann. Sci. Nat., Zool., Tom. XIV. (1882).

Kühne in Stricker's Histology, Vol. I., chap. v.

Plateau. Various Memoirs in Bull. Acad. Roy. de Belgique (1865, 1866, 1883, 1884). [Relative and Absolute Muscular Force.]

Leydig. Zum feineren Bau der Arthropoden. Müller's Archiv., 1855.

Weismann. Ueber zwei Typen contractilen Gewebes, &c. Zeits. für ration. Medicin. Bd. XV. (1862).

Structure of Insect Muscles.

The muscles of the Cockroach, when quite fresh, appear semi-transparent and colourless. If subjected to pressure or strain they are found to be extremely tender. Alcohol hardens and contracts them, while it renders them opaque and brittle.

The minute structure of the voluntary or striped muscular fibres of Vertebrates is described in common text-books.* Each fibre is invested by a transparent elastic sheath, the sarcolemma, and the space within the sarcolemma is subdivided by transverse membranes into a series of compartments. The compartments are nearly filled by as many contractile discs, broad, doubly refractive plates, which are further divisible into prismatic columns, the sarcous elements, each being as long as the contractile disc. Successive sarcous elements, continued from one compartment to another, form the primitive fibrils of the muscle. In cross-section the fibrils appear as polygonal areas bounded by bright lines. Outside the fibres, but within the sarcolemma, are nuclei, imbedded in the protoplasm, or living and formative element of the tissue.

---

* See, for example, Klein's Elements of Histology, chap. ix.

The muscular fibres of Insects present some important differences from the fibres just described. The nuclei are often found in the centre, and not on the surface of the fibres in both Insects and Crustacea. In both classes the fibrils are frequently subdivided into longitudinal strands, which have not been distinguished in Vertebrate muscles (Viallanes). The sarcolemma is often undeveloped. Lastly, Insects, like other Arthropoda, exhibit the remarkable peculiarity that not only their voluntary muscles, but all, or nearly all, the muscles of the body, even those of the digestive tube, are striated.*

General Arrangement of Insect Muscles.

The arrangement of the muscles in an Insect varies greatly according to situation and mode of action. Some of the abdominal muscles consist solely of straight parallel bundles, while the muscles of the limbs usually converge to tendinous insertions. In certain larvæ, where the segments show hardly any differentiation, the muscles form a sheet which covers the whole body, and is regularly segmented in correspondence with the exo-skeleton. As the movements of the body and limbs become more varied and more energetic, the muscles become grouped in a more complicated fashion, and the legs and wings of a flying Insect may be set in motion by a muscular apparatus almost as elaborate as that of a bird.

Muscles of the Cockroach.

The following short notes on the muscles of the Cockroach, aided by reference to the figures, will render the more noteworthy features intelligible. A very lengthy description, far beyond our space or the reader's patience, would be required to explain in detail the musculature of the head, limbs, and other specialised regions.

STERNAL MUSCLES OF ABDOMEN.—The *longitudinal sternal muscles* (fig. 34) form a nearly continuous transversely seg-

---

* The exceptions relate chiefly to the alary muscles of the pericardial septum. Lowne (Blow-fly, p. 5, and pl. v.) states that some of the thoracic muscles of that Insect are not striated.

mented sheet, covering the ventral surface between the fore-edge of the second abdominal sternum and the fore-edge of the seventh. These muscles, in conjunction with the longitudinal tergal muscles, tend to telescope the segments.

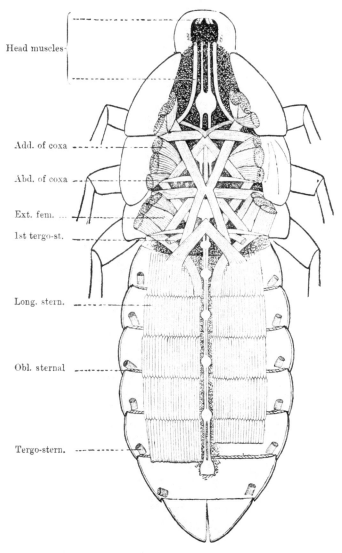

Fig. 34.—Muscles of Ventral Wall, with the Nerve-cord.   × 5.

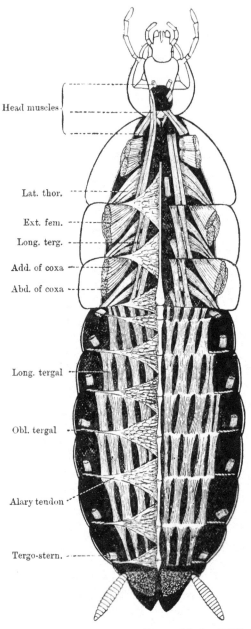

Fig. 35.—Muscles of Dorsal Wall, with the Heart and Pericardial Tendons.   × 5.

The *oblique sternal muscles* (fig. 34), which are very short, connect the adjacent edges of the sterna (2-3, 3-4, 4-5, 5-6, 6-7). They extend inwards nearly to the middle line, but, like the longitudinal sternal muscles, they are not developed beneath the nerve-cord. Acting together, the oblique sternal muscles would antagonise the longitudinal, but it is probable that they are chiefly used to effect lateral flexion of the abdomen, and that only the muscles of one side of the abdomen contract at once.

The *tergo-sternal* (or expiratory) muscles (figs. 35 and 36) form vertical pairs passing from the outer part of each abdominal sternum to the corresponding tergum. Their action is to approximate the dorsal and ventral walls, and thus to reduce the capacity of the abdomen. The first tergo-sternal muscle has its ventral insertion into the stem of the postfurca, and takes an oblique course to the first abdominal tergum.

TERGAL MUSCLES OF ABDOMEN.—The *longitudinal tergal* muscles extend from the fore part of each abdominal tergum, including the first, to the same part of the tergum next behind. They are interrupted by longitudinal spaces, so that the muscular sheet is less continuous than on the ventral surface, and has a fenestrated appearance. The direction of the fibres is slightly oblique.

Oblique tergal muscles, resembling the oblique muscles of the sterna, are also present.

In the thorax the general arrangement of the muscles is greatly modified by the altered form of the dorsal and ventral plates, and by the attachment of powerful limbs.

STERNAL MUSCLES OF THORAX.—Two tubular apodemes, lying one behind the other, project into the thorax from the ventral surface (p. 59 and fig. 27). To the foremost of these are attached three paired muscles and one median muscle. The median muscle passes to the second tubular apodeme. The anterior pair pass forwards and outwards to the base of the prothoracic leg; the next pair directly outwards to the base of the middle leg; while the posterior pair pass outwards and backwards to the arms of the medifurca. From the second tubular apodeme, in front of the metasternum, four pairs of muscles spring. Those of the anterior pass forwards and out-

wards to the coxa of the fore limb; the second pair directly
outwards to the base of the metathoracic legs; the third pair
backwards and outwards to the arms of the postfurca; the
fourth pair backwards to the second abdominal sternum.

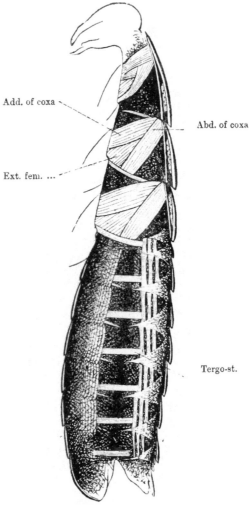

Fig. 36.—Muscles of lateral wall, &c.   × 5.

The muscles attached to the medi- and postfurca (other than
those connecting them with the tubular apodemes) are :—

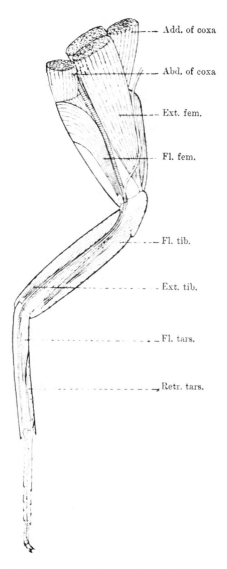

Add. of coxa

Abd. of coxa

Ext. fem.

Fl. fem.

Fl. tib.

Ext. tib.

Fl. tars.

Retr. tars.

Fig. 37.—Muscles of left mesothoracic leg, seen from behind. The muscles are—
Adductor and abductor of the coxa ; extensor and flexor of femoral joint ; flexor
and extensor of tibial joint ; flexor of tarsus ; and a retractor tarsi, which swings
the tarsus backwards, so that it points away from the head. It is opposed by
another muscle, which moves the tarsus forwards. Both muscles parallelise the
tarsus to the axis of the body, but in opposite directions.

(1) A pair passing from the posterior edge of the arms
of the medifurca to the stem of the postfurca; (2) a pair
which diverge from the stem of the postfurca and proceed to
the fore part of the second abdominal sternum; (3) a pair
passing from the posterior edge of the arms of the postfurca,
these are directed inwards and backwards, and are inserted into
the hinder part of the second abdominal sternum; (4) a pair
already mentioned, which correspond in position and action to
the tergo-sternal muscles, and spring from the stem of the postfurca, passing upwards and outwards to the sides of the first
abdominal tergum.

The muscles attached to the arms of each furca pass to other
structures in or near the middle line of the body. The pull of
such muscles must alter the slope of the two steps in the
ventral floor of the thorax (p. 58, and fig. 3, p. 12). When the
furca is drawn forwards, the step is rendered vertical or even
inclined forward, the sterna being approximated; while, on the
other hand, a backward pull brings the step into a horizontal
position, and separates the sterna.

TERGAL MUSCLES OF THORAX.—The *longitudinal tergal* muscles
are much reduced in width when compared with those of the
abdomen. Sets of obliquely placed muscles, which may be
called the *lateral thoracic* muscles, arise from near the middle of
each tergum, and converge to tendinous insertions on the fore
edge of each succeeding tergum, close to the lateral wall of the
body.

The principal muscles of the legs are figured and named, and
their action can readily be inferred from the names assigned to
them.

Insect Mechanics.

The mechanics of Insect movements require exposition and
illustration far beyond what is possible in a book like this.
Even the elaborate dissections of Lyonnet and Straus-Dürckheim
are not a sufficient basis for a thorough treatment of the subject, and until we possess many careful dissections, made by
anatomists who are bent upon mastering the action of the parts,
our views must needs be vague and of doubtful value. Zoologists

of great eminence have been led into erroneous statements when they have attempted to characterise shortly a complex animal mechanism which they did not think it worth while to analyse completely.*

The action of flight and the muscles attached to the wings are best studied in Insects of powerful flight. The female Cockroach cannot fly at all, and the male is by no means a good flier. Both sexes are, however, admirably fitted for running.

In running, two sets, each consisting of three legs, move simultaneously. A set includes a fore and hind limb of the same side and the opposite middle leg. Numbering them from before backwards, and distinguishing the right and left sides by their initial letters, we can represent the legs which work together as—

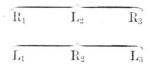

The different legs have different modes of action. The fore-leg may be compared to a grappling-iron; it is extended, seizes the ground with its claws, and drags the body towards its point of attachment. The middle leg is chiefly used to support and steady the body, but has some pushing power. The hind leg, the largest of the three, is effective in shoving, and chiefly propels the body.

Muscular Force of Insects.

The force exerted by Insects has long been remarked with surprise, and it is a fact familiar, not only to naturalists, but to all observant persons, that, making allowance for their small size, Insects are the most powerful of common animals.

* For example, Prof. Huxley, in his Anatomy of Invertebrated Animals (p. 254), says that "as the hard skeleton [of Arthropods] is hollow, and the muscles are inside it, it follows that the body, or a limb, is bent towards that side of its axis, which is opposite to that on which a contracting muscle is situated." The flexor muscles of the tail of the Crayfish, which, according to the above rule, should be extensors, the muscles of the mandibles of an Insect, and the flexors and extensors of Crustacean pincers are among the many conspicuous exceptions to this rule.

Popular books of natural history give striking and sometimes exaggerated accounts of the prodigious strength put forth by captive Insects in their efforts to escape. Thus we are told that the flea can draw 70 or 80 times its own weight.* The Cockchafer is said to be six times as strong as a horse, making allowance for size. A caterpillar of the Goat Moth, imprisoned beneath a bell-glass, weighing half a pound, which was loaded with a book weighing four pounds, nevertheless raised the glass and made its escape.

This interesting subject has been investigated by Plateau,† who devised the following experiment. The Insect to be tested was confined within a narrow horizontal channel, which was laid with cloth. A thread attached to its body was passed over a light pulley, and fastened to a small pan, into which sand was poured until the Insect could no longer raise it. Some of the results are given in the following table :—

Table of Relative Muscular Force of Insects (Plateau).

	Weight of body in grammes.	Ratio of weight lifted to weight of body.
Carabus auratus	0·703	17·4
Nebria brevicollis	0·046	25·3
Melolontha vulgaris	0·940	14·3
Anomala Frischii	0·153	24·3
Bombus terrestris	0·381	14·9
Apis mellifica	0·090	23·5

One obvious result is that within the class of Insects the relative muscular force (as commonly understood) is approximately in the inverse proportion of the weight—that is, the strength of the Insect is (by this mode of calculation) most conspicuous in the smaller species.

In a later memoir‡ Plateau gives examples from different Vertebrate and Invertebrate animals, which lead to the same general conclusion.

---

* Haller. This and other examples are taken from Rennie's Insect Transformations.

† Bull. Acad. Roy. de Belgique, 2ᵐ Sér., Tom. xx. (1865), and Tom. xxii. (1866).

‡ Loc. cit. 3ᵐ Sér., Tom. vii. (1884). Authorities for the various estimates are cited in the original memoir.

Ratio of weight drawn to weight of body (Plateau).

Horse	...	...	...	...	·5 to ·83
Man...	...	...	...	...	·86
Crab...	...	...	...	...	5·37
Insects	...	...	...	...	14·3 to 23·5

The inference commonly drawn from such data is that the muscles of small animals possess a force which greatly exceeds that of large quadrupeds or man, allowance being made for size, and that the explanation of this superior force is to be looked for in some peculiarity of composition or texture. Gerstaecker,* for example, suggests that the higher muscular force of Arthropoda may be due to the tender and yielding nature of their muscles. An explanation so desperate as this may well lead us to inquire whether we have understood the facts aright. Plateau's figures give us the ratio of the weight drawn or raised to the weight of the animal. This we may, with him, take as a measure of the *relative muscular force*. In reality, it is a datum of very little physiological value. By general reasoning of a quite simple kind it can be shown that, for muscles possessing the same physical properties, the *relative* muscular force necessarily increases very rapidly as the size of the animal decreases. For the contractile force of muscles of the same kind depends simply upon the number and thickness of the fibres, *i.e.*, upon the sectional area of the muscles. If the size of the animal and of its muscles be increased according to any uniform scale, the sectional area of a given muscle will increase as the square of any linear dimension. But the weight increases in a higher proportion, according to the increase in length, breadth, and depth jointly, or as the cube of any linear dimension.† The

---

* Klassen und Ordnungen des Thierreichs, Bd. V., pp. 61-2.

† This change in the relation of weight to strength, according to the size of the structure, has long been familiar to engineers. (See, for example, "Comparisons of Similar Structures as to Elasticity, Strength, and Stability," by Prof. James Thomson, Trans. Inst. Engineers, &c., Scotland, 1876.) The application to animal structures has been made by Herbert Spencer (Principles of Biology, Pt. II., ch. i.). The principle can be readily explained by models. Place a cubical block upon a square column. Double all the dimensions in a second model, which may be done by fitting together eight cubes like the first, and four columns, also the same as before except in length. Each column, though no stronger than before, has now to bear twice the weight.

ratio of contractile force to weight must therefore become rapidly smaller as the size of the animal increases. Plateau's second table (*see above*) actually gives a value for the relative muscular force of the Bee, in comparison with the Horse, which is only one-fourteenth of what it ought to turn out, supposing that both animals were of similar construction, and that the muscular fibres in both were equal in contractile force per unit of sectional area.*

A later series of experiments† brings out this difference in a precise form. Plateau has determined by ingenious methods what he calls the *Absolute Muscular Force*‡ of a number of Invertebrate animals (Lamellibranch Mollusca, and Crustacea), comparing them with man and other Vertebrates. His general conclusions may be shortly given as follows :—The absolute muscular force of the muscles closing the pincers of Crabs is

---

* Contractile force varies as sectional area of muscle. Let W be weight of Horse ; w, weight of Bee ; R, a linear dimension of Horse ; r, a linear dimension of Bee. Then,

$$\frac{\text{Contr. force of Horse}}{\text{Contr. force of Bee}} = \frac{\text{sect. area of muscles (Horse)}}{\text{sect. area of muscles (Bee)}} = \frac{R^2}{r^2}.$$

But since $\dfrac{W}{w} = \dfrac{R^3}{r^3}, \ \dfrac{R^2}{r^2} = \dfrac{W}{w} \times \dfrac{r}{R}.$

Therefore $\dfrac{\text{Contr. force of Horse}}{\text{Contr. force of Bee}} = \dfrac{Wr}{wR}.$

But, by definition,

$$\frac{\text{Rel. m.f. of Horse}}{\text{Rel. m.f. of Bee}} = \frac{\dfrac{\text{Contr. f. of Horse}}{W}}{\dfrac{\text{Contr. f. of Bee}}{w}} = \frac{\text{Contr. f. of Horse}}{\text{Contr. f. of Bee}} \times \frac{w}{W} =$$

$$\frac{Wr}{wR} \times \frac{w}{W} = \frac{r}{R} = \left(\frac{r^3}{R^3}\right)^{\frac{1}{3}} = \left(\frac{w}{W}\right)^{\frac{1}{3}}.$$

The weight of a horse is about 270,000 grammes, that of a bee ·09 gramme ; so that $\left(\dfrac{w}{W}\right)^{\frac{1}{3}} = \left(\dfrac{·09}{270,000}\right)^{\frac{1}{3}} = \left(·000,000,\overset{.}{3}\right)^{\frac{1}{3}} = ·0015$ (nearly) $=$ Calculated Ratio of Relative Muscular Force of Horse to that of Bee. The Observed Ratio (Plateau) is $\dfrac{·5}{23·5} = ·02128$; so that the relative muscular force of the Horse is more than fourteen times as great in comparison with that of the Bee as it would be if the muscles of both animals were similar in kind, and the proportions of the two animals similar in all respects.

† Rech. sur la Force Absolue des Muscles des Invertébrés. I^e Partie. Mollusques Lamellibranches. Bull. Acad. Roy. de Belgique, 3e Sér., Tom. VI. (1883). Do., IIe Partie. Crustacés Décapodes. Ibid., Tom. VII. (1884).

‡ *Statical muscular force* and *Specific muscular force* are synonymous terms in common use. *Contractile force per unit of sectional area* gives perhaps the clearest idea of what is meant.

low in comparison with that of Vertebrate muscles. The absolute force of the adductor muscles closing a bivalve shell may, in certain Lamellibranchs, equal that of the most powerful Mammalian muscles ; in others it falls below that of the least powerful muscles of the frog, which are greatly inferior in contractile force to Mammalian muscles. We find, therefore, that the low contractile force of Insect muscles is in harmony, and not in contrast, with common observation of their physical properties, and that the high *relative* muscular force, correctly enough attributed to them, is explicable by considerations which apply equally well to models or other artificial structures.

The comparison between the muscular force of Insects and large animals is sometimes made in another way. For example, in Carpenter's Zoology* the spring of the Cheese-hopper is described, and we are told that "the height of the leap is often from twenty to thirty times the length of the body ; exhibiting an energy of motion which is particularly remarkable in the soft larva of an Insect. A Viper, if endowed with similar powers, would throw itself nearly a hundred feet from the ground." It is here implied that the equation

$$\frac{\text{Height of Insect's leap}}{\text{Length of Insect}} = \frac{\text{Supposed ht. of Viper's leap (100 ft.)}}{\text{Length of Viper}}$$

should hold if the two animals were "endowed with similar powers."

But it is known that the work done by contraction of muscles of the same kind is proportional to the volume of the muscles ("Borelli's Law"),† and in similar animals the muscular volumes are as the weights. Therefore the equation

$$\frac{\text{Work of Insect}}{\text{Weight of Insect}} = \frac{\text{Work of Viper}}{\text{Weight of Viper}}$$

will more truly represent the imaginary case of equal leaping power. But the work = weight raised × height, and the weight raised is in both cases the weight of the animal itself. Therefore

$$\frac{\text{Wt.} \times \text{Ht.}}{\text{Wt.}} \text{ (Insect)} = \frac{\text{Wt.} \times \text{Ht.}}{\text{Wt.}} \text{ (Viper)},$$

---

* Vol. II., p. 203. The calculation here quoted is based upon an observation of Swammerdam, who relates that a Cheese-hopper, ¼ in. long, leaped out of a box 6 in. deep.

† Haughton's Animal Mechanics, 2nd ed., p. 43.

and Ht. (Insect) = Ht. (Viper). The Viper's efficiency as a leaping animal would, therefore, equal that of a Cheese-hopper if it leaped the same vertical height. Therefore, if the two animals were "endowed with similar powers," the heights to which they could leap would be equal, and not proportional to their lengths, as is assumed in the passage quoted.

Straus-Dürckheim observes that a Flea can leap a foot high, which is 200 times its own length, and this has been considered a stupendous feat. It is really less remarkable than a school-boy's leap of two feet, for it indicates precisely as great efficiency of muscles and other leaping apparatus as would be implied in a man's leap to the same height, viz., one foot.*

The Fat-body.

Adhering to the inner face of the abdominal wall is a cellular mass, which forms an irregular sheet of dense white appearance. This is the fat-body. Its component cells are polygonal, and crowded together. When young they exhibit nuclei and vacuolated protoplasm, but as they get older the nuclei disappear, the cell-boundaries become indistinct, and a fluid, loaded with minute refractive granules,† takes the place of the living protoplasm. Rhombohedral or hexagonal crystals, containing uric acid, form in the cells and become plentiful in old tissue. The salt (probably urate of soda) is formed by the waste of the proteids of the body. What becomes of it in the end we do not know for certain, but conjecture that it escapes by the blood which bathes the perivisceral cavity, that it is taken up again by the Malpighian tubules, and is finally discharged into the intestine. The old gorged cells probably burst from time to time, and the infrequency of small cells among them renders it probable that rejuvenescence takes place, the burst cells passing through a resting-stage, accompanied by renewal of their nuclei, and then repeating the cycle of change.

The segmental tubes forming the Wolffian body of Verte-brates have at first no outlet, and embryologists have hesitated

---

* In any comparison it is necessary to cite not the height cleared by the man, but the displacement during the leap of his centre of gravity.

† The granules are not shown in the figure, having been removed in the preparation of the tissue for microscopic examination.

to regard this phase of development as the permanent condition of any ancestral form.* It is, therefore, of interest to find in the fat-body of the Cockroach an example of a solid, mesoblastic, excretory organ, functional throughout life, but without efferent duct.

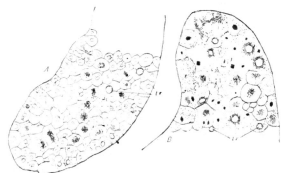

Fig. 38.—Fat-body of Cockroach, cleared with turpentine. *A*, young tissue, with distinct cell-boundaries and nuclei, a few cells towards the centre with dead contents; *B*, older ditto, loaded with urates. the cell-walls much broken down, and the nuclei gone; *tr*, tracheal tubes.　× 250.

The fat-body is eminently a metabolic tissue, the seat of active chemical change in the materials brought by the blood. Its respiratory needs are attested by the abundant air-tubes which spread through it in all directions.

The considerable bulk of the fat-body in the adult Cockroach points to the unusual duration of the perfect Insect. It is usually copious in full-fed larvæ, but becomes used up in the pupa-stage.

Extensions of the fat-body surround the nervous chain, the reproductive organs and other viscera. Sheets of the same substance lie in the pericardial sinus on each side of the heart.

The Cœlom.

The fat-body is in reality, as development shows, the irregular cellular wall of the cœlom, or perivisceral space. Through this space courses the blood, flowing in no defined vessels, but bathing all the walls and viscera. In other words, the fat-body is an aggregation of little-altered mesoblast-cells, excavated by the cœlom, the rest of the mesoblast having gone to form the muscular layers of the body-wall and of the digestive tube.

* Balfour, Embryology, Vol. II., p. 603.

CHAPTER VI.

The Nervous System and Sense Organs.

SPECIAL REFERENCES.

NEWPORT. Nervous System of Sphinx Ligustri. Phil. Trans. (1832-4). Todd's Cyclopædia, Art. "Insecta" (1839).

LEYDIG. Vom Bau des Thierischen Körpers. Bd. I. (1864). Tafeln zur. vergl. Anat. Hft. I. (1864).

BRANDT (E.). Various memoirs on the Nervous System of Insects in Horæ Soc. Entom. Ross., Bd. XIV., XV. (1879).

MICHELS. Nervensystem von Oryctes nasicornis im Larven—, Puppen—, und Käferzustande. Zeits. f. wiss. Zool., Bd. XXXIV. (1881).

DIETL. Organisation des Arthropodengehirns. Zeits. f. wiss. Zool., Bd. XXVII. (1876).

FLÖGEL. Bau des Gehirns der verschiedenen Insektenordnungen. Zeits. f. wiss. Zool., Bd. XXX. Sup. (1878).

NEWTON. On the Brain of the Cockroach. Q. J. Micr. Sci. (1879). Journ. Quekett Club (1879).

GRENACHER. Sehorgan der Arthropoden. (1879). [Origin, Structure, and Action of the Compound Eye.]

CARRIÈRE. Sehorgane der Thiere, vergl.-anat. dargestellt (1885). [Comparative Structure of various Simple and Compound Eyes.]

General Anatomy of Nervous Centres.

THE nervous system of the Cockroach comprises ganglia and connectives,* which extend throughout the body. We have, first, a supra-œsophageal ganglion, or brain, a sub-œsophageal ganglion, and connectives which complete the œsophageal ring. All these lie in the head; behind them, and extending through the thorax and abdomen, is a gangliated cord, with double connectives. The normal arrangement of the ganglia in Annulosa, one to each somite, becomes more or less modified in Insects by coalescence or suppression, and we find only eleven ganglia in the Cockroach—viz., two cephalic, three thoracic, and six abdominal.

* Yung ("Syst. nerveux des Crustacées Décapodes, Arch. de Zool. exp. et gén.," Tom. VII., 1878) proposes to name *connectives* the longitudinal bundles of nerve-fibres which unite the ganglia, and to reserve the term *commissures* for the transverse communicating branches.

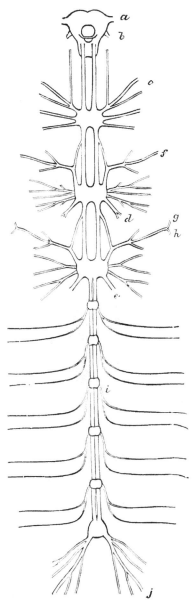

Fig. 39.—Nervous System of Female Cockroach, × 6. *a*, optic nerve ; *b*, antennary nerve ; *c*, *d*, *e*, nerves to first, second, and third legs ; *f*, to wing-cover ; *g*, to second thoracic spiracle ; *h*, to wing ; *i*, abdominal nerve ; *j*, to cerci.

The nervous centres of the head form a thick, irregular ring, which swells above and below into ganglionic enlargements, and leaves only a small central opening, occupied by the œsophagus. The tentorium separates the brain or supra-œsophageal ganglion from the sub-œsophageal, while the connectives traverse its central plate. Since the œsophagus passes above the plate, the investing nervous ring also lies almost wholly above the tentorium.

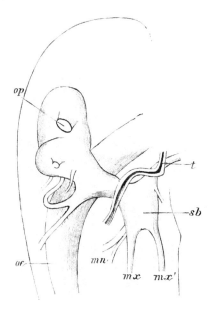

Fig. 40.—Side view of Brain of Cockroach, × 25. *op*, optic nerve ; *oe*, œsophagus; *t*, tentorium ; *sb*, sub-œsophageal ganglion ; *mn*, *mx*, *mx'*, nerves to mandible and maxillæ. Copied from E. T. Newton.

The brain is small in comparison with the whole head; it consists of two rounded lateral masses or hemispheres, incompletely divided by a deep and narrow median fissure. Large optic nerves are given off laterally from the upper part of each hemisphere; lower down, and on the front of the brain, are the two gently rounded antennary lobes, from each of which proceeds an antennary nerve; while from the front and upper part of each hemisphere a small nerve passes to the so-called "ocellus," a transparent spot lying internal to the antennary socket on each side in the suture between the clypeus and the epicranium. The sub-œsophageal ganglion gives off branches to the mandibles, maxillæ, and labrum. While, therefore, the supra-œsophageal is largely sensory, the sub-œsophageal ganglion is the masticatory centre.

The œsophageal ring is double below, being completed by the connectives and the sub-œsophageal ganglion; also by a smaller transverse commissure, which unites the connectives, and applies itself closely to the under-surface of the œsophagus.*

Two long connectives issue from the top of the sub-œsophageal ganglion, and pass between the tentorium and the submentum on their way to the neck and thorax. The three thoracic ganglia are large (in correspondence with the important appendages of this part of the body) and united by double connectives. The six abdominal ganglia have also double connectives, which are bent in the male, as if to avoid stretching during forcible elongation of the abdomen. The sixth abdominal ganglion is larger than the rest, and is no doubt a complex, representing several coalesced posterior ganglia; it supplies large branches to the reproductive organs, rectum, and cerci.

Internal Structure of Ganglia.

Microscopic examination of the internal structure of the nerve-cord reveals a complex arrangement of cells and fibres. The connectives consist almost entirely of nerve-fibres, which, as in Invertebrates generally, are non-medullated. The ganglia include (1) rounded, often multipolar, nerve-cells; (2) tortuous and extremely delicate fibres collected into intricate skeins; (3) commissural fibres, and (4) connectives. The chief fibrous tracts are internal, the cellular masses outside them. A relatively thick, and very distinct neurilemma, probably chitinous, encloses the cord. Its cellular matrix, or chitinogenous layer,

---

* This commissure, which has been erroneously regarded as characteristic of Crustacea, was found by Lyonnet in the larva of Cossus, by Straus-Dürckheim in Locusta and Buprestis, by Blanchard in Dytiscus and Otiorhynchus, by Leydig in Glomeris and Telephorus, by Dietl in Gryllotalpa, and by Liénard in a large number of other Insects and Myriapods, including Periplaneta. See Liénard, "Const. de l'anneau œsophagien," Bull. Acad. Roy. de Belgique, 2° Sér., Tom. XLIX., 1880.

is distinguished by the elongate nuclei of its constituent cells.*
Tracheal trunks pass to each ganglion, and break up upon and
within it into a multitude of fine branches.

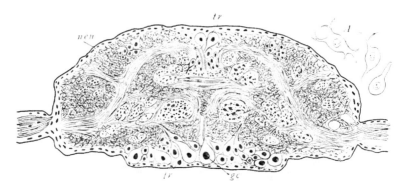

Fig. 41.—Transverse section of Third Thoracic Ganglion. *neu*, neurilemmar cells ;
gc, ganglionic cells ; *tr*, tracheal tubes ; *A*, ganglionic cells, highly magnified.
× 75.

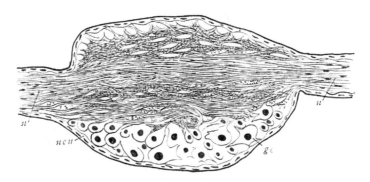

Fig. 42.—Longitudinal vertical section of Third Thoracic Ganglion. *n*, connective.
The other references as in fig. 41.   × 75.

Bundles of commissural fibres pass from the ganglion cells of
one side of the cord to the peripheral nerves of the other.
There are also longitudinal bands which blend to form the
connectives, and send bundles into the peripheral nerves. Of

---

* We have not been able to distinguish in the adult Cockroach the *double* layer of
neurilemmar cells noticed by Leydig and Michels in various Coleoptera.

the peripheral fibres, some are believed to pass direct to their place of distribution, while others traverse at least one complete segment and the corresponding ganglion before separating from the cord.

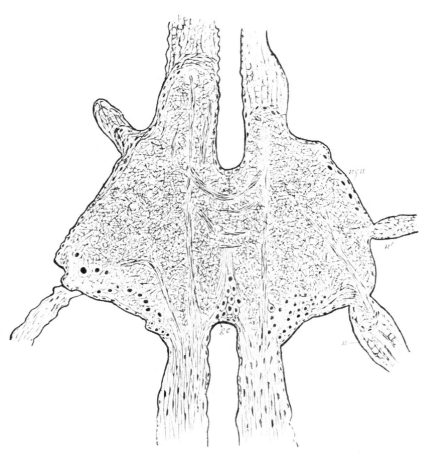

Fig. 43.– Longitudinal horizontal section of Third Thoracic Ganglion. *n*, peripheral nerves. The other references as before. × 75.

Many familiar observations show that the ganglia of an Insect possess great physiological independence. The limbs of decapitated Insects, and even isolated segments, provided that they contain uninjured ganglia, exhibit unmistakable signs of life.

Median Nerve-Cord.

Lyonnet,[*] Newport,[†] and Leydig[‡] have found in large Insects a system of median nerves, named *respiratory* (Newport) or *sympathetic* (Leydig). These nerves do not form a continuous cord extending throughout the body, but take fresh origin in each segment from the right and left longitudinal commissures alternately. The median nerve lies towards the dorsal side of the principal nerve-cord, crosses over the ganglion next behind, and receives a small branch from it. Close behind the ganglion it bifurcates, the branches passing outwards and blending with the peripheral nerves. Each branch, close to its origin, swells into a ganglionic enlargement. The median nerve and its branches differ in appearance and texture from ordinary peripheral nerves, being more transparent, delicate, and colourless. They are said to supply the occlusor muscles of the stigmata. In the Cockroach the median nerves are so slightly developed in the thorax and abdomen (if they actually exist) that they are hardly discoverable by ordinary dissection. We have found only obscure and doubtful traces of them, and these only in one part of the abdominal nerve-cord. The stomato-gastric nerves next to be described appear to constitute a peculiar modification of that median nerve-cord which springs from the circum-œsophageal connectives.

Stomato-gastric Nerves.

In the Cockroach the stomato-gastric nerves found in so many of the higher Invertebrates are conspicuously developed. From the front of each œsophageal connective, a nerve passes forwards upon the œsophagus, outside the chitinous crura of the tentorium. Each nerve sends a branch downwards to the labrum, and the remaining fibres, collected into two bundles, join above the œsophagus to form a triangular enlargement, the

[*] Traité Anat., p. 201, pl. ix., fig. 1.

[†] Phil. Trans., 1834, p. 401, pl. xvi.

[‡] Vom Bau des Thierischen Körpers, pp. 203, 262; Taf. z. vergl. Anat., pl. vi., fig. 3.

frontal ganglion. From this ganglion a recurrent nerve passes backwards through the œsophageal ring, and ends on the dorsal surface of the crop (·3 inch from the ring), in a triangular

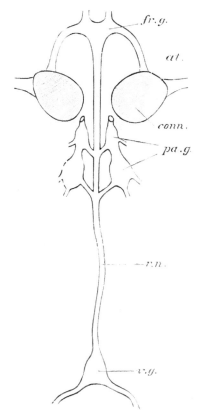

Fig. 44.—Stomato-gastric Nerves of Cockroach. *fr.g.*, frontal ganglion; *at.*, antennary nerve; *conn.*, connective; *pa.g.*, paired ganglia; *r.n.*, recurrent nerve; *v.g.*, ventricular ganglion.

ganglion, from which a nerve is given off outwards and backwards on either side. Each nerve bifurcates, and then breaks up into branches which are distributed to the crop and gizzard.* Just behind the œsophageal ring, the recurrent nerve forms a

* The stomato-gastric nerves of the Cockroach have been carefully described by Koestler (Zeits. f. wiss. Zool., Bd. XXXIX., p. 592).

plexus with a pair of nerves which proceed from the back of the brain. Each nerve forms two ganglia, one behind the other, and each ganglion sends a branch inwards to join the recurrent nerve. Fine branches proceed from the paired nerves of the œsophageal plexus to the salivary glands.

The stomato-gastric nerves differ a good deal in different insects; Brandt* considers that the paired and unpaired nerves are complementary to each other, the one being more elaborate, according as the other is less developed. A similar system is found in Mollusca, Crustacea, and some Vermes (*e.g.*, Nemerteans). When highly developed, it contains unpaired ganglia and nerves, but may be represented only by an indefinite plexus (earthworm). It always joins the œsophageal ring, and sends branches to the œsophagus and fore-part of the alimentary canal. The system has been identified with the sympathetic, and also with the vagus of Vertebrates, but such correlations are hazardous; the first, indeed, may be considered as disproved.

Internal Structure of Brain.

The minute structure of the brain has been investigated by Leydig, Dietl, Flögel, and others, and exhibits an unexpected complexity. It is as yet impossible to reduce the many curious details which have been described to a completely intelligible account. The physiological significance, and the homologies of many parts are as yet altogether obscure. The comparative study of new types will, however, in time, bridge over the wide interval between the Insect-brain and the more familiar Vertebrate-brain, which is partially illuminated by physiological experiment. Mr. E. T. Newton has published a clear and useful description† of the internal and external structure of the brain of the Cockroach, which incorporates what had previously been ascertained with the results of his own investigations. He has also described ‡ an ingenious method of combining a number of successive sections into a dissected model of the

* " Mem. Acad. Petersb.," 1835.
† " Q. J. Micr. Sci.," 1879, pp. 340-356, pl. xv., xvi.
‡ " Journ. Quekett Micr. Club," 1879.

brain. Having had the advantage of comparing the model with
the original sections, we offer a short abstract of Mr. Newton's
memoir as the best introduction to the subject. He describes
the central framework of the Cockroach brain as consisting of
two solid and largely fibrous trabeculæ, which lie side by side
along the base of the brain, becoming smaller at their hinder
ends; they meet in the middle line, but apparently without
fusion or exchange of their fibres. Each trabecula is continued
upwards by two fibrous columns, the cauliculus in front, and the
peduncle behind; the latter carries a pair of cellular disks, the

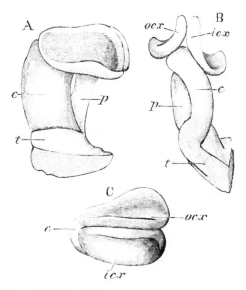

Fig. 45.—A, lobes of the brain of the Cockroach, seen from within; *c*, cauliculus;
p, peduncle; *t*, trabecula. B, ditto, from the front; *ocx*, outer calyx; *icx*, inner
calyx. C, ditto, from above. Copied from E. T. Newton.

calices (the cauliculus, though closely applied to the calices, is
not connected with them); these disks resemble two soft cakes
pressed together above, and bent one inwards, and the other
outwards below. The peduncle divides above, and each branch
joins one of the calices of the same hemisphere.

This central framework is invested by cortical ganglionic
cells, which possess distinct nuclei and nucleoli. A special
cellular mass forms a cap to each pair of calices, and this

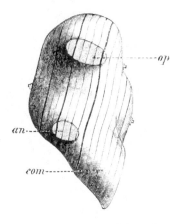

Fig. 46.—Model of Cockroach Brain, constructed from slices of wood representing successive sections.

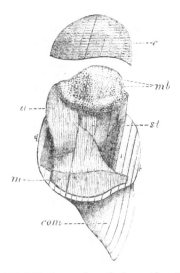

Fig. 47.—Right half of Model-brain seen from the inner side, with the parts dissected away, so as to show the anterior nervous mass (*caulicalus*). *a*; the median mass (*trabecula*). *m*; the mushroom-bodies (*calices*), *mb*; and their stems (*peduncles*), *st*. The cellular cap, *c*, has been raised, so as to display the parts below : *com*, is a part of the connective uniting the brain and infra-œsophageal ganglia. [Figs. 45–48 are taken from Mr. E. T. Newton's paper in "Journ. Quekett Club," 1879.]

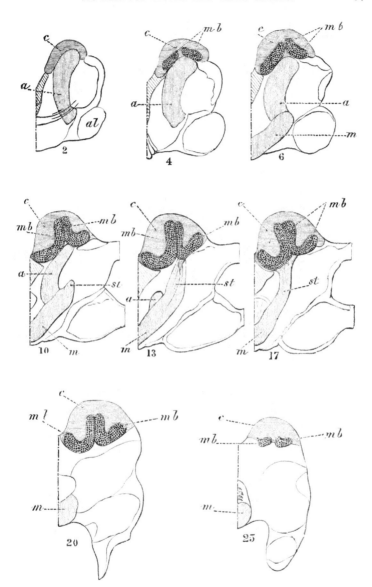

Fig. 48.—Diagrammatic outlines of sections of the Brain of a Cockroach. Only one side of the brain is here represented. The numbers indicate the position in the series of thirty-four sections into which this brain was cut. *al*, antennary lobe; *mb*, mushroom bodies (*calices*), with their cellular covering, *c*, and their stems (*peduncles*), *st*; *a*, anterior nervous mass (*cauliculus*); *m*, median nervous mass (*trabecula*). From E. T. Newton.

consists of smaller cells without nucleoli. Above the meeting-place of the trabeculæ is a peculiar laminated mass, the *central body*, which consists of a network of fibres continuous with the neighbouring ganglionic cells, and enclosing a granular substance. The antennary lobes consist of a network of fine fibres

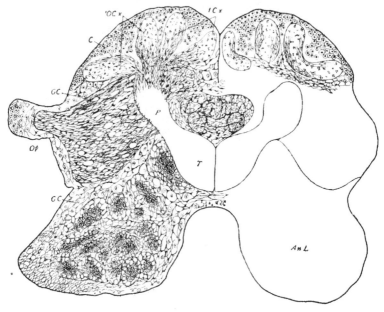

Fig. 49.—Frontal section of Brain of Cockroach. *C*, cellular layer beneath neurilemma; *I Cx*, inner calix ; *O Cx*, outer calix ; *G C*, ganglion-cells ; *P*, peduncle ; *T*, trabecula ; *Op*, optic nerve ; *An L*, antennary lobe. × 24.

enclosing ganglion cells, and surrounded by a layer of the same. It is remarkable that no fibrous communications can be made out between the calices and the cauliculi, or between the trabeculæ and the œsophageal connectives.

Sense Organs. The Eye of Insects.

The sense organs of Insects are very variable, both in position and structure. Three special senses are indicated by transparent and refractive parts of the cuticle, by tense membranes with modified nerve-endings, and by peculiar sensory rods or filaments upon the antennæ. These are taken to be the organs respectively of sight, hearing, and smell. Other sense organs, not as yet fully elucidated, may co-exist with these. The maxillary palps of the Cockroach, for example, are continually used in exploring movements, and may assist the animal to select its food; the cerci, where these are well-developed, and the halteres of Diptera, have been also regarded as sense organs of some undetermined kind, but this is at present wholly conjecture.*

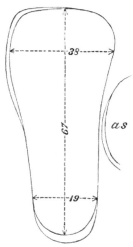

Fig. 50.—Plan of Eye of Cockroach, showing the number of facets along the principal diameters. *as*, antennary socket.

The compound eyes of the Cockroach occupy a large, irregularly oval space (see fig. 50) on each side of the head. The total number of facets may be estimated at about 1,800. The number is very variable in Insects, and may either greatly exceed that found in the Cockroach, or be reduced to a very small one indeed. According to Burmeister, the Coleopterous genus Mordella possesses more than 25,000 facets. Where the facets are very numerous, the compound eyes may occupy nearly the whole surface of the head, as in the House-fly Dragon-fly, or Gad-fly.

Together with compound eyes, many Insects are furnished also with simple eyes, usually three in number, and disposed in

* It is to be remarked that unusually large nerves supply the cerci of the Cockroach.

a triangle on the forehead. The white fenestræ, which in the Cockroach lie internal to the antennary sockets, may represent two simple eyes which have lost their dioptric apparatus. In many larvæ only simple eyes are found, and the compound eye is restricted to the adult form; in larval Cockroaches, however, the compound eye is large and functional.

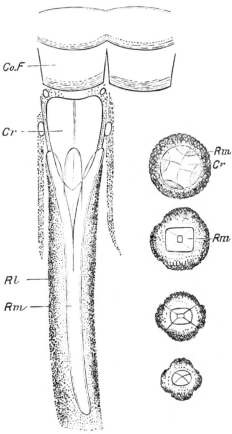

Fig. 51.—One element of the Compound Eye of the Cockroach, × 700. *Co. F.* corneal facets; *Cr,* crystalline cones; *Rm,* nerve-rod (rhabdom); *Rl,* retinula of protoplasmic fibrils. To the right are transverse sections at various levels. Copied from Grenacher.

Each facet of the compound eye is the outermost element of a series of parts, some dioptric and some sensory, which forms one of a mass of radiating rods or fibres. The facets are transparent, biconvex, and polygonal, often, but not quite regularly, hexagonal. In many Insects the deep layer of each facet is separable, and forms a concavo-convex layer of different texture from the superficial and biconvex lens. The facets, taken together, are often described as the cornea; they represent the chitinous cuticle of the integument. The subdivision of the cornea into two layers of slightly different texture suggests an achromatic correction, and it is quite possible, though unproved, that the two sets of prisms have different dispersive powers. Beneath the cornea we find a layer of crystalline cones, each of which rests by its base upon the inner surface of a facet, while its apex is directed inwards towards

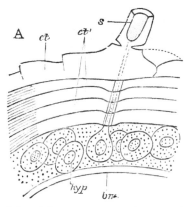

Fig. 52.—Diagram of Insect Integument, in section. *bm*, basement-membrane; *hyp*, hypodermis, or chitinogenous layer; *ct, ct'*, chitinous cuticle; *s*, a seta.

the brain. The crystalline cones are transparent, refractive, and coated with dark pigment; in the Cockroach they are comparatively short and blunt. Behind each cone is a nerve-rod (rhabdom), which, though outwardly single for the greater part of its length, is found on cross-section to consist of four components (rhabdomeres)* ; these diverge in front, and receive the tip of a cone, which is wedged in between them; the nerve-rods are densely pigmented. The rhabdom is invested by a protoplasmic sheath, which is imperfectly separated into

* The number in Insects varies from eight to four, but seven is usual; four is the usual number in Crustacea.

segments (retinulæ), corresponding in number with the rhabdomeres. Each retinula possesses at least one nucleus. The
retinulæ were found by Leydig to possess a true visual purple.
To the hinder ends of the retinulæ are attached the fibres of
the optic nerve, which at this point emerges through a "fenestrated membrane."

In the simple eye the non-faceted cornea and the retinula are
readily made out, but the crystalline cones are not developed

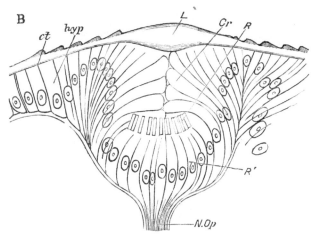

Fig. 53.—Section through Eye of Dytiscus-larva, showing the derivation of the
parts from modified hypodermic cells.   *L*, lens ;   *Cr*, crystalline cones ;   *R*, nerve-
rods ;   *N. Op.* optic nerve.   From Grenacher.

as such.   The morphological key to both structures is found in
the integument, of which the whole eye, simple or compound, is
a modification.   A defined tract of the chitinous cuticle becomes
transparent, and either swells into a lens (fig. 53), or becomes
regularly divided into facets (fig. 55), which are merely the
elaboration of imperfectly separated polygonal areas, easily
recognised in the young cuticle of all parts of the body.   Next,
the chitinogenous layer is folded inwards, so as to form a cup,
and this, by the narrowing of the mouth, is transformed into a
flask, and ultimately into a solid two-layered cellular mass (fig.
53).   The deep layer undergoes conversion into a retina, its
chitinogenous cells developing the nerve-rods as interstitial
structures, while the superficial layer, which loses its functional

importance in the simple eye, gives rise by a similar process of interstitial growth to the crystalline cones of the compound eye (fig. 55). The basement-membrane, underlying the chitin-ogenous cells, is transformed into the fenestrated membrane. The nerve-rods stand upon it, like organ pipes upon the sound-board, while fibrils of the optic nerve and fine tracheæ pass through its perforations. The mother-cells of the crystalline cones and nerve-rods are largely replaced by the interstitial substances they produce, to which they form a sheath; they are often loaded with pigment, and the nuclei of the primitive-cells can only be distinguished after the colouring-matter has been discharged by acids or alkalis.

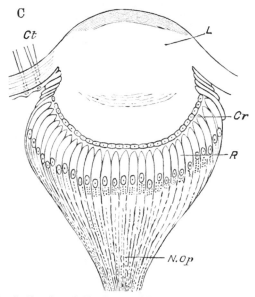

Fig. 54.—Section through Simple Eye of Vespa.   The references as above.
Simplified from Grenacher.

Dr. Hickson* has lately investigated the minute anatomy of the optic tract in various Insects. He finds, in the adult of the higher Insects, three distinct ganglionic swellings, consisting of a network of fine fibrils, surrounded by a sheath of crowded nerve-cells. Between the ganglia the fibres usually decussate. In the Cockroach, and some other of the lower Insects, the

* "Q. J. Micr. Sci.," 1885.

outermost ganglion is undeveloped. The fibres connecting the
second ganglion with the eye take a straight course in the
young Cockroach, but partially decussate in the adult.

All the parts between the crystalline cones and the true optic
nerve are considered by Hickson to compose the retina of
Insects, which, instead of ending at the fenestrated-membrane,
as has often been assumed, includes the ganglia and decussating
fibres of the optic tract. The layer of retinulæ and rhabdoms
does not form the whole retina, but merely that part which, in
the vertebrate eye, is known as the layer of rods and cones.

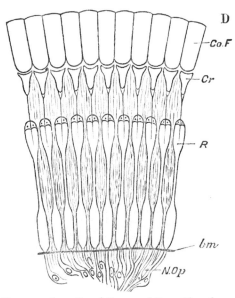

Fig. 55.—Diagrammatic section of Compound Eye. The references as above.

As to the way in which the compound eye renders distinct
vision possible, there is still much difference of opinion. A
short review of the discussion which has occupied some of the
most eminent physiologists and histologists for many years
past will introduce the reader to the principal facts which have
to be reconciled.

The investigation, like so many other trains of biological
inquiry, begins with Leeuwenhoeck (Ep. ad Soc. Reg. Angl. iii.),
who ascertained that the cornea of a shardborne Beetle, placed

in the field of a microscope, gives images of surrounding objects, and that these images are inverted. When the cornea is flattened out for microscopic examination, the images (e.g., of a window or candle-flame) are similar, and it has been too hastily assumed that a multitude of identical images are perceived by the Insect. The cornea of the living animal is, however, convex, and the images formed by different facets cannot be precisely identical. No combined or collective image is formed by the cornea. When the structure of the compound eye had been very inadequately studied, as was the case even in Cuvier's time (Leçons d'Anat. Comp., xii., 14), it was natural to suppose that all the fibres internal to the cornea were sensory, that they formed a kind of retina upon which the images produced by the facets were received, and that these images were transmitted to the brain, to be united, either by optical or mental combination, into a single picture. Müller,* in 1826, pointed out that so simple an explanation was inadmissible. He granted that the simple eye, with its lens and concave retina, produces a single inverted image, which is able to affect the nerve-endings in the same manner as in Vertebrates. But the compound eye is not optically constructed so as to render possible the formation of continuous images. The refractive and elongate crystalline cones, with their pointed apices and densely pigmented sides, must destroy any images formed by the lenses of the cornea. Even if the dioptric arrangement permitted the formation of images, there is no screen to receive them.† Lastly, if this difficulty were removed, Müller thought it impossible for the nervous centres to combine a great number of inverted partial images. How then can Insects and Crustaceans see with their compound eyes? Müller answered that each facet transmits a small pencil of rays travelling in the direction of its axis, but intercepts all others. The refractive lens collects the rays, and the pigmented as well as refractive crystalline cone further concentrates the pencil, while it stops out all rays which diverge appreciably from the axis. Each element of the compound eye transmits a single impression of greater or less brightness, and

---

* Exner has since determined by measurement and calculation the optical properties of the eye of Hydrophilus. He finds that the focus of a corneal lens is about 3mm. away, and altogether behind the eye.

† Zur vergl. Phys. des Gesichtsinnes.

the brain combines these impressions into some kind of picture, a picture like that which could be produced by stippling. It may be added that the movements of the insect's head or body would render the distance and form of every object in view much readier of appreciation. No accommodation for distance would be necessary, and the absence of all means of accommodation ceases to be perplexing. Such is Müller's theory of what he termed "mosaic vision." Many important researches, some contradictory, some confirmatory of Müller's doctrine,* have since been placed on record, with the general result that some modification of Müller's theory tends to prevail. The most important of the new facts and considerations which demand attention are these :—

Reasons have been given for supposing that images are formed by the cornea and crystalline cones together. This was first pointed out by Gottsche (1852), who used the compound eyes of Flies for demonstration. Grenacher has since ascertained that the crystalline cones of Flies are so fluid that they can hardly be removed, and he believes that Gottsche's images were formed by the corneal facets alone. He finds, however, that the experiment may be successfully performed with eyes not liable to this objection, *e.g.*, the eyes of nocturnal Lepidoptera. A bit of a Moth's eye is cut out, treated with nitric acid to remove the pigment, and placed on a glass slip in the field of the microscope. The crystalline cones, still attached to the cornea, are turned towards the observer, and one is selected whose axis coincides with that of the microscope. No image is visible when the tip of the cone is in focus, but as the cornea approaches the focus, a bristle, moved about between the mirror and the stage, becomes visible. This experiment is far from decisive. No image is formed where sensory elements are present to receive and transmit it. Moreover, the image is that of an object very near to the cornea, whereas all observations of living Insects show that the compound eye is used for far sight, and the simple eye for near sight. Lastly, the treatment with acid, though unavoidable, may conceivably affect the

---

* A critical history of the whole discussion is to be found in Grenacher's "Sehorgan der Arthropoden" (1879), from which we take many historical and structural details.

result. It is not certain that the cones really assist in the production of the image, which may be due to the corneal facets alone, though modified by the decolorised cones.

Grenacher has pointed out that the composition of the nerve-rod furnishes a test of the mosaic theory. According as the percipient rod is simple or complex, we may infer that its physiological action will be simple or complex too. The adequate perception of a continuous picture, though of small extent, will require many retinal rods; on the other hand, a single rod will suffice for the discrimination of a bright point. What then are the facts of structure? Grenacher has ascertained that the retinal rods in each element of the compound eye rarely exceed seven, and often fall as low as four—further, that the rods in each group are often more or less completely fused so as to resemble simple structures, and that this is especially the case with Insects of keen sight.*

Certain facts described by Schultze tell on the other side. Coming to the Arthropod eye, fresh from his investigation of the vertebrate retina, Schultze found in the retinal rods of Insects the same lamellar structure which he had discovered in Vertebrata. He found also that in certain Moths, Beetles, and Crustacea, a bundle of extremely fine fibrils formed the outer extremity of each retinal or nerve-rod. This led him to reject the mosaic theory of vision, and to conclude that a partial image was formed behind every crystalline cone, and projected upon a multitude of fine nerve-endings. Such a retinula of delicate fibrils has received no physiological explanation, but it is now known to be of comparatively rare occurrence; it has no pigment to localise the stimulus of light; and there is no reason to suppose that an image can be formed within its limits.

The optical possibility of such an eye as that interpreted to us by Müller has been conceded by physicists and physiologists so eminent as Helmholz and Du Bois Reymond. Nevertheless, the competence of any sort of mosaic vision to explain the precise and accurate perception of Insects comes again and again into question whenever we watch the movements of a

---

* Flies, whose eyes are in several respects exceptional, have almost completely separated rods, notwithstanding their quick sight.

House-fly as it avoids the hand, of a Bee flying from flower to flower, or of a Dragon-fly in pursuit of its prey. The sight of such Insects as these must range over several feet at least, and within this field they must be supposed to distinguish small objects with rapidity and certainty. How can we suppose that an eye without retinal screen, or accommodation for distance, is compatible with sight so keen and discriminating? The answer is neither ready nor complete, but our own eyesight shows how much may be accomplished by means of instruments far from optically perfect. According to Aubert, objects, to be perceived as distinct by the human eye, must have an angular distance of from 50″ to 70″, corresponding to several retinal rods. Our vision is therefore mosaic too, and the retinal rods which can be simultaneously affected comprise only a fraction of those contained within the not very extensive area of the effective retina. Still we are not conscious of any break in the continuity of the field of vision. The incessant and involuntary movements of the eyeball, and the appreciable duration of the light-stimulus partly explain the continuity of the image received upon a discontinuous organ. Even more important is the action of the judgment and imagination, which complete the blanks in the sensorial picture, and translate the shorthand of the retina into a full-length description. That much of what we see is seen by the mind only is attested by the inadequate impression made upon us by a sudden glimpse of unfamiliar objects. We need time and reflection to interpret the hints flashed upon our eyes, and without time and reflection we see nothing in its true relations. The Insect-eye may be far from optical perfection, and yet, as it ranges over known objects, the Insect-mind, trained to interpret colour, and varying brightness, and parallax, may gain minute and accurate information. Grant that the compound eye is imperfect, and even rude, if regarded as a camera; this is not its true character. It is intended to receive and interpret flashing signals; it is an optical telegraph.

Plateau* has recently submitted the seeing powers of a number of different Insects to actual experiment. The two windows of a room five metres square were darkened. An

* Bull. de l'Acad. Roy. de Belgique, 1885.

aperture fitted with ground glass was then arranged in each window. At a distance of four metres from the centre of the space between the windows captive Insects were from time to time liberated. One of the windows was fenced with fine trellis, so as to prevent the passage of the Insect, or otherwise altered in form, but the size of the aperture could be increased at pleasure, so as exactly to make up for any loss of light caused thereby, the brightness of the two openings being compared by a photometer.

It was found that day-flying Insects require a tolerably good light; in semi-obscurity they cannot find their way, and often refuse to fly at all. By varnishing one or other set in Insects possessing both simple and compound eyes, it was found that day-flying Insects provided with compound eyes do not use their simple eyes to direct their course. When the light from one window was sensibly greater than that from the other, the Insect commonly chose the brightest, but the existence of bars, close enough to prevent or to check its passage, had no perceptible effect upon the choice of its direction. Alterations in the shape of one of the panes seemed to be immaterial, provided that the quantity of light passing through remained the same, or nearly the same. Plateau concludes that Insects do not distinguish the forms of objects, or distinguish them very imperfectly.

It is plain, and Plateau makes this remark himself, that such experiments upon the power of unaided vision in Insects, give a very inadequate notion of the facility with which an Insect flying at large can find its way. There the animal is guided by colour, smell, and the actual or apparent movements of all visible objects. Exner has pointed out how important are the indications given by movement. Even in man, the central part of the retina is alone capable of precise perception of form, but a moving object is observed by the peripheral tract. Plateau (from whom this quotation is made) adds that most animals are very slightly impressed by the mere form of their enemies, or of their prey, but the slightest movement attracts their notice. The sportsman, the fisherman, and the entomologist cannot fail to learn this fact by repeated and cogent proofs.

Sense of Smell in Insects.

The existence of a sense of smell in Insects has probably never been disputed. Many facts of common observation prove that carrion-feeders, for example, are powerfully attracted towards putrid animal substances placed out of sight. The situation of the olfactory organs has only been ascertained by varied experiments and repeated discussion. Rosenthal, in 1811, and Lefebvre, in 1838, indicated the antennæ as the organs of smell, basing their conclusions upon physiological observations made upon living insects. Many entomologists of that time were inclined to regard the antennæ as auditory organs.* Observations on the minute structure of the antennæ were made by many workers, but for want of good histological methods and accurate information concerning the organs of smell in other animals, these proved for a long time indecisive. It was by observation of living insects that the point was actually determined.

Hauser's experiments, though by no means the first, are the most ,instructive which we possess. He found that captive insects, though not alarmed by a clean glass rod cautiously brought near, became agitated if the same rod had been first dipped in carbolic acid, turpentine, or acetic acid. The antennæ performed active movements while the rod was still distant, and after it was withdrawn the insect was observed to wipe its antennæ by drawing them through its mouth. After the antennæ had been extirpated or coated with paraffin, the same insects became indifferent to strong-smelling substances, though brought quite near. Extirpation of the antennæ prevented flies from discovering putrid flesh, and hindered or prevented copulation in insects known to breed in captivity.

Following up these experiments by histological investigation of many insects belonging to different orders, Hauser clearly established the following points, which had been partially made known before :—

The sensory elements of the antennæ are lodged in grooves or pits, which may be filled with fluid. The nerve-endings are associated with peculiar rods, representing modified chitino-

---

* References to the literature of the question are given by Hauser in Zeits. f. wiss. Zool., Bd. XXXIV., and by Plateau in Bull. Soc. Zool. de France, Tom. X.

genous cells. The number of grooves or pits may be enormous. In the male of the Cockchafer, Hauser estimates that there are 39,000 in each antenna. He remarks that in all cases where the female Insect is sluggish and prone to concealment, the male has the antennæ more largely developed than the female.

Sense of Taste in Insects.

F. Will* gives an account of many authors who have investigated with more or less success the sense organs of various Insects. He relates also the results of his own experiments, and gives anatomical details of the sensory organs of the mouth in various Hymenoptera.

Wasps, flying at liberty, were allowed to visit and taste a packet of powdered sugar. This was left undisturbed for some hours, and then replaced by alum of the same appearance. The Wasps attacked the alum, but soon indicated by droll movements that they perceived the difference. They put their tongues in and out and cleansed them from the ill-tasted powder. Two persisted at the alum till they rolled on the table in agony, but they soon recovered and flew away. In a few hours the packet was quite deserted. After a day's interval, during which the sugar lay in its usual place, powdered, and of course perfectly tasteless, dolomite was substituted. The wasps licked it diligently and could not be persuaded for a long time that it could do nothing for them. Similar experiments were made with other substances, and Insects whose antennæ and palps had been removed were subjected to trial. The result clearly proved that a sense of taste existed, and that its seat is in the mouth.† Peculiar nerve-endings, such as Meinert and Forel had previously found in Ants, were found in abundance on the labium, the paraglossæ, and the inner side of the maxillæ of the Wasp. Some lay in pits, through the bases of which single nerves emerged, and swelled into bulbs, or passed into peculiar conical sheaths. Interspersed among the gustatory nerve-endings were setæ of various kinds, some protective, some tactile, and others intended to act as guiding-hairs for the saliva.

* Zeits. f. wiss. Zool., 1885.

† Will confirms, by his own experiments (p. 685), Plateau's conclusion (*Supra*, p.46), that the maxillary and labial palps have nothing to do with the choice of food.

Will observes that the organs described satisfy the essential conditions of a sense of taste. The nerve-endings pass free to the surface, and are thus directly accessible to chemical stimulus. Further, they are so placed that they and the particles of food which get access to them are readily bathed by the saliva. Moistened or dissolved in this fluid, the sapid properties of food are most fully developed.

The sensory pits and bulbs appropriated to taste are believed to be unusually abundant in the social Hymenoptera.

Sense of Hearing in Insects.

The auditory organs of Insects and other Arthropoda are remarkable for the various parts of the body in which they occur. Thus they have been found in the first abdominal segment of Locusts, and in the tibia of the fore-leg of Crickets and Grasshoppers, and more questionable structures with peculiar nerve-endings have been described as occurring in the hinder part of the abdomen of various larvæ (*Ptychoptera, Tabanus, &c*). The auditory organ of Decapod Crustacea is lodged in the base of the antennule, that of Stomapods in the tail, while an auditory organ has been lately discovered on the underside of the head of the Myriopod *Scutigera*.

Auditory organs are best developed in such Insects as produce sounds as a call to each other. The Cockroach is dumb, and it is, therefore, not a matter of surprise that no structure which can be considered auditory should have ever been detected in this Insect.[*]

The sensory hairs of the skin have been already noticed (p. 31).

---

[*] For a popular account of auditory organs in Insects, see Graber's Insekten, Vol. I., page 287 ; also J. Müller, Vergl. Phys. d. Gesichssinn, p. 439 ; Siebold, Arch. f. Naturg., 1844 ; Leydig, Müller's Arch. 1855 and 1860 ; Hensen, Zeits. f. wiss. Zool., 1866 ; Graber, Denkschr. der Akad. der wiss. Wien, 1875 ; and Schmidt, Arch. f. mikr. Anat., 1875.

CHAPTER VII.

The Alimentary Canal and its Appendages.

SPECIAL REFERENCES.

CHOLODKOWSKY. Zur Frage über den Bau und über die Innervation der Speichel-drüsen der Blattiden. Horæ Soc. Entom. Rossicæ, Tom. XVI. (1881). [Salivary Glands of Cockroaches.]

SCHINDLER. Beiträge zur Kenntniss der Malpighi'schen Gefässe der Insekten. Zeits. f. wiss. Zool., Bd. XXX. (1878). [Malpighian Tubules of Insects.]

CHUN. Ueber den Bau, die Entwickelung, und physiologische Bedeutung der Rectaldrüsen bei den Insekten. Abh. der Senkenbergischen Naturforschers Gesell-schaft, Bd. X. (1876). [Rectal Glands of Insects.]

LEYDIG. Lehrbuch der Histologie, &c., and VIALLANES. (Loc. cit. supra, chap. iv.) [Histology of Alimentary Canal.]

BASCH. Untersuchungen über das Chylopoëtische und Uropoëtische System der Blatta orientalis. Kais. Akad. der Wissenschaften. (Math—Nat. Classe.), Bd. XXXIII. (1858). [Digestive and Excretory Organs of Blatta.]

SIRODOT. Recherches sur les Sécrétions chez les Insectes. Ann. Sci. Nat., 4ᵉ Série, Zool., Tom. X. (1859). [Digestive and Excretory Organs of Oryctes, &c.]

JOUSSET DE BELLESME. Recherches expérimentales sur la digestion des Insectes et en particulier de la Blatte (1875).

PLATEAU. Recherches sur les Phénomènes de la Digestion chez les Insectes. Mem. de l'Acad. Roy. de Belgique, Tom. XLI. (1874). [Now the principal authority on the Digestion of Insects. The other physiological memoirs cited (Nos. 5, 6, 7) are chiefly of historical interest.]

PLATEAU. Note additionelle. Bull. Acad. Roy. de Belgique, 2ᵉ Sér., Tom. XLIV. (1877). [Contains some corrections of importance.]

The Alimentary Canal.

THE alimentary canal of the Cockroach measures about 2¾ inches in length, and is therefore about 2¾ times the length of the body. In herbivorous Insects the relative length of the alimentary canal may be much greater than this; it is five

I

times the length of the body in Hydrophilus. Parts of the
canal are specialised for different digestive offices, and their
order and relative size are given in the following table :—

Œsophagus and crop	·95 in.
Gizzard	·1
Chylific stomach	·5
Small intestine	·1
Colon	·875
Rectum	·25
	2·775

Fig. 56.—Alimentary Canal of Cockroach.   × 2.

The principal appendages of the alimentary canal are the
salivary glands, the cæcal diverticula of the stomach, and the
Malpighian tubules.

Considered with respect to its mode of formation, the alimentary canal of all but the very simplest animals falls into three sections—viz., (1) the mesenteron, or primitive digestive cavity, lined by hypoblast; (2) the stomodæum, or mouth-section, lined by epiblast, continuous with that of the external surface; and (3) the proctodæum, or anal section, lined by epiblast folded inwards from the anus, just as the epiblast of the stomodæum is folded in from the mouth. The mesenteron of the Cockroach is very short, as in other Arthropoda, and includes only the chylific stomach with its diverticula. The mouth, œsophagus, and crop form the stomodæum, while the proctodæum begins with the Malpighian tubules, and extends thence to the anus. Both stomodæum and proctodæum have a chitinous lining, which is wanting in the mesenteron. At the time of moult, or a little after, this lining is broken up and passed out of the body.

The mouth of the Cockroach is enclosed between the labrum in front, and the labium behind, while it is bounded laterally by the mandibles and first pair of maxillæ. The chitinous

Ce C

Mo Mi

Fig. 57.—Section of Wall of Crop. *Cc*, chitinous layer; *C*, chitinogenous cells; *Mi*, inner muscular layer; *Mo*, outer do.   × 275.

lining is thrown into many folds, some of which can be obliterated by distension, while others are permanent and filled with solid tissues. The lingua is such a permanent fold, lying like a tongue upon the posterior wall of the cavity and reaching as far as the external opening. The thin chitinous surface of the lingua is hairy, like other parts of the mouth, and stiffened by special chitinous rods or bands. The salivary ducts open by a common orifice on its hinder surface. Above, the mouth leads into a narrow gullet or œsophagus, with longitudinally folded walls, which traverses the nervous ring, and then passes through the occipital foramen to the neck and thorax. Here it gradually dilates into the long and capacious crop, whose large rounded end occupies the fore-part of the abdomen. When empty, or half-empty, the wall of the crop contracts, and is thrown into longitudinal folds, which disappear on distension. Numerous tracheal tubes ramify upon its outer surface, and appear as fine white threads upon a greenish-grey ground.

Three layers can be distinguished in the wall of the crop— viz., (1) the muscular, (2) the epithelial, and (3) the chitinous layer.* The muscular layer consists of annular and longitudinal fibres, crossing at right angles. (See fig. 58.) In most animals the muscles of organic life, subservient to nutrition and reproduction, are very largely composed of plain or unstriped fibres. In Arthropoda (with the exception of the anomalous Peripatus) this is not generally the case, and the muscular fibres of the alimentary canal belong to the striped variety. The

Fig. 58.—Wall of Crop, in successive layers. References as in fig. 57. × 250.

epithelium rests upon a thin structureless basement-membrane, which is firmly united in the œsophagus and crop to the muscular layer and the epithelium. The epithelium consists of scattered nucleated cells, rounded or oval. These epithelial cells, homologues of the chitinogenous cells of the integument, secrete the transparent and structureless chitinous lining. Hairs (setæ) of elongate, conical form, and often articulated at the base, like the large setæ of the outer skin, are abundant.

* Here, as generally in the digestive tube of the adult Cockroach, the peritoneal layer is inconspicuous or wanting. It occasionally becomes visible—e.g., in the outer wall of the Malpighian tubules, and in the tubular prolongation of the gizzard.

In the œsophagus they are very long, and grouped in bundles along sinuous transverse lines. In the crop the hairs become shorter, and the sinuous lines run into a polygonal network. The points of the hairs are directed backwards, and they no doubt serve to guide the flow of saliva towards the crop.

The gizzard has externally the form of a blunt cone, attached by its base to the hinder end of the crop, and produced at the other end into a narrow tube ($\frac{1}{4}$ to $\frac{1}{3}$ in. long), which projects into the chylific stomach. Its muscular wall is thick, and consists of many layers of annular fibres, while the internal cavity is nearly closed by radiating folds of the chitinous lining. Six of the principal folds, the so-called "teeth," are much stronger than the rest, and project so far inwards that they nearly meet. They vary in form, but are generally triangular in cross section and irregularly quadrilateral in side view.

Fig. 59.—Transverse section of Gizzard of Cockroach. The chitinous folds are represented here as symmetrical. See next figure. × 30.

Between each pair are three much less prominent folds, and between these again are slight risings of the chitinous lining. A ridge runs along each side of the base of each principal tooth, and the minor folds, as well as part of the principal teeth, are covered with fine hairs. The central one of each set of secondary folds is produced behind into a spoon-shaped process, which extends considerably beyond the rest, and gradually subsides till it hardly projects from the internal surface of the gizzard. Behind each large tooth (*i.e.*, towards the chylific

stomach) is a rounded cushion set closely with hairs, and
between and beyond these are hairy ridges. (See fig. 61.) The
whole forms an elaborate machine for squeezing and straining
the food, and recalls the gastric mill and pyloric strainer of the

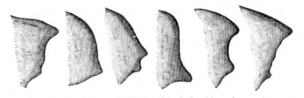

Fig. 60.—The Six Primary Folds (teeth) of the Gizzard, seen in profile.

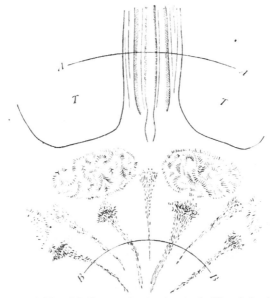

Fig. 61.—Part of Gizzard laid open, showing two teeth (*T*) and the intermediate
folds, as well as the hairy pads below. *A—A* and *B—B* are lines of section
(see figs. 62 and 63). × 50.

Crayfish. The powerful annular muscles approximate the teeth
and folds, closing the passage, while small longitudinal muscles,
which can be traced from the chitinous teeth to the cushions,
appear to retract these last, and open a passage for the food.*

* Plateau has expressed a strong opinion that neither in the stomach of Crustacea
nor in the gizzard of Insects have the so-called teeth any masticatory character.
He compares them to the psalterium of a Ruminant, and considers them strainers
and not dividers of the food. His views, as stated by himself, will be found
on p. 131.

The gizzard ends below, as we have already mentioned, in a narrow cylindrical tube which is protruded into the chylific stomach for about one-third of an inch.   Folds project from the wall of this tube, and reduce its central cavity to an irregular star-like figure.   Below it ends in free processes slightly different from each other in size and shape.   The chitinous

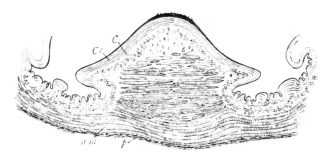

Fig. 62.—Section through one tooth and two intermediate spaces (see figure 61, *A—A*). *Cc*, chitinous cuticle ; *C*, chitinogenous layer; *am*, annular muscles; *p*, peritoneal layer.   × 75.

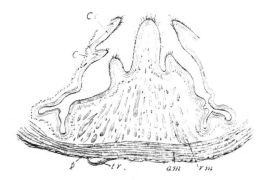

Fig. 63.—Section through one principal hairy ridge and two intermediate spaces (see fig. 61, *B—B*) ; *rm*, radiating muscles ; *tr*, trachea.   The other references as before.   × 75.

lining and the chitinogenous layer beneath pass to the end of the tube and are then reflected upon its outer wall, ascending till they meet the lining epithelium of the cæcal tubes.   Between the wall of the gizzard-tube and its external reflected layer, tracheal tubes, fat-cells, and longitudinal muscles are enclosed.

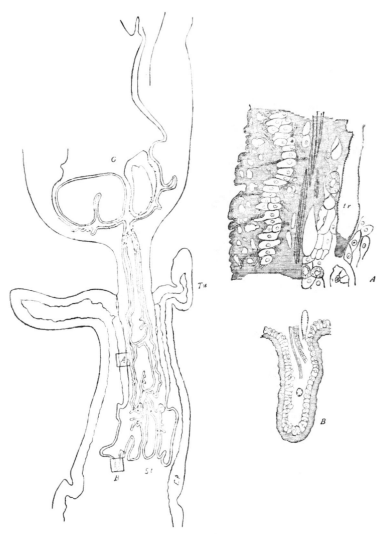

Fig. 64.—Longitudinal section through Gizzard and fore-part of Chylific Stomach. *G*, gizzard ; *Tu*, cæcal tube ; *St*, stomach ; *Ep*, its lining epithelium.   *A* and *B* are enlarged in the side figures.   × 35.

A.—The Reflected Chitinogenous Layer of the Tubular Gizzard.   *Tr*, tracheal tube.   × 400.

B.—One of the Tubular Extensions of the same, enclosing muscles and tracheæ.   × 400.

The chylific stomach is a simple cylindrical tube, provided at
its anterior end with eight (sometimes fewer) cæcal tubes, and
opening behind into the intestine.   Its muscular coat consists of
a loose layer of longitudinal fibres, enclosing annular fibres.
Internal to these is a basement membrane, which supports an
epithelium consisting of elongate cells which are often clustered

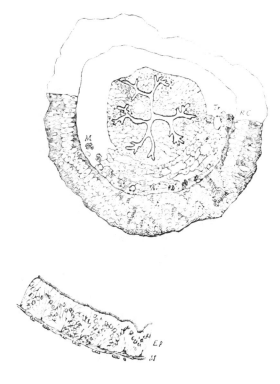

Fig. 65.—Transverse section of tubular prolongation of Gizzard, within the Chylific
    Stomach, part of which is shown at its proper distance.   *R C*, reflected
    chitinogenous layer ;   *Tr*, tracheal tube ;   *M*, cross section of muscle ;   *Ep*,
    epithelium of chylific stomach.   × 100.

into regular eminences, and separated by deep cavities.   The
epithelium forms no chitinous lining in the chylific stomach or
cæcal tubes ; and this peculiarity, no doubt, promotes absorption
of soluble food in this part of the alimentary canal.   Short
processes are given off from the free ends of the epithelial cells,
as in the intestines of many Mammalia and other animals.

Between the cells a reticulum is often to be seen, especially
where the cells have burst; it extends between and among all
the elements of the mucous lining, and probably serves, like
the very similar structure met with in Mammalian intestines,*
to absorb and conduct some of the products of digestion.

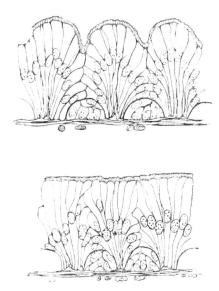

Fig. 66.—Epithelium of Chylific Stomach. In the upper figure the digestive surface
is indented, while in the lower figure it is flat. Both arrangements are
common, and may be seen in a single section. The epithelial buds are shown
below, and again below these the annular and longitudinal muscles. × 220.

Different epithelial cells may be found in all the stages
noticed by Watney—viz., (1) with divided nuclei; (2) small,
newly produced cells at the base of the epithelium; (3) short
and broad cells, overtopped by the older cells around; (4) dome-
shaped masses of young cells, forming "epithelial buds";†
(5) full-grown cells, ranging with those on either side, so as to
form an unbroken and uniform series. The regeneration of the

---

* See Watney, Phil. Trans., 1877, Pt. II. The "epithelial buds" described and
figured in this memoir are also closely paralleled in the chylific stomach of the
Cockroach.

† These epithelial buds have been described as glands, and we only saw their
significance after comparing them with Dr. Watney's account.

tissue is thus provided for. The cells come to maturity and burst, when new cells, the product of the epithelial buds, take their place.

The epithelium of the chylific stomach is continued into the eight cæcal tubes, where it undergoes a slight modification of form.

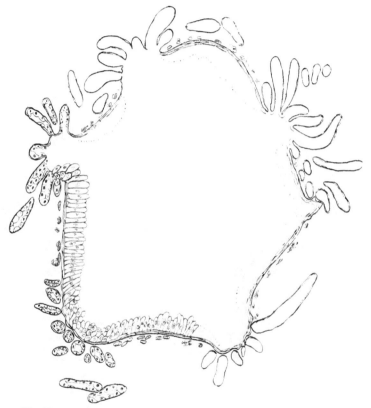

Fig. 67.—Section of Chylific Stomach, showing the six bundles of Malpighian tubules. × 70.

At the hinder end of the chylific stomach is a very short tube about half the diameter of the stomach, the small intestine. At its junction with the chylific stomach are attached, in six bundles, 60 or 70 long and fine tubules, the Malpighian tubules.* The small intestine has the same general

* Development shows that these tubules belong to the proctodæum, and not to the mesenteron.

structure as the œsophagus and crop; its chitinous lining is hairy, and thrown into longitudinal folds which become much more prominent in the lower part of the tube. The junction of the small intestine with the colon is abrupt, and a strong annular fold assumes the character of a circular valve (fig. 68).

From the circular valve the colon extends for nearly an inch. Its diameter is somewhat greater than that of the chylific stomach, and uniform throughout, except for a lateral diverticulum or cæcum, which is occasionally but not constantly present

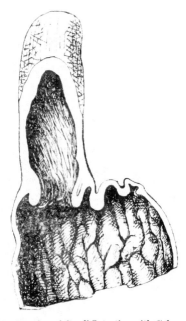

Fig. 68.—Junction of Small Intestine with Colon.   × 15.

towards its rectal end. The fore part of the colon is thrown into a loose spiral coil. A constriction divides the colon from the next division of the alimentary canal, the rectum.

The rectum is about $\frac{1}{4}$ inch long, and is dilated in the middle when distended. Six conspicuous longitudinal folds project into the lumen of the tube. These folds are characterised by an unusual development of the epithelium, which is altogether wanting in the intermediate spaces, where the chitinous lining blends with the basement-membrane, both being thrown into sharp longitudinal corrugations. Between the six epithelial bands and the muscular layer are as many triangular spaces, in which ramify tracheal tubes and fine nerves for the supply of the epithelium. The chitinous layer is finely setose. The muscular layer consists of annular fibres strengthened externally by longitudinal fibres along the interspaces between the six primary folds.*

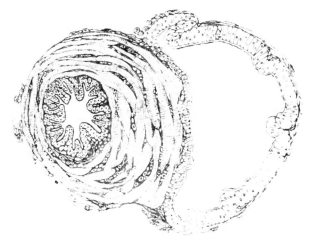

Fig. 69.—Transverse section of Small Intestine and Colon, close to their junction. × 50.

The corrugated and non-epitheliated interspaces may be supposed to favour distension of the rectal chamber, while the great size of the cells of the bands of epithelium is perhaps due to their limited extent. Leydig† attributed to these rectal bands a respiratory function, and compared them to the epithelial folds of the rectum of Libellulid larvæ, which, as is well known, respire by admitting fresh supplies of water into this cavity. It is an obvious objection that Cockroaches and other Insects in which the rectal bands are well developed do not take water into the intestine at all. Gegenbaur has there-

* The epithelial bands of the rectum of Insects were first discovered by Swammerdam in the Bee (Bibl. Nat., p. 455, pl. xviii., fig. 1). Dufour called them muscular bands (Rech. sur les Orthoptères, &c., p. 369, fig. 44).

† "Lehrbuch der Histologie," p. 337.

fore modified Leydig's hypothesis. He suggests (Grundzüge
d. Vergl. Anat.) that the functional rectal folds of Dragon-flies
and the non-functional folds of terrestrial Insects are both
survivals of tracheal gills, which were the only primitive organs
of respiration of Insects. The late appearance of the rectal
folds and the much earlier appearance of spiracles is a serious
difficulty in the way of this view, as Chun has pointed out. It
seems more probable that the respiratory appendages of the
rectum of the Dragon-fly larvæ are special adaptations to
aquatic conditions of a structure which originated in terrestrial
Insects, and had primarily nothing to do with respiration.

Fig. 70.—Transverse section of Rectum.   × 50.

The number of the rectal bands (six) is worthy of remark.
We find six sets of folds in the gizzard and small intestine of
the Cockroach, six bundles of Malpighian tubules, with six
intermediate epitheliated bands. There are also six longitudinal
bands in the intestine of the Lobster and Crayfish.   The
tendency to produce a six-banded stomodæum and proctodæum
may possibly be related to the six theoretical elements (two
tergal, two pleural, two sternal,) traceable in the Arthropod
exoskeleton, of which the proctodæum and stomodæum are
reflected folds.

The anus of the Cockroach opens beneath the tenth tergum, and between two "podical" plates. Anal glands, such as occur in some Beetles, have not been discovered in Cockroaches.

Appendages. The Salivary Glands.

The three principal appendages of the alimentary canal of the Cockroach are outgrowths of the three primary divisions of the digestive tube; the salivary glands are diverticula of the stomodæum, the cæcal tubes of the mesenteron, and the Malpighian tubules of the proctodæum.

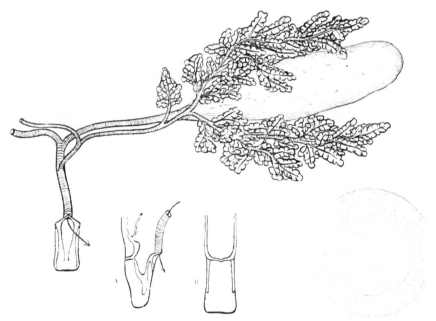

Fig. 71.—Salivary Glands and Receptacle, right side. The arrow marks the opening of the common duct on the back of the lingua. A, side view of lingua; B, front view of lingua.

A large salivary gland and reservoir lie on each side of the œsophagus and crop. The gland is a thin foliaceous mass about ⅓ in. long, and composed of numerous acini, which are grouped into two principal lobes. The efferent ducts form a trunk, which receives a branch from a small accessory lobe, and then unites with its fellow. The common glandular duct thus

formed opens into the much larger common receptacular duct,
formed by the union of paired outlets from the salivary reservoirs. The common salivary duct opens beneath the lingua.
Each salivary reservoir is an oval sac with transparent walls,
and about half as long again as the gland. The ducts and
reservoirs have a chitinous lining, and the ducts exhibit a
transverse marking like that of a tracheal tube. When
examined with high powers the wall of the salivary gland
shows a network of protoplasm with large scattered nuclei,
resting upon a structureless chitinous membrane.

The salivary glands are unusually large in most Orthoptera.*
In other orders they are of variable occurrence and of very
unequal development.

The Cœcal Tubes.

There are eight (sometimes fewer) cæcal tubes arranged in a
ring round the fore end of the chylific stomach ; they vary in
length, the longer ones, which are about equal to the length of
the stomach itself, usually alternating with shorter ones, though
irregularities of arrangement are common. The tubes are
diverticula of the stomach and lined by a similar epithelium.
In the living animal they are sometimes filled with a whitish
granular fluid.

Similar cæcal tubes, sometimes very numerous and densely
clustered, are attached to the stomach in many Crustacea and
Arachnida. The researches of Hoppe Seyler, Krukenberg,
Plateau, and others have established the digestive properties
of the fluid secreted in them, which agrees with the pancreatic
juice of Vertebrates.

The Malpighian Tubules.

The Malpighian tubules mark the beginning of the small
intestine, to which they properly belong. They are very
numerous (60-70) in the Cockroach, as in Locusts, Earwigs, and
Dragon-flies ; and unbranched, as in most Insects. They are
about ·8 inch in length, and ·002 inch in transverse diameter,
so that they are barely visible to the naked eye as single

* Except in Dragon-flies and Ephemeræ.

threads. In larvæ about one-fifth of an inch long, Schindler* found only eight long tubules, the usual number in Thysanura, Anoplura, and Termes; but the grouping into six masses, so plainly seen in the adult, throws some doubt upon this observation. In the adult Cockroach the long threads wind about the abdominal cavity and its contained viscera.

In the wall of a Malpighian tubule there may be distinguished (1) a connective tissue layer, with fine fibres and nuclei; within this, (2) a basement-membrane, between which

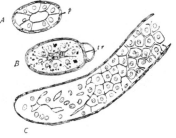

Fig. 72.—Malpighian Tubules of Cockroach. *A*, transverse section of young tubule; *p*, its connective-tissue or "peritoneal" layer; *B*, older tubule, crowded with urates; *tr*, tracheal tube; *C*, tubule cut open longitudinally, showing three states of the lining epithelium.   × 200.

and the connective tissue layer runs a delicate, unbranched tracheal tube; (3) an epithelium of relatively large, nucleated cells, in a single layer, nearly filling the tube, and leaving only a narrow, irregular central canal. Transverse sections show from four to ten of these cells at once. The tubules appear transparent or yellow-white, according as they are empty or full; sometimes they are beaded or varicose; in other cases, one half is coloured and the other clear. The opaque contents consist partly of crystals, which usually occur singly in the epithelial cells, or heaped up in the central canal. Occasionally, they form spherical concretions with a radiate arrangement. They contain uric acid, and probably consist of urate of soda.†

* Zeitsch. f. wiss. Zool., Bd. XXX.

† The contents of the Malpighian tubules may be examined by crushing the part in a drop of dilute acetic acid, or in dilute sulphuric acid (10 per cent.). In the first case a cover-slip is placed on the fluid, and the crystals, which consist of oblique rhombohedrons, or derived forms, are usually at once apparent. If sulphuric acid is used, the fluid must be allowed to evaporate. In this case they are much more elongated, and usually clustered. The murexide reaction does not give satisfactory indications with the tubules of the Cockroach.

In the living Insect the tubules remove urates from the blood
which bathes the viscera; the salts are condensed and crystal-
lised in the epithelial cells, by whose dehiscence they pass into
the central canals of the tubules, and thence into the intestine.

The Malpighian tubules develop as diverticula from the
proctodæum, which is an invagination of the outer integument
and its morphological equivalent.   They are, therefore, similar
in origin to urinary organs opening upon the surface of the
body and developed as invaginations of the integument, like
the "shell-glands" of lower Crustacea, and the "green glands"
of Decapod Crustacea.   The segmental organs of *Peripatus*,
Annelids, and Vertebrates do not appear to be possible equiva-
lents of the excretory organs of Arthropods.   They arise, not
as involutions, but as solid masses of mesoblastic tissue, or as
channels constricted off from the peritoneal cavity, and their
ducts have only a secondary connection with the outside of the
body or with the alimentary canal.

Digestion of Insects.

The investigation of the digestive processes in Insects is
work of extreme difficulty, and it is not surprising that much
yet remains to be discovered.   Plateau has, however, succeeded
in solving some of the more important questions, which, before
his time, had been dealt with in an incomplete or otherwise
unsatisfactory way.   The experiments of Basch, though now
superseded by Plateau's more trustworthy results, deserve
notice as first attempts to investigate the properties of the
digestive fluids of Insects.

Basch set out with a conviction that where a chitinous lining
is present, the epithelium of the alimentary canal secretes chitin
only, and that proper digestive juices are only elaborated in
the chylific stomach, or in the salivary glands.   The tests
applied by him seemed to show that the saliva, as well as the
contents of the œsophagus and crop, had an acid reaction, while
the contents of the chylific stomach were neutral at the beginning of the tube and alkaline further down.   From this he
concluded that the supposed deep-seated glands of the chylific
stomach secreted an alkaline fluid, which neutralised the acidity

of the saliva. Finding that the epithelial cells of the stomach were often loaded with oil-drops, he concluded that absorption, at least of fats, takes place here. The chylific stomach, carefully emptied of its contents, was found to convert starch into sugar at ordinary temperatures. The saliva of the Cockroach gave a similar result, and when a weak solution of hydrochloric acid was added, Basch thought that the mixture could digest blood-fibrin at ordinary temperatures.

Plateau's researches upon *Periplaneta americana*,[*] modified by subsequent experiments upon *P. orientalis*,[†] and by still more recent observations, lead him to the following conclusions[‡] :—

1.—The saliva of the Cockroach changes starch into glucose; but the saliva is not acid, it is either neutral (*P. orientalis*) or alkaline (*P. americana*). Any decided acidity found in the crop is due to the ingestion of acid food; but a very faint acidity may occur, which results from the presence in the crop of a fluid secreted by the cæcal diverticula of the mesenteron.

2.—The glucose thus formed is absorbed in the crop, and no more is formed in the succeeding parts of the digestive tube.

3.—The function of the gizzard is that of a grating or strainer. It has no power of trituration. If the animal consumes vegetable food rich in cellulose, a substance not capable of digestion in the crop, the fragments are found unaltered as to form and size in the mesenteron. If it is supplied with plenty of farinaceous food, such as meal or flour, the saliva is not adequate to the complete solution and transformation of the starch, and the intestine is found full of uninjured starch granules, which must have traversed the gizzard without crushing.

4.—The cæcal diverticula secrete a feebly acid fluid. To demonstrate its acidity an extremely sensitive litmus solution, capable of indicating one part in twenty thousand of hydrochloric acid, must be used. The fluid secreted by the cæca emulsifies fats, and converts albuminoids into peptones.

In all Insects digestion is effected in the following way (which is particularly easy of demonstration in *Carabus* and

[*] Bull. Acad. Roy. de Belgique, 1876.

[†] Ib., 1877.

[‡] We are indebted to Prof. Plateau for the statement of his views given in the text.

Dytiscus). The crop is filled with food coarsely divided by the mandibles, and the gizzard being shut to prevent further passage, the fluid secretion of the cæca ascends to the crop, and there acts upon the food. Digestion is effected in the crop, and not beyond it. This is clear beyond doubt. In Decapod Crustacea also it is very easy to prove that the fluid secreted by the so-called liver ascends into the stomach (which corresponds to the crop, together with the gizzard of the Insect). To satisfy ourselves on this point we have only to open a Crayfish during active digestion.

When digestion in the crop is finished, the gizzard relaxes, and the contents of the crop, now in a semi-fluid condition, pass into the mesenteron, which is devoid of chitinous lining, and particularly fitted for absorption.

5.—There are no absorbent vessels properly so called, and Plateau has long thought that the products of digestion pass by osmosis directly through the walls of the digestive tube, to mix with the blood in the perivisceral space. If we may rely upon what is now known of the process in Vertebrates, we should be led to modify this explanation. It is very likely that in Insects, as in Vertebrates, absorption is effected by the protoplasm of the epithelial cells, which select and appropriate certain subtances formed out of the dissolved food. Not only do the epithelial cells transmit to the neighbouring blood-currents the materials which they have previously absorbed, but they subject certain kinds to further elaboration. The protoplasm of the epithelial cells of Vertebrates is capable of forming fat. Thus, a mixture of soap and glycerine, injected into the intestine of a Vertebrate, is absorbed by the lacteals in the form of oil-drops. Modern physiologists allow, too, that part of the peptone is similarly changed into albumen, without transport to a distance, by the activity of the epithelial lining.

These facts explain why Plateau was unable to isolate the secretion of the epithelium of the chylific stomach of Insects. The cells are not secretory, but absorbent; and the secretion vainly sought for does not actually exist.

CHAPTER VIII.

The Organs of Circulation and Respiration.

SPECIAL REFERENCES.

VERLOREN. Mém. sur la Circulation dans les Insectes. Mém. cour. par l'Acad. Roy. de Belgique, Tom. XIX. (1847). [Structure of Circulatory Organs in a number of different Insects.]

GRABER. Ueb. den Propulsatorischen Apparat der Insekten. Arch. f. mikr. Anat., Bd. IX. (1872). [Heart and Pericardium.]

LEYDIG. Larve von Corethra plumicornis. Zeits. f. wiss. Zool., Bd. III. (1852). [Valves in Heart.]

LANDOIS, H. Beob. üb. das Blut der Insekten. Zeits. f. wiss. Zool., Bd. XIV. (1864). [Blood of Insects.]

JAWOROWSKI. Entw. des Rückengefässes, &c., bei Chironomus. Sitzb. der k. Akad. der Wiss. Wien., Bd. LXXX. (1879). [Minute Structure and Development of Heart.]

LANDOIS, H., and THELEN. Der Tracheenverschluss bei den Insekten. Zeits. f. wiss. Zool., Bd. XVII. (1867). [Stigmata.]

PALMEN. Zur Morphologie des Tracheensystems (1877). [Morphology of Stigmata and Tracheal Gills.]

MACLEOD. La Structure des Trachées et la Circulation Péritrachéenne. (Brussels, 1880.)

LUBBOCK. Distribution of Tracheæ in Insects. Trans. Linn. Soc., Vol. XXIII. (1860).

RATHKE. Untersuch. üb. den Athmungsprozess der Insekten. Schr. d. Phys. Oek. Gesellsch. zu Königsberg. Jahrg. I. (1861). [Experiments and Observations on Insect-respiration.]

PLATEAU. Rech. Expérimentales sur les Mouvements Respiratoires des Insectes. Mém. de l'Acad. Roy. de Belgique, Tom. XLV. (1884). Preliminary notice in Bull. Acad. Roy. de Belgique, 1882.

LANGENDORFF. Studien üb. die Innervation der Athembewegungen.—Das Athmungscentrum der Insekten. Arch. f. Anat. u. Phys. (1883). [Respiratory Centres of Insects.]

Circulation of Insects.

A VERY long chapter might be written upon the views advanced by different writers as to the circulation of Insects. Malpighi first discovered the heart or dorsal vessel in the young Silkworm. His account is tolerably full and remarkably free from mistakes. The heart of the Silkworm, he tells us, extends the whole length of the body, and its pulsations are externally visible in young larvæ. He supposed that contraction is effected by muscular fibres, but these he could not distinctly see. The tube, he says, has no single large chamber, but is formed of many little hearts (*corcula*) leading one into another. The number of these he could not certainly make out, but believed that there was one to each segment of the body. During contraction each chamber became more rounded, and when contraction was specially energetic, the sides of the tube appeared to meet at the constrictions. The flow of blood, he ascertained, was forward, the rhythm not constant. No arteries were seen to be given off from the heart.* Swammerdam thought that his injections ascertained the existence of vessels branching out from the heart,† but this proved to be a mistake. Lyonnet added many details of interest to what was previously known. He came to the conclusion that there was no system of vessels connected with the heart, and even doubted whether the organ so named was in effect a heart at all. Marcel de Serres maintained that it was merely the secreting organ of the fat-body. Cuvier and Dufour doubted whether any circulation, except of air, existed in Insects. This was the extreme point of scepticism, and naturalists were drawn back from it by Herold,‡ who repeated and confirmed the views held by the seventeenth-century anatomists, and insisted upon the demonstrable fact that the dorsal vessel of an Insect does actually pulsate and impel a current of fluid. Carus, in 1826, saw the blood flowing in definite channels in the wings, antennæ, and legs. Straus-Durckheim followed up this discovery by demonstrating the contractile and valvular structures of the dorsal vessel. Blanchard affirmed that a complex system of vessels accompanied the air tubes throughout the body, occupying peritracheal spaces supposed to exist between the inner and outer walls of the tracheæ. This peritracheal circulation has not withstood critical inquiry,§ and it might be pronounced wholly imaginary, except for the fact that air tubes and nerves are found here and there within the veins of the wings of Insects.

* Dissert. de Bombyce, pp. 15, 16 (1669).

† Biblia Naturæ, p. 410.

‡ Schrift. d. Marburg. Naturf. Gesellschaft, 1823.

§ See, for a full account of this discussion, MacLeod sur la Structure des Trachées, et la Circulation Péritrachéenne (1880). The peritracheal circulation was refuted by Joly (Ann. Sci. Nat., 1849).

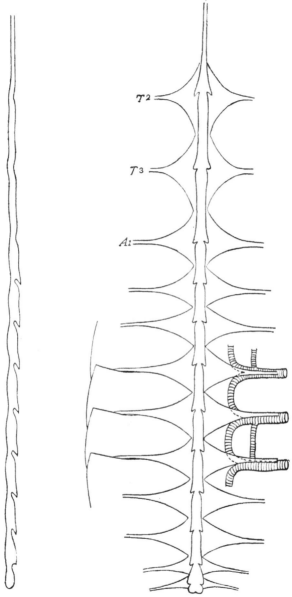

Fig. 73.—Heart, Alary Muscles, and Tracheal Arches, seen from below ; to the left is a side view of the heart. T^2, T^3, A^1, alary muscles attached to the second thoracic, third thoracic, and first abdominal terga.   × 6.   Fig. 35 (p. 74) is not quite correct as to the details of the heart.   The thoracic portion should be chambered, and additional chambers and alary muscles represented at the end of the abdomen.   These omissions are rectified in the present figure.

Heart of the Cockroach.

The heart of the Cockroach is a long, narrow tube, lying immediately beneath the middle line of the thorax and abdomen. It consists of thirteen segments (fig. 73), which correspond to three thoracic and ten abdominal somites. Each segment, as a rule, ends behind in a conspicuous fold which projects backwards from the dorsal surface; immediately in front of this are two lateral lobes. The median lobe passes into the angle between two adjacent terga, and is continuous with the dorsal wall of the segment next behind, from which it is separated only by a deep constriction, while the lateral folds

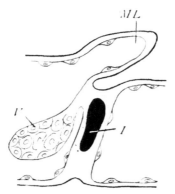

Fig. 74.—Diagram to show the interventricular valves and lateral inlets of the Heart. *ML*, median lobe ; *V*, valve ; *I*, lateral inlet.

conceal paired lateral inlets,* which lead from the pericardial space to the hinder end of each chamber of the heart. Immediately in front of each constriction is the interventricular valve, a pear-shaped mass of nucleated cells, hanging down from the upper wall of the heart, and inclining forward below. The position of this valve indicates that during systole it closes upon the constricted boundary between two chambers, thus shutting off at once the inlets and the passage into the chambers behind. In this way the progressive and rhythmical contraction of the chambers impels a steady forward current of blood, allowing an

---

* It may be observed that Graber, who has paid close attention to the heart of Insects, describes the inlets (*e. g.*, in *Dytiscus*) as situated, not at the hinder end, but in the middle of each segment. We have not been able to discover such an arrangement in the heart of the Cockroach.

intermittent stream to enter from the pericardial space, but preventing regurgitation.

The wall of the heart includes several distinct layers. There are (1) a transparent, structureless intima, only visible when thrown into folds; (2) a partial endocardium, of scattered, nucleated cells, which passes into the interventricular valves; (3) a muscular layer, consisting of close-set annular, and distant longitudinal fibres. The annular muscles are slightly interrupted at regular and frequent intervals, and are imperfectly

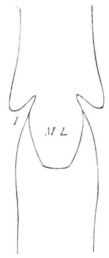

Fig. 75.—Junction of two chambers of the Heart, seen from above. *ML*, median lobe ; *I*, lateral inlet.

joined along the middle line above and below, so as to indicate (what has been independently proved) that the heart arises as two half-tubes, which afterwards join along the middle. Elongate nuclei are to be seen here and there among the muscles. The adventitia (4), or connective tissue layer, is but slightly developed in the adult Cockroach.

Within the muscular layer is a structure which we have failed to make out to our own satisfaction. It presents the appearance of regular but imperfect rings, which do not extend over the upper third of the heart. They probably meet in a ventral suture, but this and other details are hard to make out, owing to the transparency of the parts. The rings stain with

difficulty, and we have not observed nuclei belonging to them.
Each extends over more than one bundle of annular muscles.

The difficulty of investigating a structure so minute and
delicate as the heart of an Insect may explain a good deal of the
discrepancy noted on comparing various published descriptions.
Perhaps the most obvious peculiarity which distinguishes the
heart of the Cockroach, is the subdivision of the thoracic portions into three chambers, which, though less prominent in side-
view than the abdominal chambers, are, nevertheless, perfectly
distinct. The number of abdominal chambers is also unusually
high ; but it is so easy to overlook the small chambers at the
posterior end of the abdomen, that the number given in some
of the species may have been under-estimated.

Pericardial Diaphragm and Space.

The heart lies in a pericardial chamber, which is bounded
above by the terga and the longitudinal tergal muscles; below
by a fenestrated membrane, the pericardial diaphragm. The
intermediate space, which is of inconsiderable depth, is nearly
filled by a cellular mass laden with fat, and resembling the
fat-body.

The pericardial diaphragm, or floor of the pericardium, is
continuous, except for small oval openings scattered over its
surface. It consists of loosely interwoven fibres, interspersed
with elongate nuclei (connective-tissue corpuscles) and connected by a transparent membrane. Into the diaphragm are
inserted pairs of muscles, which, from their shape and supposed
continuity with the heart, have been named alæ cordis, or alary
muscles.* These are bundles of striated muscle, about ·003 in.
wide, which arise from the anterior margin of each tergum.
In the middle of the abdomen every alary muscle passes
inwards for about ·04 in., without breaking-up or widening,
and then spreads out fanwise upon the diaphragm. The
fibres unite below the heart with those of the fellow-muscle, and
also join, close to the heart, those of the muscles in front and
behind. The alary muscles are often said to distend the heart
rhythmically by drawing its walls apart, but this cannot be

* Lyonnet.

true. They do not pass into the heart at all. Even if they did, a pull from opposite sides upon a flexible, cylindrical tube, would narrow and not expand its cavity. Moreover, direct observation* shows that the heart continues to beat after all the alary muscles have been divided, and even after it has been cut in pieces. These facts suggest that the heart of Insects is innervated by ganglia upon or within it, and indeed transparent larvæ, such as *Corethra* or *Chironomus*, exhibit paired cells, very like simple ganglia, along the sides of the heart.

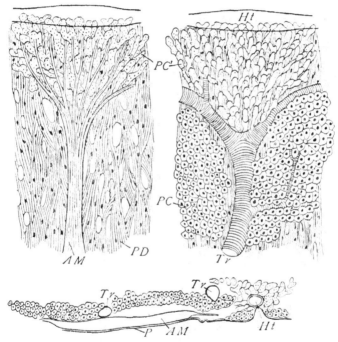

Fig. 76.—Heart and Pericardial Diaphragm. On the right, as seen from above ; on the left, as seen from below ; the bottom figure represents a transverse section. *Ht*, heart ; *PD*, pericardial diaphragm ; *AM*, alary muscle ; *Tr*, tracheal tube ; *PC*, pericardial fat-cells ; *PC*¹, multinucleate fat-cells.

Scattered over the upper surface of the pericardial diaphragm are groups of cells, similar to the fat-masses of the perivisceral space. Over the fan-like expansions of the alary muscles are

* Brandt, Ueb. d. Herz der Insekten u. Muscheln. Mél. Biol. Bull. Acad. St. Petersb. Tom. VI. (1866).

different fat-cells, which form branched and multinucleate lobes, and radiate in the same direction as the underlying muscles.

Tracheal trunks, arising close to the stigmata, ascend upon the tergal wall towards the heart. They overlie the alary muscles, and end near the heart by bifurcation, sending one branch forward and another backward to meet corresponding branches of adjacent trunks. A series of arches is thus formed by the dorsal tracheæ on each side of the heart. Occasionally an arch is subdivided into two smaller parallel tubes. A few branches of distribution are given off to the fat-cells of the pericardium.

Graber has explained the action of the pericardial diaphragm and chamber in the following way.* When the alary muscles contract, they depress the diaphragm, which is arched upwards when at rest. A rush of blood towards the heart is thereby set up, and the blood streams through the perforated diaphragm into the pericardial chamber. Here it bathes a spongy or cavernous tissue (the fat-cells), which is largely supplied with air tubes, and having been thus aerated, passes immediately forwards to the heart, entering it at the moment of diastole, which is simultaneous with the sinking of the diaphragm.

In the Cockroach the facts of structure do not altogether justify this explanation. The fenestræ of the diaphragm are mere openings without valves. The descent of a perforated non-valvular plate can bring no pressure to bear upon the blood, for it is not contended that the alary muscles are powerful enough to change the figure of the abdominal rings. Moreover, we find comparatively few tracheal tubes in the pericardial chamber, and can discover no proof that in the Cockroach the fat-cells adjacent to the heart have any special respiratory character. The diaphragm appears to give mechanical support to the heart, resisting pressure from a distended alimentary canal, while the sheets of fat-cells, in addition to their proper physiological office, may equalise small local pressures, and prevent displacement. The movement of the blood towards the heart must (we think) depend, not upon the alary muscles, but upon the far more powerful muscles of the abdominal wall, and upon the pumping action of the heart itself.

* Arch. f. mikr. Anat., Bd. IX. (1872); Insekten, ch. x.

Circulation of the Cockroach.

The pulsations of the heart are rhythmical and usually frequent, the number of beats in a given time varying with the species, the age, and especially with the degree of activity or excitement of the Insect observed.*

Cornelius † watched the pulsations in a white Cockroach immediately after its change of skin, and reckoned them at eighty per minute; but he remarks that the Insect was restless, and that the beats were probably accelerated in consequence.

In the living Insect a wave of contraction passes rapidly along the heart from behind forwards; and the blood may under favourable circumstances be seen to flow in a steady, backward stream along the pericardial sinus, to enter the lateral aperture of the heart. The peristaltic movement of the dorsal vessel may often be observed to set in at the hinder end of the tube before the preceding wave has reached the aorta.

From the heart a slender tube (the aorta) passes forward to the head. It lies upon the dorsal surface of the œsophagus, which it accompanies as far as the supra-œsophageal ganglia. In many Insects the thoracic portion of the dorsal vessel is greatly narrowed and non-valvular, forming the aorta of most writers on Insect Anatomy. The aorta often dips downward near its origin, but in the Cockroach the thoracic portion of the vessel keeps nearly the same level as the abdominal. It gives off no lateral branches, but suddenly ends immediately in front of the œsophageal ring in a trumpet-shaped orifice,‡ by which the blood passes at once into a lacunar system which occupies the perivisceral space. Here the blood bathes the digestive and reproductive organs, receives the products of digestion, which are not transmitted by lacteals, but discharged at once into the blood; here, too, it gives up its urates to the excretory tubules, and its superfluous fats to the finely-divided lobules of the fat-body. The form of the various appendages of the alimentary

---

* Newport, in Todd's Cyclopædia of Anatomy and Physiology, Art. Insecta, pp. 981-2.

† Beitr. zur näheren Kenntuiss von Periplaneta orientalis, p. 19.

‡ The termination of the aorta has been described by Newport, in *Sphinx* (Phil. Trans., 1832, Pt. I., p. 385) *Vanessa, Meloe, Blaps* and *Timarcha*. (Todd's Cycl., Art. "Insecta," p. 978.)

canal (salivary glands, cæcal tubes, and Malpighian tubules), as well as of the testes, ovaries, and fat-body, is immediately connected with the passive behaviour of the fluid upon which their nutrition depends. Instead of being compact organs injected at every pulsation by blood under pressure, they are diffuse, tubular, or branched, so as to expose as large a surface as possible to the sluggish stream in which they float.

From the perivisceral space the blood enters the pericardial sinus by the apertures in its floor, and returns thence by the lateral inlets into the heart.

No satisfactory injections of the circulatory channels can be made in Insects, on account of the large lacunæ, or cavities without proper wall, which are interposed between the heart and the extremities of the body. In the wings and other transparent organs the blood has been seen to flow along definite channels, which form a network, and resemble true blood vessels in their arrangement. Whether they possess a proper wall has not been ascertained. It is observed that in such cases the course of the blood is generally forwards along the anterior, and backwards along the posterior, side of the appendage. The direction of the current is not, however, quite constant, and the same cross branch may at different times transmit blood in different directions.[*]

Blood of the Cockroach.

The blood of the Cockroach may be collected for examination by cutting off one of the legs, and wiping the cut end with a cover-slip. It abounds in large corpuscles, each of which consists of a rounded nucleus invested by protoplasm. Amœboid movements may often be observed, and dividing corpuscles are occasionally seen. Crystals may be obtained by evaporating a drop of the blood without pressure ; they form radiating clusters of pointed needles. The fresh-drawn blood is slightly alkaline ; it is colourless in the Cockroach, but milky, greenish, or reddish in some other Insects. The quantity varies greatly, according to the nutrition of the individual : after a few days' starvation, nearly all the blood is absorbed. Larvæ contain much more blood, in proportion to their weight, than other Insects.

[*] Moseley, Q. J. Micr. Sci. (1871).

Respiratory Organs of Insects.

The respiratory organs of Insects consist of ramified tracheal tubes, which communicate with the external air by stigmata or spiracles. Of these spiracles the Cockroach has ten pairs— eight in the abdomen and two in the thorax. The first thoracic spiracle lies in front of the mesothorax, beneath the edge of the tergum ; the second is similarly placed in front of the metathorax. The eight abdominal spiracles belong to the first eight somites ; each lies in the fore part of its segment, and hence, apparently, in the interspace between two terga and two sterna. The first abdominal spiracle is distinctly dorsal in position.

The disposition of the spiracles observed in the Cockroach is common in Insects, and, of all the recorded arrangements, this approaches nearest to the plan of the primitive respiratory system of Tracheata, in which there may be supposed to be as many spiracles as somites.* The head never carries spiracles except in *Smynthurus*, one of the Collembola (Lubbock). Many larvæ possess only the first of the three possible thoracic spiracles ; in perfect Insects this is rarely or never met with (*Pulicidæ?*), but either the second, or both the second and third, are commonly developed. Of the abdominal somites, only the first eight ever bear spiracles, and these may be reduced in burrowing or aquatic larvæ to one pair (the eighth), while all disappear in the aquatic larva of *Ephemera*.

From the spiracles, short, wide air-tubes pass inwards, and break up into branches, which supply the walls of the body and all the viscera. Dorsal branches ascend towards the heart on the upper side of the alary muscles ; each bifurcates above, and its divisions join those of the preceding and succeeding segments, thus forming loops or arches. The principal ventral branches take a transverse direction, and are usually connected by large longitudinal trunks, which pass along the

---

* The oldest Tracheate actually known to bear spiracles is the Silurian Scorpion of Gothland and Scotland (Scudder, in Zittel's Palæontologie, p. 738). We need not say that this is very far removed from the primitive Tracheate which morphological theory requires. The existing *Peripatus* makes a nearer approach to the ideal ancestor of all Tracheates, if we suppose that all Tracheates had a common ancestor of any kind, which is not as yet beyond doubt.

sides of the body; the Cockroach, in addition to these, possesses smaller longitudinal vessels, which lie close to the middle line, on either side of the nerve-cord.* The ultimate branches form an intricate network of extremely delicate tubes, which penetrates or overlies every tissue.

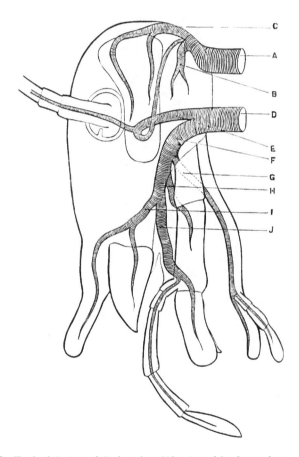

Fig. 77.—Tracheal System of Cockroach. Side view of head seen from without, introducing the chief branches of the left half. × 15.

* The longitudinal air-tubes are characteristic of the more specialised Tracheata. In Araneidæ, many Julidæ, and Peripatus each spiracle has a separate tracheal system of its own.

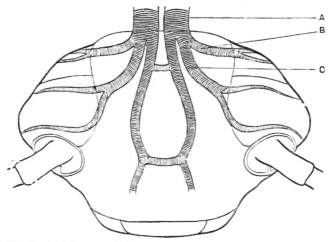

Fig. 78.—Tracheal System of Cockroach.   Top and front of head seen from
without.   × 15.

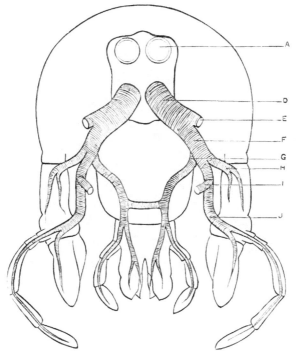

Fig. 79.—Tracheal System of Cockroach.   Back of head, seen from the front, the
fore half being removed.   × 15.   The letters A—J indicate corresponding
branches in figs. 77, 78, and 79.

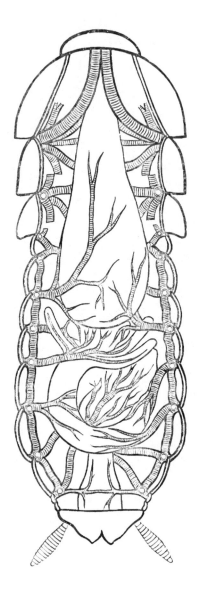

Fig. 80.—Tracheal System of Cockroach. The dorsal integument removed and the viscera in place. × 5.

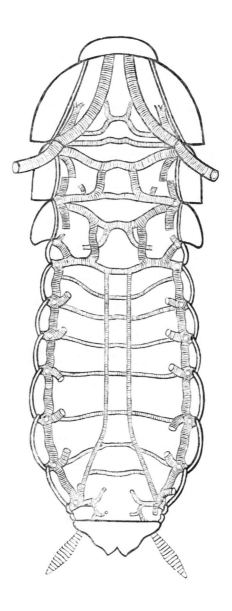

Fig. 81.—Tracheal System of Cockroach. The viscera removed to show the ventral tracheal communications. × 5.

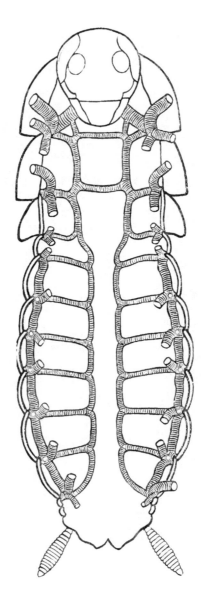

Fig. 82.—Tracheal System of Cockroach.   The ventral integument and viscera
      removed to show the dorsal tracheal communications.   × 5.

Tracheal Tubes.

The accompanying figures sufficiently explain the chief features of the tracheal system of the Cockroach, so far as it can be explored by simple dissection. Leaving them to tell their own tale, we shall pass on to the minute structure of the air-tubes, the spiracles, and the physiology of Insect respiration.

The tracheal wall is a folding-in of the integument, and agrees with it in general structure. Its inner lining, the intima, is chitinous, and continuous with the outer cuticle. It is secreted by an epithelium of nucleated, chitinogenous cells, and outside this is a thin and homogeneous basement membrane. The integument, the tracheal wall, and the inner layers of nearly the whole alimentary canal are continuous and equivalent structures. The lining of the larger tracheal tubes at least is shed at every moult, like that of the stomodæum and proctodæum.

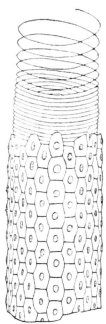

Fig. 83.—Tracheal tube with its epithelium and spiral thread. Slightly altered from a figure given by Chun (Rectal-drüsen bei den Insekten, pl. iv., fig. 1).

Tracheal Thread.

In the finest tracheal tubes ('0001 in. and under) the intima is to all appearance homogeneous. In wider tubes it is strengthened by a spiral thread, which is denser, more refractive, and more flexible than the intervening membrane. The thread projects slightly into the lumen of the tube, and is often branched. It is interrupted frequently, each length making but a few turns round the tube, and ending in a point. The thread of a branch is never continued into a main trunk. Both the thread and the intervening membrane become invisible or faint when the tissue is soaked with a transparent fluid, so as

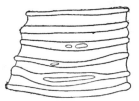

Fig. 84.—Intima (chitinous lining) of a large tracheal tube. The spiral thread divides here and there. Copied from MacLeod, loc. cit., fig. 9.

to expel the air. Both, but especially the thread, absorb colouring matter with difficulty. The thread, from its greater thickness, offers a longer resistance to solvents, such as caustic alkalies, and also to mechanical force ; it can therefore be readily unrolled, and often projects as a loose spiral from the end of a torn tube, while the membrane breaks up or crumbles away.*

The large tracheal tubes close to the spiracles are without spiral thread, and the intima is here subdivided into polygonal

* Investigators are not yet agreed as to the minute structure of the tracheal thread. Chun (Abh. d. Senkenberg. Naturf. Gesells., Bd. X., 1876) considers it an independent chitinous formation, not a mere thickening of the intima. He describes the thread as solid. The intima itself is, he believes, divisible in the larger tubes into an inner and an outer layer, into both of which the thread is sunk. Macloskie (Amer. Nat., June, 1884) describes the spiral as a fine tubule, opening by a fissure along its length. He regards it as a hollow crenulation of the intima, and continuous therewith. Packard (Amer. Nat. Mag., May, 1886) endeavours to show that the thread is not spiral, but consists of parallel thickenings of the intima. He is unable to find proof of the tubular structure, or of the external fissure. We have specially examined the trachea of the Cockroach, and find that the thread can readily be unwound for several turns. It is truly spiral.

areas, each of which is occupied by a reticulation of very fine threads. This structure may be traced for a short distance between the turns of the spiral thread.

The chitinogenous layer of the tracheal tubes is single, and consists of polygonal, nucleated cells, forming a mosaic pattern, but becoming irregular and even branched in the finest branches. The cell walls are hardly to be made out without staining. Externally, the chitinogenous cells rest upon a delicate basement membrane.

Where a number of branches are given off together, the tracheal tube may be dilated. Fine branches, such as accompany nerves, are often sinuous. In the very finest branches the tube loses its thread, the chitinogenous cells become irregular, and the intima is lost in the nucleated protoplasmic mass which replaces the regular epithelium of the wider tubes.*

The Spiracles.

The spiracles of the Cockroach are by no means of complicated structure, but their small size, and the differences between one spiracle and another, are difficulties which cost some pains to overcome.

The first thoracic spiracle (fig. 85) is the largest in the body. It lies in front of the mesothorax, between the bases of the first and second legs. It is placed obliquely, the slit being inclined downwards and backwards, and is closed externally by a large, slightly two-lobed valve, attached by its lower border. The aperture immediately within the valve divides into two nearly equal cavities, each of which leads to a separate tracheal trunk ; and between these cavities is a septum, thickened on its free edge, against which the margin of the valve appears to close. A special occlusor muscle arises from the integument below the spiracle, and is inserted into a chitinous process which projects inwardly from the centre of the valve. A second muscle, whose connections and mode of action we have not been able to make out satisfactorily, lies beneath the first, and is inserted into the thickened edge of the septum.

---

* It has been supposed that these irregular cells of the tracheal endings pass into those of the fat-body, but the latter can always be distinguished by their larger and more spherical nuclei.

The second thoracic spiracle (fig. 86) lies in front of the metathorax, between the bases of the second and third legs. It is
much smaller and simpler than the first. Its valve is nearly
semi-circular, and the free border is strengthened on its deep
surface by a chitinous rim, which terminates beyond the end of
the hinge of the valve in a process which gives insertion to the
occlusor muscle.

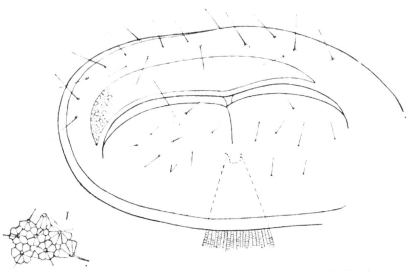

Fig. 85.—First Thoracic Spiracle (left side), seen from the outside. × 70. *V*, valve;
I, setose lining of valve (mouth of tracheal tube) × 230. The occlusor muscle is
shown. The arrow indicates the direction of air entering the spiracle. In the
natural position this spiracle is set obliquely, the slit being inclined downwards
and backwards. (*P. americana.*)

The abdominal spiracles present quite a different plan of
structure. The external orifice is permanently open, owing to
the absence of valves, but communication with the tracheal trunk
may be cut off at pleasure by an internal occluding apparatus.
The external orifice leads into a shallow oval cup, which communicates with the tracheal trunk by a narrow slit, or internal
aperture of the spiracle. The chitinous cuticle, surrounding
this internal aperture, is richly provided with setæ, which are
turned towards the opening.* Fig. 87 *C* represents a spiracle

* In the first abdominal spiracle the setæ are developed only on that lip which
carries the bow.

seen from within, and shows that the slit divides the cup into two unequal lips, the smaller of which inclines away from the middle line of the body, is movable, and is strengthened on its deep surface by a curved chitinous rod, the "bow" of Landois.

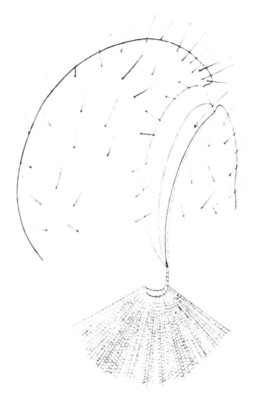

Fig. 86.—Second Thoracic Spiracle (left side), seen from the outside. × 70. *V*, lower (movable) valve. The occlusor muscle is shown. The arrow indicates the direction of air entering the spiracle. (*P. americana.*)

From the opposite lip, a pouch is thrown out, which serves for the attachment of the occlusor muscle. The muscle is inserted into the extremity of the bow, and when it contracts, the bow is pulled over into the position shown in fig. 87*D*, and the opening is closed. The antagonist muscle, which exists in all the abdominal spiracles, is shown in fig. 88 ; it arises from the supporting plate of the spiracle, and is inserted opposite to the occlusor, into the extremity of the bow.

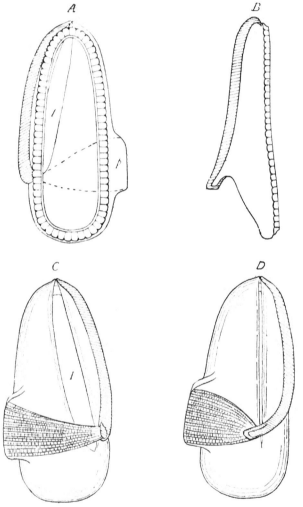

Fig. 87.—Four views of the First Abdominal Spiracle (left side).   × 70.   The bow is shaded in all the figures.   (*P. americana.*)

A—The spiracle, seen from the outside; *p*, lateral pouch; *I*, internal aperture.

B—   Do.,   side view.

C—   Do.,   seen from the inside, the aperture open.   The occlusor muscle is shown.

D—The spiracle, seen from the inside, the aperture shut.

Each of the eight abdominal spiracles is constructed on this plan ; the first merely differs from the others in its larger size and dorsal position, being carried upon the lateral margin of the first abdominal tergum, whereas the others are placed on the side of the body, each occupying an interspace between two

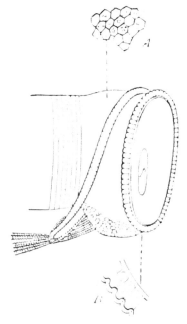

Fig. 88.—Abdominal Spiracle (left side) in side view, showing the bow : × 70 ; p, lateral pouch of spiracle, seen from within. The tesselated structure of the spiracle and trachea is shown at A (× 230), and the margin of the external aperture at B (× 230). (P. americana.)

terga and two sterna.   The bow is of about the same length in all ; hence the apparent disproportion in the figures of different spiracles.   The external aperture of the abdominal spiracles is oval or elliptical, placed vertically and directed backwards.

We have already pointed out that the wall of the air-tube, for a short distance from the spiracular orifice, has a tesselated instead of a spiral marking.   In the thoracic spiracles the tesselated cells are grouped round regularly placed setæ (fig. 85 I).   The chitinous cuticle within the opening is crowded with fine setæ, which are often arranged so as to form a fringe on one or both sides of the internal aperture.   (Supra, p. 152.)

Mechanism of Respiration.

In animals with a complete circulation, aërated blood is diffused throughout the body by means of arteries and capillaries, which deliver it under pressure at all points. Such animals usually possess a special aërating chamber (lung or gill), where oxygen is made to combine with the hæmoglobin of the blood. It is otherwise with Insects. Their blood escapes into great lacunæ, where it stagnates, or flows and ebbs sluggishly, and a diffuse form of the internal organs becomes necessary for their free exposure to the nutritive fluid. The blood is not injected into the tissues, but they are bathed by it, and the compact kidney or salivary gland is represented in Insects by tubules, or a thin sheet of finely divided lobules. By a separate mechanism, air is carried along ramified passages to all the tissues. Every organ is its own lung.

We must now consider in more detail how air is made to enter and leave the body of an Insect. The spiracles and the air-tubes have been described, but these are not furnished with any means of creating suction or pressure ; and the tubes themselves, though highly elastic, are non-contractile, and must be distended or emptied by some external force. Many Insects, especially such as fly rapidly, exhibit rhythmical movements of the abdomen. There is an alternate contraction and dilatation, which may be supposed to be as capable of setting up expirations and inspirations as the rise and fall of the diaphragm of a Mammal. In many Insects, two sets of muscles serve to contract the abdomen—viz., muscles which compress or flatten, and muscles which approximate or telescope the segments.* In the Cockroach the second set is feebly developed, but the first is more powerful, and causes the terga and sterna alternately to approach and separate with a slow, rhythmical movement ; in a Dragon-fly or Humble-bee the action is much more conspicuous, and it is easy to see that the abdomen is bent as well as depressed at each contraction. No special muscles exist for dilating the abdomen, and this seems to depend entirely upon the elasticity of the parts. It was

---

* This subject is treated at greater length in Prof. Plateau's contribution on Respiratory Movements of Insects. (*Infra*, p. 159.)

long supposed that, when the abdomen contracted, air was
expelled from the body, and the air passages emptied ; that
when the abdomen expanded again by its own elasticity, the
air passages were refilled, and that no other mechanism was
needed. Landois pointed out, however, that this was not
enough. Air must be forced into the furthest recesses of the
tracheal system, where the exchange of oxygen and carbonic
acid is effected more readily than in tubes lined by a dense
intima. But in these fine and intricate passages the resistance
to the passage of air is considerable, and the renewal of the air
could, to all appearance, hardly be effected at all if the inlets
remained open. Landois accordingly searched for some means
of closing the outlets, and found an elastic ring or spiral, which
surrounds the tracheal tube within the spiracle. By means of
a special muscle, this can be made to compress the tube, like
a spring clip upon a flexible gas pipe. When the muscle
contracts, the passage is closed, and the abdominal muscles can
then, it is supposed, bring any needful pressure to bear upon
the tracheal tubes, much in the same way as with ourselves,
when we close the mouth and nostrils, and then, by forcible
contraction of the diaphragm and abdominal walls, distend the
cheeks or pharynx. Landois describes the occluding apparatus
of the Cockroach as completely united with the spiracle. It
consists, according to him, of two curved rods, the " bow " and
the " band," one of which forms each lip of the orifice. From
the middle of the band projects a blunt process for the attachment of the occlusor muscle, which passes thence to the
extremity of the bow. The concave side of each rod is fringed
with setæ, and turned towards the opening, which lies between
the two. Upon this description of the spiracles of the Cockroach we have to remark that there is no occluding apparatus
at all in the thoracic spiracles, which are provided with
external valves. In the abdominal spiracles the bow is perfectly distinct, but the " band " of Landois has no separate
existence. Though the actual mechanism in this Insect does
not altogether agree with Landois' description, it is capable
of performing the physiological office upon which he justly
lays so much stress—viz., the closing of the outlets of the
tracheal system, in order that pressure may be brought upon
the contained air.

The injection of air by muscular pressure into a system of very fine tubes may, however, appear to the reader, as it formerly did to ourselves, extremely difficult or even impossible. Can any pressure be applied to tubes within the body of an Insect which will force air along the passages of (say) ·0001 in. diameter ? It may well seem that no pressure would suffice to distend these minute tubules, in which the actual replacement of carbonic acid by oxygen takes place, but that the air would either contract to a smaller volume or burst the tissues.

If we question the physical possibility of Landois' explanation, an alternative is still open to us. The late Prof. Graham has applied the principle of Diffusion to the respiration of animals, and has shown how by a diffusion-process the carbonic acid produced in the remote cavities would be moved along the smaller tubes, and emptied into wider tubes, from which it could be expelled by muscular action. The carbonic acid is not merely exchanged for oxygen, but for a larger volume of oxygen (O 95 : CO_2 81) ; and there is consequently a tendency to accumulation within the tubes, which is counteracted by the elasticity of the air vessels, as well as by special muscular contractions.[*]

Whether diffusion or injection by muscular pressure is the chief means of effecting the interchange of gases between the outer air and the inner tissues of the Insect, is a question to be dealt with by physical enquiry.

If we suppose two reservoirs of different gases at slightly different pressures to be connected by a capillary tube of moderate dimensions, such as one of the larger tracheæ of the Cockroach, transference by the molecular movements of diffusion would be small compared with that effected by the flow of the gas in mass. But if the single tube were replaced by a number of others, of the same total area, but of the fineness (say) of the pores in graphite, the flow of the gas would be stopped, and the transference would be effected by diffusion only. We may next consider tubes of intermediate fineness, say a tracheal tubule of the Cockroach at the point

* Phil. Mag., 1833. Reprinted in "Researches," p. 44. Graham expressly applies the law of diffusion of gases to explain the respiration of Insects. Sir John Lubbock quotes and comments upon the passage in his paper on the Distribution of the Tracheæ in Insects. (Linn. Trans. Vol. XXIII.)

where the spiral thread ceases, and where the exchange of gases through the wall of the tubule becomes comparatively unobstructed. Such a tubule is about ·0001 in. diameter. If we may extend to such tubules the laws which hold good for the flow of gases in capillary tubes of much greater diameter, the quantity of air which might be transmitted in a given time by muscular pressure of known amount can be determined. Suppose the difference of pressure at the two ends of the tubule to be one-hundredth of an atmosphere, and further, that the tubule is a quarter of an inch long and ·0001 in. diameter. The tubule would then be cleared out every four seconds. Such a flow of air along innumerable tubules might well suffice for the respiratory needs of the Cockroach. Without laying too much stress upon this calculation, for which exact data are wanting, we may be satisfied that an appreciable quantity of air may be made by muscular pressure to flow along even the finer air passages of an Insect.*

Respiratory Movements of Insects.

By FÉLIX PLATEAU, Professor in the University of Ghent.

The respiratory movements of large Insects are in general very apparent, and many observers have said something about what they have seen in various species. It is only since the publication of Rathke's memoir, however, that precise views have been gained as to the mechanism of these movements. This remarkable work, treating of the respiratory movements in Insects, the movable skeletal plates, and the respiratory muscles characteristic of all the principal groups, filled an important blank in our knowledge. But, notwithstanding the skill displayed in this research, many questions still remained unanswered, which required more exact methods than mere observation with the naked eye or the simple lens.

The writer, who was followed a year later by Langendorff, conceived the idea of studying, by such graphic methods as are now familiar, the respiratory movements of perfect Insects. He

* For an explanation of the physical principles involved in this discussion, and for the calculation (based upon our own assumptions), we are indebted to Mr. A. W. Rücker, F.R.S.

has made use of two modes of investigation. The first, or graphic method, in the strict sense of the term, consisted in recording upon a revolving cylinder of smoked paper the respiratory movements, transmitted by means of very light levers of Bristol board, attached to any selected part of the Insect's exoskeleton. Unfortunately, this plan is only applicable to insects of more than average size. A second method, that of projection, consisted in introducing the Insect, carried upon a small support, into a large magic lantern fitted with a good petroleum lamp. When the amplification does not exceed 12 diameters, a sharp profile may be obtained, upon which the actual displacements may be measured, true to the fraction of a millimetre. Placing a sheet of white paper upon the lantern screen, the outlines of the profile are carefully traced in pencil so as to give two superposed figures, representing the phases of inspiration and expiration respectively. By altering the position of the Insect, so as to obtain profiles of transverse section, or of the different parts of the body, and, further, by gluing very small paper slips to parts whose movements are hard to observe, the successive positions of the slips being then drawn, complete information is at last obtained of every detail of the respiratory movements : nothing is lost.

This method, similar to that employed by the English physiologist, Hutchinson,[*] is valuable, because it enables us, with a little practice, to investigate readily the respiratory movements of very small Arthropods, such as Flies or Lady-birds. It has this advantage over all others, that it leaves no room for errors of interpretation.

Not satisfied with mere observation by such means as these, of the respiratory movements of Insects, the writer has also studied the muscles concerned, and, in common with other physiologists (Faivre, Barlow, Luchsinger, Dönhoff, and Langendorff), has examined the action of the various nervous centres upon the respiratory organs. The results at which he has arrived may be summarised as follows :—

1. There is no close relation between the character of the respiratory movements of an Insect and its position in the zoological system. Respiratory movements are similar only

[*] J. Hutchinson, Art. Thorax, Todd's Cycl. of Anat. and Phys.

when the arrangement of the abdominal segments, and especially when the disposition of the attached muscles are almost identical. Thus, for example, the respiratory movements of a Cockroach are different from those of other Orthoptera, but resemble those of Hemiptera Heteroptera.

2. The respiratory activity of resting Insects is localised in the abdomen. V. Graber has expressed this fact in a picturesque form, by saying that in Insects the chest is placed at the hinder end of the body.

3. In most cases the thoracic segments do not share in the respiratory movements of an Insect at rest. Among the singular exceptions to this rule is the Cockroach (*P. orientalis*), in which the terga of the meso- and meta-thoracic segments perform movements exactly opposite in direction to those of the abdomen. (See fig. 89, *Ms. th*, *Mt. th.*)

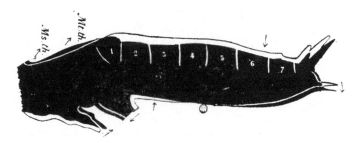

Fig. 89.—Profile of Cockroach (*P. orientalis*). The black surface represents the expiratory contour, while the inspiratory is indicated by a thin line. The arrows show the direction of the expiratory movement. *Ms. th.*, mesothorax; *Mt. th.*, metathorax. Reduced from a magic-lantern projection.

4. Leaving out of account all details and all exceptions, the respiratory movements of Insects may be said to consist of alternate contraction and recovery of the figure of the abdomen in two dimensions—viz., vertical and transverse. During expiration the diameters in question are reduced, while during respiration they revert to their previous amounts. The transverse expiratory contraction is often slight, and may be imperceptible. On the other hand, the vertical expiratory contraction is never absent, and usually marked. In the Cockroach (*P. orientalis*) it amounts to one-eighth of the depth of the abdomen (between segments 2 and 3).

5. Three principal types of respiratory mechanism occur in Insects, and these admit of further subdivision :—

(*a*) Sterna usually stout and very convex, yielding but little. Terga mobile, rising and sinking appreciably. To this class belong all Coleoptera, Hemiptera Heteroptera, and Blattina (Orthoptera).

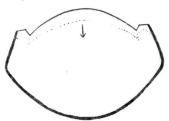

Fig. 90.—Transverse section of Abdomen, Lamellicorn Beetle.   The position of the terga and sterna after an inspiration, is indicated by the thick line ; the dotted line shows their position after an expiration, and the arrow marks the direction of the expiratory movement.

In the Cockroach (*Periplaneta*) the sterna are slightly raised during expiration.   (See figs. 89 and 91.)

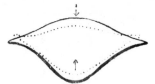

Fig. 91.—Transverse section of Abdomen, Cockroach (*P. orientalis*).

(*b*) Terga well developed, overlapping the sterna on the sides of the body, and usually concealing the pleural membrane, which forms a sunk fold.   The terga and sterna approach and recede alternately, the sterna being almost always the more mobile.   To this type belong Odonata, Diptera, aculeate Hymenoptera, and Acridian Orthoptera. (Fig. 92.)

(*c*) The pleural membrane, connecting the terga with the sterna, is well developed and exposed on the sides of the body.   The terga and sterna approach and recede alternately, while the pleural zone simultaneously becomes depressed or returns to its original figure.   To this type the writer assigns the Locustidæ, the Lepidoptera and the true Neuroptera (excluding Phryganidæ).   (Fig. 93.)

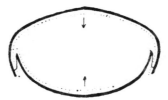

Fig. 92.—Transverse section of Abdomen, Bee (*Bombus*).

6. Contrary to the opinion once general, changes in length of the abdomen, involving protrusion of the segments and subsequent retraction, are rare in the normal respiration of Insects. Such longitudinal movements extend throughout one entire group only—viz., the aculeate Hymenoptera. Isolated examples occur, however, in other zoological divisions.

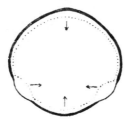

Fig. 93.—Transverse section of Abdomen, Hawk Moth (*Sphingina*).

7. Among Insects sufficiently powerful to give good graphic tracings, it can be shown that the inspiratory movement is slower than the expiratory, and that the latter is often sudden.

8. In most Insects, contrary to what obtains in Mammals, only the expiratory movement is active; inspiration is passive, and effected by the elasticity of the body-wall.

9. Most Insects possess expiratory muscles only. Certain Diptera (*Calliphora vomitoria* and *Eristalis tenax*) afford the simplest arrangement of the expiratory muscles. In these types they form a muscular sheet of vertical fibres, connecting the terga with the sterna, and underlying the soft elastic membrane which unites the hard parts of the somites. One of the

most frequent complications arises by the differentiation of this sheet of vertical fibres into distinct muscles, repeated in every segment, and becoming more and more separated as the sterna increase in length. (See the tergo-sternal muscles of the Cockroach, fig. 36, p. 76.) Special inspiratory muscles occur in Hymenoptera, Acridiidæ, and Phryganidæ.

10. The abdominal respiratory movements of Insects are wholly reflex. Like other physiologists who have examined this side of the question, the writer finds that the respiratory movements persist in a decapitated Insect, as also after destruction of the cerebral ganglia or œsophageal connectives; further, that in Insects whose nervous system is not highly concentrated (e.g., Acridiidæ and Dragon-flies), the respiratory movements persist in the completely-detached abdomen; while all external influences which promote an increased respiratory activity in the uninjured animal, have precisely the same action upon Insects in which the anterior nervous centres have been removed, upon the detached abdomen, and even upon isolated sections of the abdomen.

The view formerly advocated by Faivre, that the metathoracic ganglia play the part of special respiratory centres, must be entirely abandoned. All carefully performed experiments on the nervous system of Arthropoda have shown that each ganglion of the ventral chain is a motor centre, and in Insects a respiratory centre, for the somite to which it belongs. This is what Barlow calls the "self-sufficiency" of the ganglia.

The writer has made similar observations upon the respiration of Spiders and Scorpions;* but to his great surprise he has been unable either by direct observation, or by the graphic method, or by projection, to discover the slightest respiratory movement of the exterior of the body. This can only be explained by supposing that inspiration and expiration in Pulmonate Arachnida are intra-pulmonary, and affect only the proper respiratory organs. The fact is less surprising because of the wide zoological separation between Arachnida and Insects.

* De l'absence de mouvements respiratoires perceptibles chez les Arachnides (Archives de Biologie de Van Beneden et Van Bambeke, 1885.)

Respiratory Activity of Insects.

The respiratory activity of Insects varies greatly. Warmth, feeding, and movement are found to increase the frequency of their respirations, and also the quantity of carbonic acid exhaled. In Liebe's[*] experiments a Carabus produced ·24 mgr. of carbonic acid per hour in September, but only ·09 mgr. per hour in December. A rise of temperature raised the product temporarily to twice its previous amount ; but when the same insect was kept under experiment for several days without food, the amount fell in spite of its increased warmth. Treviranus[†] gives the carbonic acid exhaled by a Humble-bee as varying from 22 to 174, according as the temperature varied from 56° to 74° F.

Larvæ often breathe little, especially such as lie buried in wood, earth, or the bodies of other animals. The respiration of pupæ is also sluggish, and not a few are buried beneath the ground or shrouded in a dense cocoon or pupa-case. Muscular activity originates the chief demand for oxygen, and accordingly Insects of powerful flight are most energetic in respiration.

A rise of temperature proportionate to respiratory activity has been observed in many insects. Newport[‡] tells us how the female Humble-bee places herself on the cells of pupæ ready to emerge, and accelerates her inspirations to 120 or 130 per minute. During these observations he found in some instances that the temperature of a single Bee was more than 20° above that of the outer air.

Some Insects can remain long without breathing. They survive for many hours when placed in an exhausted receiver, or in certain irrespirable gases. Cockroaches in carbonic acid speedily become insensible, but after twelve hours' exposure to the pure gas they revive, and appear none the worse. H. Müller[§] says that an Insect, placed in a small, confined space, absorbs *all* the oxygen. In Sir Humphry Davy's " Consolations in Travel "[‖] is a description of the Lago dei

---

[*] Ueb. d. Respiration der Tracheaten. Chemnitz (1872).
[†] See table in Burmeister's " Manual," Eng. trans. p. 398.
[‡] Art. " Insecta," Cyc. Anat. and Phys., p. 989.
[§] Pogg. Ann. 1872, Hft. 3.
[‖] Works, Vol. IX., p. 287. This passage has been cited by Rathke.

Tartari, near Tivoli, a small lake whose waters are warm and saturated with carbonic acid. Insects abound on its floating islands; though water birds, attracted by the abundance of food, are obliged to confine themselves to the banks, as the carbonic acid disengaged from the surface would be fatal to them, if they ventured to swim upon it when tranquil.

Origin of Tracheal Respiration.

Kowalewsky, Bütschli, and Hatschek have described the first stages of development of the tracheal system. Lateral pouches form in the integument; these send out anterior and posterior extensions, which anastomose and form the longitudinal trunks. The tracheal ramifications are not formed by a process of direct invagination, but by the separation of chitinogenous cells, which cohere into strings, and then form irregular tubules. The cells secrete a chitinous lining, and afterwards lose their distinct contours, fusing to a continuous tissue, in which the individual cells are indicated only by their nuclei, though by appropriate re-agents the cell boundaries can be defined.

The ingenious hypothesis propounded by Gegenbaur, that the tracheal tubes of Insects were originally adapted to aquatic respiration, and that the stigmata arose as the scars of disused tracheal gills, has been discussed in chap. iv. Semper has suggested[*] that tracheæ may be modified segmental organs, but the most probable view of their origin is that put forth by Moseley,[†] that they arose as ramified cutaneous glands. In *Peripatus* the openings are distributed irregularly over the body; the external orifices lead to pits, from which simple tubes, with but slight spiral markings, extend into the deeper tissues.

[*] Arbeiten a. d. Zool. Zoot. Inst. Würzburg. Bd. II., 1874.
[†] Phil. Trans., 1874, p. 757.

CHAPTER IX.

REPRODUCTION.

SPECIAL REFERENCES.

BRANDT, A. Ueber die Eiröhren der Blatta (Periplaneta) orientalis. Mem. Acad. St. Petersb. Ser. 7, Vol. XXI. (1874). [Ovarian Tubes of Cockroach.]

LACAZE-DUTHIERS. Rech. sur l'armure génitale femelle des Insectes Orthoptères. Ann. Sci. Nat., Zool., 3ᵉ Sér., Tom. XVII. (1852). [External reproductive organs of female Orthoptera.]

BERLESE. Ricerde sugli organi genitali degli Ortotteri. Atti della R. Acad. dei Lincei. Ser. 3, Vol. XI. (1882). [Genital Organs of European Orthoptera.]

KADYI. Beitr. zur Vorgänge beim. Eierlegen der Blatta Orientalis. Vorläufige Mittheilung. Zool. Anz., 1879, p. 632. [Formation of egg-capsules of Cockroach.]

BREHM. Comparative structure of the reproductive organs in Blatta germanica and Periplaneta orientalis. Mem. Soc. Ent. St. Petersb., Tom. VIII. (1880). In Russian. [Male organs only.]

RAJEWSKY. Ueber die Geschlechtsorgane von Blatta orientalis, &c. Nachr. d. kais. Gesellsch. d. Moskauer Universität., Bd. XVI. (1875). [Testes of Cockroach. The original paper is in Russian; an abstract is given in Hofmann and Schwalbe's Jahresbericht, 1875, p. 425.]

BÜTSCHLI. Bau u. Entwickelung d. Samenfäden bei Insekten u. Crustaceen. Zeits. f. wiss. Zool., Bd. XXI., pp. 402–414; 526–534. Pl. xl. xli. (1871). [Spermatozoa and spermatogenesis in the Cockroach.]

LA VALETTE ST. GEORGE. Spermatologische Beiträge. II. *Blatta germanica.* Arch. f. mikr. Anat., Bd. XXVII. (1886). [Spermatogenesis in *B. germanica.*]

MORAVITZ. Quædam ad anat. Blattæ germanicæ pertinentia. Dissertatio inauguralis. Dorpat. (1853). [An excellent early account of the anatomy of *B. germanica*, including a description of the male and female organs. The figures are not trustworthy.]

Female Reproductive Organs.

The ovaries of the two sides of the body are separated, as in most Insects, and consist on each side of eight tubes, four dorsal and four ventral, which open into the inner side of a common oviduct. The two oviducts unite behind, and form a very short uterus. Tracheæ and fat-cells tie the ovarian tubes

of each side together into a spindle-shaped bundle. Each tube
is about ·4 in. long, and has a beaded appearance, owing to the
eggs which distend its elastic wall. It gradually tapers in
front; then suddenly narrows to a very small diameter; and
lastly, joins with the extremities of the other tubes to form a
slender solid filament, which passes towards the heart, and
becomes lost in the fat-body. The wall of an ovarian tube
consists of a transparent elastic membrane, lined by epithelium,
and invested externally by a peritoneal layer of connective
tissue.

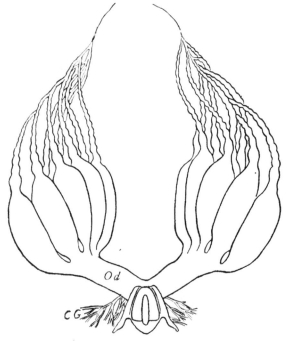

Fig. 94.—Female Reproductive Organs.   *Od*, oviduct ; *CG*, colleterial gland.   × 14.

The epithelium of an ovarian tube presents some remarkable
peculiarities which disguise its true character. High up in the
tube, the narrow lumen is occupied by a clear protoplasm, in
which nuclei, but no cell walls, can be discerned. Where the
tube suddenly widens, large rounded and nucleated masses of
protoplasm appear, interspersed with nuclei entangled in a

network of protoplasm. Passing down the tube, the large cells, which can now be recognised as eggs, arrange themselves in a single row, to the number of about twenty. They are at first polygonal or squarish, but gradually become cylindrical, and finally oval. Between and around the eggs the nuclei gradually arrange themselves into one-layered follicles, which are attached, not to the wall of the tube, but to the eggs, and travel downwards with them. As the eggs descend, the yolk which they contain increases rapidly, and the germinal vesicle

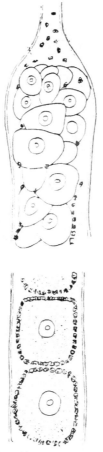

Fig. 95.—Ovarian Tube (acetic acid preparation), showing scattered nuclei (upper figure), which ultimately form follicles around the ova (lower figure). Copied from Brandt, *loc. cit.*

and spot (nucleus and nucleolus), which were at first very
plain, disappear. A vitelline membrane is secreted by the
inner surface, and a chitinous chorion by the outer surface of
the egg-follicle.

The lowest egg in an ovarian tube is nearly or altogether of
the full size ; it is of elongate-oval figure, and slightly curved,
the convexity being turned towards the uterus. It is filled
with a clear albuminous fluid, which mainly consists of yolk.
The chorion now forms a transparent yellowish capsule, which
under the microscope appears to be divided up into very many
polygonal areas, defined by rows of fine dots. These areas
probably correspond to as many follicular cells. The convex
surface of the chorion is perforated by numerous micropyles,
fine pores through which it is probable the spermatozoa gain
access to the interior of the egg.

The uterus has a muscular wall and a chitinous lining. Two
repeatedly branched colleterial glands open into its under side.
Of these the left is much the larger, and overlies the other.
It consists of many dichotomous tubes, some of which are a
little dilated at their blind ends. The gland is much entangled
with fat-cells, which make it difficult to unravel. The right
gland is probably of no functional importance ; the left gland
is filled with a milky substance, containing many crystals and
a coagulable fluid, out of both of which the egg-capsule is
formed.*

At its hinder end the uterus opens by a median vertical slit,
which lies in the 8th sternum, into a genital pouch which
represents part of the external integument, folded back far into
the interior of the abdomen. (See fig. 96.) Upon the dorsal
wall of the genital pouch the orifice of the spermatheca is
situated.† This is a short tube dilated at the end, and wound

---

* The crystals have been supposed to consist of oxalate of lime (Duchamp, Rev.
des sci. nat. Montpellier, Tom. VIII.). Hallez observes that they are prismatic, with
rhombic base, the angles truncated. They are insoluble in water and weak nitric
acid, but dissolve rapidly in strong sulphuric acid without liberation of gas, and still
more rapidly in caustic potash. (Compt. Rend., Aug., 1885.)

† It is usually stated that the spermatheca of the Cockroach opens into the
uterus, as it does in most other Insects, but this is not true. Locusts and Grasshoppers have the outlet of the spermatheca placed as in the Cockroach ; in other
European Orthoptera, it lies upon the dorsal wall of the uterus. (Berlese, loc. cit.,
p. 273.)

into a spiral of about one turn. From the tube a cæcal process is given off, which may correspond with the accessory gland attached to the duct of the spermatheca in many Insects (*e.g.*, Coleoptera, Hymenoptera, and some Lepidoptera). The spermatheca is filled during copulation, and is always found to contain

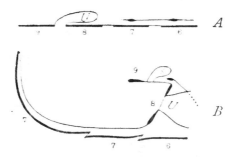

Fig. 96.—Diagram to show the theoretical (upper figure) and actual position of the hinder abdominal sterna in the female Cockroach. *U*, uterus; *s*, spermatheca. The nerve-cord is introduced into both figures.

spermatozoa in the fertile female.[*] The spermatozoa are no doubt passed into the genital pouch from time to time, and there fertilise the eggs descending from the ovarian tubes.

The external reproductive organs of the female Cockroach belong to the 7th, 8th, and 9th somites. The 7th sternum is incompletely divided into anterior and posterior sections, and the posterior section is split into lateral halves. These are joined by a flexible membrane, which admits of the wide separation of the halves, when copulation or the passage of the large egg-capsule renders it necessary. The vertical faces of the membrane, which are pressed together when the parts are at rest, are stiffened by chitinous thickenings.

If the succeeding sterna retained their proper place, as they do in some Orthoptera (*e.g.*, the Mole Cricket), the 8th and 9th sterna would project beyond the 7th, while the rectum would

---

[*] It is a striking proof of the sagacity of Malpighi, that he should have observed in the Silkworm the spermatophore of the male ("in spiram circumvolutum persimile semen") and the spermatheca of the female. His reasoning as to the function of the spermatheca wanted nothing but microscopic evidence of the actual transference of spermatozoa to establish it in all points. Audouin and Siebold supplied what was wanting nearly two centuries later, but they mistook the spirally wound spermatophore for a broken-off penis, and Stein (Weibl. Geschlechtsorgane der Käfer, p. 85) first arrived at the complete proof of Malpighi's explanation.

open beneath the last tergum, and the uterus between the 8th
and 9th sterna. In the adult female Cockroach, however, the
8th and 9th somites are telescoped into the 7th, and completely
hidden by it. Their terga are reduced to narrow bands. The
8th sternum forms a semi-transparent plate which slopes downwards and backwards, and is pierced by a vertical slit, the
outlet of the uterus. The upper edge of this sternum is hinged

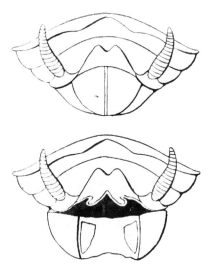

Fig. 97.—Hinder end of abdomen of female Cockroach. In the upper figure the
halves of the 7th sternum are closed ; in the lower figure they are open.

upon the projecting basis of the anterior gonapophyses (to be
described immediately), and the parts form a kind of spring
joint, ordinarily closed, but capable of being opened wide upon
occasion. The 9th sternum is a small median crescentic plate,
distinct from the 8th ; it supports the spermatheca, whose duct
traverses an oval plate which projects from the fore-edge of
the sternum.

By the telescoping of the 8th and 9th somites the sterna
take the position shown in fig. 96B, and a new cavity, the
genital pouch, is formed by invagination. This receives the
extremity of the body of the male during copulation, while it
serves as a mould in which the egg-capsule is cast during
oviposition. Its chitinous lining resembles that of the outer

integument. The uterus opens into its anterior end, which is bounded by the 8th sternum; the spermatheca opens into its roof, which is supported by the 9th sternum and the gonapophyses; while its floor is completed by the 7th sternum and the infolded chitinous membrane.

Fig. 98.—External Reproductive Organs of Female. T^{x}, &c., terga; S^{7}, &c., sterna; G, anterior gonapophysis; G^{1}, its base; g, posterior gonapophyses; Od, oviduct; sp, spermatheca; R, rectum. The upper figure shows the parts in oblique profile; the left lower figure is an oblique view from before of the outlet of the uterus, the anterior gonapophyses being cut short; the right lower figure shows the gonapophyses. Arrows indicate the outlet of the oviduct and uterus.

A pair of appendages (anterior gonapophyses) are shown by the development of the parts to belong to the 8th somite.

They are slender, irregularly bent, and curved inwards at the
tips. A small, forked, chitinous slip connects them with both
the 8th and 9th terga, but their principal attachment is to the
upper (properly, posterior) edge of the 8th sternum.   The
anterior gonapophyses expand at their bases into broad horizontal plates, which form part of the roof of the genital pouch.

Two pairs of appendages, belonging to the 9th somite, form
the posterior gonapophyses.   The outer pair are relatively
large, soft, and curved : the inner narrow, hard, and straight.*

The anterior gonapophyses form the lower, and the posterior
the upper jaw of a forceps, which in many Insects can be
protruded beyond the body.   Some of the parts are often armed
with teeth, and the primary use of the apparatus is to bore
holes in earth or wood for the reception of the eggs.   Hence
the apparatus is often called the *ovipositor*.   It forms a prominent appendage of the abdomen in such Insects as Crickets,
Saw-flies, Sirex, and Ichneumons.   The sting of the Bee is a
peculiar adaptation of the same organ to a very different
purpose.   In the Cockroach the ovipositor is used to grasp the
egg-capsule, while it is being formed, filled with eggs, and
hardened ; and the notched edge (fig. 5, p. 23) is the imprint
of the inner posterior gonapophyses, made while the capsule is
still soft.   The shape of the parts in the male and female
indicates that the ovipositor is passive in copulation, and is
then raised to allow access to the spermatheca.

Male Reproductive Organs.

The male reproductive organs of Insects, in spite of very
great superficial diversity, are reducible to a common type,
which is exemplified by certain Coleoptera.   The essential parts
are (1) the *testes*, which in their simplest form are paired,
convoluted tubes ; more commonly they branch into many
tubules or vesiculæ, while they may become consolidated into a

---

* The descriptions and figures of the reproductive appendages of female Orthoptera by Lacaze-Duthiers (Ann. Sci. Nat., 1852) are so often consulted, that it may
be useful to explain how we understand and name the same parts. In pl. xi., fig. 2,
8′ and 9′ are the 8th and 9th terga ; the anterior gonapophyses are seen to be
attached to them below ; *a* (figs. 2 and 4) is the base of the same appendage, but the
twisted ends are incorrect ; the 8th sternum is seen at the back (figs. 2 and 4) ;
a′ represents the outer, *f* the inner pair of posterior gonapophyses.

single organ ; (2) long coiled *rasa deferentia*, opening into or close to (3) paired *vesiculæ seminales*, which discharge into (4) the *ejaculatory duct*, a muscular tube, with chitinous lining, by which the spermatozoa are forcibly expelled. Opening into the vesiculæ seminales, the ejaculatory duct, or by a distinct external orifice, may be found (5) *accessory glands*, very variable in form, size, and number. More than one set may occur in the same Insect. To these parts, which are rarely deficient, are very often appended an external armature of hooks or claspers.

The male Cockroach will be found to agree with this description. It presents, however, two peculiarities which are uncommon, though not unparalleled. In the first place the testes are functional only in the young male. They subsequently shrivel, and are functionally replaced by the vesiculæ seminales and their appendages, where the later transformations of the sperm-cells are effected. The atrophied testes are nevertheless sufficiently large in the adult to be easily made out. Secondly, the accessory glands are numerous, and differ both in function and insertion. Two sets are attached to the vesiculæ seminales, and the fore end of the ejaculatory duct (*utriculi majores* and *breviores*); another large conglobate gland opens separately to the exterior. We shall now describe the structure of these parts in more detail.*

The testes may be found in older larvæ or adults beneath the fifth and sixth terga of the abdomen. They lie in the fat-body, from which they are not very readily distinguished. Each testis consists of 30–40 rounded vesicles attached by short tubes to the vas deferens.† The wall of the testis

---

* We propose to notice here the chief differences which we have found between the figures of Brehm (*loc. cit.*), which are the fullest and best we have seen, and our own dissections.

Figs. 10, 11 (pp. 169–70). The ejaculatory duct and duct of the conglobate gland are made to end in the penis (*infra*, p. 178).

Figs. 14, 15 (p. 173). These figures seem to us erroneous in many respects, such as the median position of the penis and titillator.

Fig. 16 (p. 174). The pair of hooks marked *E* are too small, and there are additional plates at the base, which are not figured (see our fig. 102). *F* (of our fig.) is omitted.

† In *Blatta germanica* the testes are functional throughout life. They consist of four lobes each. The vasa deferentia are much shorter than in *P. orientalis*.

consists of a peritoneal layer and an epithelium, which is folded inwards along transverse lines. The cells of the epithelium give rise to spermatocysts,* which enclose sperm cells. By

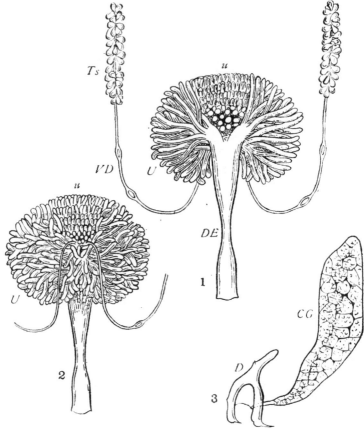

Fig. 99.—1. Male Organs, ventral view. *Ts*, testis ; *VD*, vas deferens ; *DE*, ductus ejaculatorius ; *U*, utriculi majores ; *u*, utriculi breviores. 2. Do., dorsal view, showing termination of vasa deferentia. 3. Conglobate gland, and its duct. × 8.

division of the nuclei of the sperm cells spermatozoa are formed, which have at first nucleated heads and long tails.

* The spermatocysts are peculiar to Insects and Amphibia. They arise by division of the spermatospores, or modified epithelial cells, and form hollow cysts, within which sperm cells (or spermatoblasts) are developed by further division. The sperm cells are usually placed radiately around the wall of the spermatocyst. They escape by dehiscence, and are transformed into spermatozoa.

Subsequently the enlarged heads disappear. The spermatozoa move actively. In adult males the testes undergo atrophy, but can with care be discovered in the enveloping fat-body.

The vasa deferentia are about ·25 inch in length. They pass backwards from the testes, then turn downwards on each side of the large intestine, and finally curve upwards and forwards, entering the vesiculæ seminales on their dorsal side. Each vas deferens divides once or twice into branches, which immediately reunite ; in the last larval stage the termination of the passage dilates into a rounded, transparent vesicle.

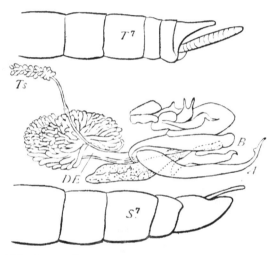

Fig. 100.—Male Organs, side view. T^7, seventh tergum ; S^7, seventh sternum ; *Ts*, *DE*, as before. *A*, *B*, see fig. 102. × 8.

The vesiculæ seminales are simple, rounded lobes in the pupa (fig. 101), but their appearance is greatly altered in the adult by the development of two sets of utricles (modified accessory glands). The longer utricles (*utriculi majores*) open separately into the sides of the vesiculæ ; nearer to the middle line are the shorter and more numerous *utriculi breviores*, which open into the fore part of the vesiculæ.

The utricles form the "mushroom-shaped gland" of Huxley, which was long described as the testis. In the adult male the utricles are usually distended with spermatozoa, and of a brilliant opaque white.

The ejaculatory duct is about ·15 inch long, and overlies the 6th–9th sterna. It is wide in front, where it receives the paired outlets of the vesiculæ seminales. Further back it narrows, and widens again near to its outlet, which we find to be between the external chitinous parts, and not into the penis, as described by Brehm. The duct possesses a muscular wall for the forcible ejection of its contents, and in accordance with its origin as a folding-in of the outer surface, it is provided with a chitinous lining. In the adult the fore part of the duct may be distended with spermatozoa.

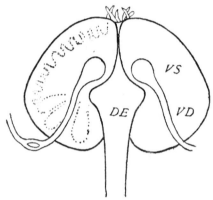

Fig. 101.—Vesiculæ Seminales and Ductus Ejaculatorius of Pupa. *VD*, vas deferens. × 28.

The ejaculatory duct is originally double (p. 194), and its internal cavity is still subdivided in the last larval stage or so-called " pupa."

Upon the ventral surface of the ejaculatory duct lies an accessory gland of unknown function ; it is "composed of dichotomous, monilated tubes, lined by a columnar epithelium, all bound together by a common investment into a flattened, elongated mass." * The duct of this gland does not enter the penis, as described by Brehm, but opens upon a double hook, which forms part of the external genital armature (fig. 99, 3). It may be convenient to distinguish this as the "conglobate gland."†

* Huxley, Anat. Invert. Animals, p. 416.

† The term "accessory gland," used by Huxley and others, is already appropriated to glands which we believe to be represented by the utricles of the Cockroach, and which have only a general correspondence with the gland in question.

The external reproductive organs of the male Cockroach are concealed within the 9th sternum. The so-called penis (fig. 102) is long, slender, and dilated at the end. It is not perforated, and we do not understand its use, though it probably conveys the semen.

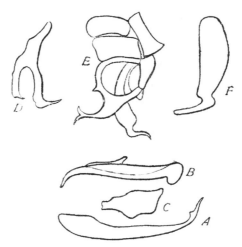

Fig. 102.—External Male Organs, separated. The lettering agrees with Brehm's figures. *A*, titillator ; *B*, penis ; *C—F*, hooks and plates. × 8.

The "titillator" (Brunner von Wattenwyl) is a solid curved hook with a hollow base. Besides these, are several odd-shaped, unsymmetrical pieces (fig. 102, *C, D, E, F*), moved by special muscles. A pair of styles (see figs. 32–3 and 103) project from the hinder edge of the 9th sternum. These paired and unpaired appendages are believed to open the genital pouch of the female, but we do not understand their action in detail.*

Brehm observes that the male reproductive organs of the Cockroach are most nearly paralleled by those of the Mantidæ. A free penis occurs in all Orthoptera, except Acridiidæ and Phasmidæ.

The male organs of the House Cricket will be found much easier to understand than those of the Cockroach. The testes are of irregular, oval figure, the vasa deferentia very long,

---

* Similar organs, forming a male genital armature, have been described in various Insects. See Burmeister, Man. of Entomology, p. 328 (Eng. Transl.); Siebold, Anat. of Invertebrates ; Gosse in Linn. Trans., Ser. 2, Vol. II. (1883); Burgess on Milk-weed Butterfly, Ann. Mem. Bost. Soc. Nat. Hist.; &c.

tortuous, and enlarged towards the middle of their length. The vesiculæ seminales bear many utriculi majores et breviores. The penis is of simple form, and dilated at the end. The titillator is broad, but produced into a slender prong, which projects beyond the penis. A pair of subanal styles is found, but the unpaired hooklets are wanting or very inconspicuous.

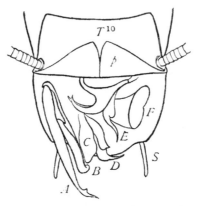

Fig. 103.—The Tenth Tergum reflected to show the external male organs *in situ.* T^{10}, tenth tergum ; *p*, podical plates ; *A—F*, as in fig. 102 ; *S*, sub-anal styles. × 8.

Very little is known about the act of copulation among Cockroaches, and the opportunities of observation are few. The following account is given by Cornelius (*loc. cit.*, p. 22) :—

"The male and female Cockroaches associate in pairs, the females being generally quiet. The male, on the contrary, bustles about the female, runs round her, trailing his extended abdomen on the ground, and now and then raises his wings. If the female moves away, the male stops the road. At last, when the female has become perfectly still, the male goes in front of her, brings the end of his abdomen towards her, then moves backwards, and pushes his whole length under the female. The operation is so rapid that it is impossible to give an exact account of the circumstances. Then the male creeps out from beneath the female, raises high both pairs of wings, depresses them again, and goes off, while the female usually remains quiet for some time."

CHAPTER X.

DEVELOPMENT.

SPECIAL REFERENCES.

RATHKE. Zur Entwickelungsgesch. der *Blatta germanica*. Meckel's Arch. of Anat. u. Phys., Bd. VI. (1832).

BALFOUR. Comparative Embryology, 2 vols. (1880–1).

GRABER. Insekten, Vol. II. (1879).

LUBBOCK. Origin and Metamorphoses of Insects (1874).

KOWALEWSKY. Embryol. Studien an Würmern u. Arthropoden. Mém. Ac. Petersb. Sér. VII., Vol. XVI. (1871).

WEISMANN. Entw. der Dipteren. Zeits. f. wiss. Zool., Bde. XIII., XIV. (1863–4).

METSCHNIKOFF. Embryol. Studien. an Insecten. Ib., Bd. XVI. (1866).

BÜTSCHLI. Entwicklungsgeschichte der Biene. Ib., Bd. XX. (1870).

BOBRETZKY. Bildung d. Blastoderms u. d. Keimblätter bei den Insecten. Ib., Bd. XXXI. (1878).

NUSBAUM. Rozwój przewodów organów pteiowych u owadów (Polish). Kosmos. (1884). [Development of Sexual Outlets in Insects.]

———— Struna i struna Leydig'a u owadów (Polish). Kosmos (1886). [Chorda and Leydig's chorda in Insects.]

The Embryonic Development of the Cockroach.[*]

BY JOSEPH NUSBAUM, MAGISTER OF ZOOLOGY, WARSAW.

THE development of the Cockroach is by no means an easy study. It costs some pains to find an accessible place in which the females regularly lay their eggs, and the opaque capsule renders it hard to tell in what stage of growth the contained embryos will be found. Accordingly, though the development of the Cockroach has lately attracted some observers, the

---

[*] In the following description it is to be understood that the observations have been made upon *Blatta germanica*, except where *P. orientalis* is expressly named.

inexperienced embryologist will find it more profitable to examine the eggs of Bees, of Aphides, or of such Diptera as lay their eggs in water.

The Cockroach is developed, like most animals, from fertilised eggs.* The eggs of various animals differ much in size and form, but always contain a formative plasma or egg-protoplasm, a germinal vesicle (*nucleus*), and a germinal spot (*nucleolus*). Besides these essential parts, eggs also always contain a greater or less quantity of food-yolk, which serves for the supply of the developing embryo. The quantity of this yolk may be small, and its granules are then uniformly dispersed through the egg-protoplasm; or very considerable, in which case the protoplasm and yolk become more or less sharply defined. Eggs of the first kind are known as *holoblastic*, those of the second kind as *meroblastic*, names suggested by the complete or partial segmentation which these kinds of eggs respectively undergo. When the food-yolk is very abundant it does not at first (and in some cases does not at any time) exhibit the phenomena of growth, such as cell-division. If, on the other hand, the yolk is scanty and evenly dispersed through the egg-protoplasm, the segmentation proceeds regularly and completely. The eggs of Arthropoda, including those of the Cockroach, are meroblastic.

The eggs of the Cockroach (*P. orientalis*) are enclosed (see p. 23) sixteen together in stout capsules of horny consistence. They are adapted to the form of the capsule, laterally compressed, convex on the outer, and concave on the inner side. The ventral surface of the embryo lies towards the inner, concave surface of the egg. Each egg is provided with a very thin brownish shell (*chorion*), whose surface is ornamented with small six-sided projections. In young eggs, still enclosed within the ovary, the nucleus (*germinal vesicle*) and nucleolus (*germinal spot*) can be plainly seen, but by the time they are ready for deposition within the capsule, so large a quantity of food-yolk, at first finely—afterwards coarsely—granular, accumulates within them, that the germinal vesicle and spot cease to be visible.

* Fertilisation consists essentially in the union of an egg-nucleus (female nucleus) with a sperm-nucleus (male nucleus). From this union the first segmentation-nucleus is derived.

Since the yolk of the newly-laid egg of the Cockroach is of a consistence extremely unfavourable to hardening and microscopic investigation, I have not been able to obtain transverse sections of the germinal vesicle, nor to study the mode of its division (segmentation). If, however, we may judge from what other observers have found in the eggs of Insects more suitable for investigation than those of the Cockroach, we shall be led to conclude that a germinal vesicle, with a germinal spot surrounded by a thin layer of protoplasm, lies within the nutritive yolk of the Cockroach egg. From this protoplasm all the cells of the embryo are derived.

The germinal vesicle, together with the surrounding protoplasm, undergoes a process of division or segmentation. Some of the cells thus formed travel towards the surface of the egg to form a thin layer of flattened cells investing the yolk, the so-called *blastoderm*, while others remain scattered through the yolk, and constitute the yolk-cells (fig. 107).

On the future ventral side of the embryo (and therefore on the concave surface of the egg) the cells of the blastoderm become columnar, and here is formed the so-called ventral plate, the first indication of the embryo. This is a long narrow flattened structure (fig. 104). It is wider in front where the head

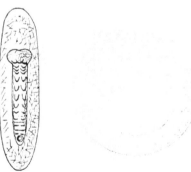

Fig. 104.—Ventral Plate of *Blatta germanica*, with developing appendages, seen from below. × 20.

segment is situated; further back it becomes divided by many transverse lines into the primitive segments. The total number of segments in the ventral plate of Insects is usually seventeen.*

* Balfour, Embryology, Vol. I., p. 337.

Indications of the appendages appear very early. They give rise to an unpaired labrum, paired antennæ, mandibles, and maxillæ (two pairs). The first and second pair of maxillæ have originally, according to Patten,* two and three branches respectively. Behind the mouth-parts are found three rudimentary legs. Upon all the abdominal segments, according to Patten, rudimentary limbs are formed; but these soon disappear, except one pair, which persists for a time in the form of a knobbed stalk;

Fig. 105.—Ventral Plate of *B. germanica*, side view.   × 20.

subsequently this, too, completely disappears. Three or four of the hindmost segments curve under the ventral surface of the embryo, and apparently (?) give rise to the modified segments and appendages of the extremity of the abdomen (fig. 105). The ventral plate lies at first directly beneath the egg membrane (chorion), but afterwards becomes sunk in the yolk, so that a

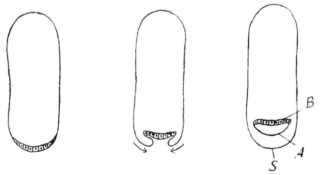

Fig. 106.—Diagram to illustrate the formations of the Embryonic Membranes. *A*, amnion ; *S*, serous envelope ; *B*, blastoderm.

portion of the yolk makes its way between the ventral plate and the chorion. Whilst this portion of the yolk is perfectly homogeneous, the remainder, placed internally to it, becomes coarsely granular, and encloses many roundish cavities and

* Q. J. Micr. Sci., Vol. XXIV., page 596 (1884).

yolk-cells. The middle region of the body is more deeply sunk
in the yolk than the two ends, and the embryo thus assumes a
curved position (fig. 105).

This curvature of the embryo is closely connected with the
formation of the embryonic membranes. On either side of the
ventral plate a fold of the blastoderm arises, and these folds
grow towards each other beneath the chorion. Ultimately they
meet along the middle line of the ventral plate (fig. 106),
and thus form a double investment, the outer layer being the
serous envelope, the inner the *amnion*. Between the two the
yolk passes in, as has been explained above (fig. 107).

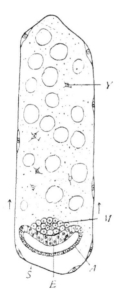

Fig. 107.—Transverse section through young Embryo of *B. germanica*.
E, epiblast; *M*, mesoblast; *Y*, yolk-cells.

At the same time that the embryonic membranes are forming,
the embryonic layers make their appearance. The ventral
plate, which was originally one-layered, forms the *epiblast* or
outer layer of the embryo, and from this are subsequently
derived the middle layer (*mesoblast*) and the deep layer
(*hypoblast*).

As to the origin of the mesoblast most observers have found[*] that a long groove (the *germinal groove*) appears in the middle line of the ventral plate (fig. 108), which bulges into the

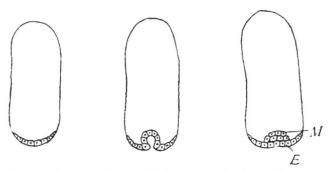

Fig. 108.—Diagram to illustrate the formation of the Germinal Layers.
E, epiblast ; *M*, mesoblast.

yolk, gradually detaches itself from the epiblast, and completes itself into a tube. The lumen of this tube soon becomes filled with cells, and the solid cellular mass thus formed divides into two longitudinal tracts, which lie right and left of the middle line of the ventral plate beneath the epiblast, and are known as the *mesoblastic bands*. In the Cockroach I was able to satisfy myself that in this Insect also, the mesoblast, in all probability, arises by the formation and closure of a similar groove of the epiblast. *M* (fig. 108) represents the stage in which the lumen of the groove has disappeared, and the mesoblast forms a solid cellular mass.

The origin of the hypoblast in Insects has not as yet been clearly determined. Two quite different views on this subject have found support. Some observers (Bobretsky, Graber, and others) maintain that the hypoblast originates in the yolk-cells, which form a superficial layer investing the rest of the yolk. Others (especially Kowalewsky[†]) believe that the process is altogether different. According to the latest observations of the eminent embryologist just named, upon the development of the *Muscidæ*, the germinal groove gives rise, not only to the

[*] Kowalewsky in *Hydrophilus*, Graber in *Musca* and *Lina*, Patten in *Phryganidæ*, myself in *Meloe*, &c.

[†] Biolog. Centrablatt. Bd. VI., No. 2 (1886).

two mesoblastic bands, but also, in its central region, to the hypoblast. This makes its appearance, however, not as a continuous layer, but as two hourglass-shaped rudiments, one at the anterior, the other at the posterior end of the ventral plate. These rudiments have their convex ends directed away from each other, while their edges are approximated and gradually meet so as to form a continuous hypoblast beneath the mesoblast. Although I have not been able completely to satisfy myself as to the mode of formation of the hypoblast in the Cockroach, I have observed stages of development which lead me to suppose that it proceeds in this Insect in a manner similar to that observed by Kowalewsky in *Muscidæ*. The hourglass-shaped rudiments of the hypoblast become pushed upwards by those foldings-in of the epiblast which form towards the anterior and posterior ends of the embryo, and give rise to the stomodæum and proctodæum.*

The stage of development in which the germinal groove appears, by the folding inwards of the epiblast, has been observed in many other animals, and is known as the Gastræa-stage. In all higher types (Vertebrates, the higher Worms, Arthropoda, Echinodermata) the mesoblast and hypoblast are formed in the folded-in part of the Gastræa in a manner similar to that observed in Insects.

The yolk-cells, which some observers have supposed to form the hypoblast, are believed by Kowalewsky to have no other function except that of the disintegration and solution of the yolk. I can, however, with confidence affirm that in the Cockroach these cells take part in the formation of permanent tissues (see below).

Each of the two mesoblastic bands which lie right and left of the germinal groove divides into many successive somites, and each of these becomes hollow. Every such somite consists of an inner (dorsal) one-layered and an outer (ventral) many-layered wall, the latter being in contact with the epiblast. The cavities of all the somites unite to form a common cavity, the *cœlom* or perivisceral space of the Cockroach. The cœlom, like the cavities in which it originates, is bounded by two layers of mesoblast—an inner, the so-called *splanchnic* or visceral layer,

* These terms are explained on p. 115.

which lies on the outer side of the hypoblast, and an outer *somatic* or parietal layer, beneath the epiblast.   There are accordingly four layers in the Cockroach-embryo—viz., (1) *epiblast*, from which the integument and nervous system are developed ; (2) *somatic layer of mesoblast*, mainly converted into the muscles of the body-wall ; (3) *splanchnic layer of mesoblast*, yielding the muscular coat of the alimentary canal ; and (4) *hypoblast*, yielding the epithelium of the mesenteron.

Scattered yolk-cells associate themselves with the mesoblast cells, so that the constituents of the mesoblast have a two-fold origin.   Fig. 109 shows that the yolk-cells are large, finely

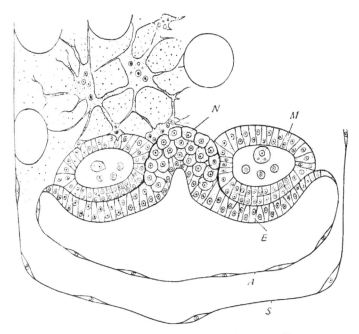

Fig. 109.—Transverse sections of Embryo of *B. germanica*, with rudimentary nervous system (Oc. 4, Obj. D.D. Zeiss). *N*, nervous system ; *M*, mesoblastic somites.

granular, and provided with many (3–6) nuclei and nucleoli. They send out many branching protoplasmic threads, which connect the different cells together, and thus form a cellular network.   Certain cells separate themselves from the rest, apply themselves to the walls of the somites, and form a provisional

diaphragm (fig. 110, *D*) consisting of a layer of flattened cells ;*
other cells (fig. 109) pass into and through the walls of the
somites, and reach their central cavity, where they increase in
number and blend with the mesoblast cells.   What finally
becomes of them I cannot say; perhaps they form the fat-body.

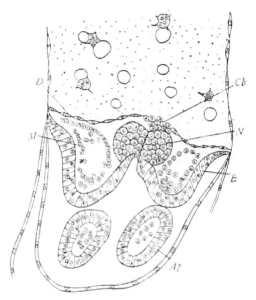

Fig. 110.—Transverse section through ventral region of Embryo of *B. germanica*. The
  nerve-cord has by this time detached itself from the epiblast, *E*. *D* is the temporary
  diaphragm ; *Ch*, temporary cellular band, from which the neurilemma proceeds;
  Ap, appendages in section ; *M*, mesoblast ; *N*. nerve-cord. (Oc. 4. Obj. BB.
  Zeiss).

The ventral plate occupies, as I have explained, the future
ventral surface of the Insect, and here only at first both the
embryonic membranes are to be met with.   On the sides and
above the yolk is invested by the serous envelope alone.   The
ventral plate, however, gradually extends upwards upon the
sides of the egg, in the directions of the arrows (fig. 107), and
finally closes upon the dorsal surface of the embryo, so as completely to invest the whole yolk.   Every segment of the
embryo shows at a certain stage numerous clusters of spherical
granules, which according to Patten (loc. cit.) are composed of
urates (fig. 111, *S*).

  * Cf. Korotneff, Embryol. der Gryllotalpa. Zeits. f. wiss. Zool. (1885).

We shall now proceed to consider the development of the several organs of the Cockroach.

Nervous System.—Along the middle line of the whole ventral surface there is formed a somewhat deep groove-like infolding of the epiblast, bounded on either side by paired solid thickenings, which detach themselves from the epiblast (fig. 110, *N*) and constitute the double nervous chain. In many other Insects a median cord (from which are derived the transverse interganglionic commissures) forms along the bottom of the nervous fold. This secondary median fold is very inconspicuous and

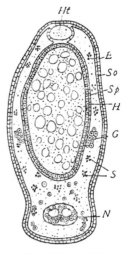

Fig. 111.—Transverse section of older Embryo of *B. germanica* (abdomen). *E*. Epiblast; *H*, hypoblast; *Ht*, heart; *G*, reproductive organs; *S*, spherical granules.

slightly developed in the Cockroach, so that the transverse commissures between the developing ganglia are mainly contributed by the cellular substance of the lateral nervous band. The brain is formed out of two epiblastic thickenings which occupy shallow depressions. The so-called *inner neurilemma,* which surrounds the ventral nerve-cord, is developed as follows:— Along the ventral nerve-cord, and between its lateral halves, a small solid cellular band (fig. 110, *Ch*) is developed out of the mesoblastic diaphragm described above. This grows round the ventral nerve-cord on all sides (fig. 112, *N'*), passing also inwards between the central fibrillar tract and the outer cellular layer, and thus forming the thin membrane which invests the central nervous mass (fig. 112, *N''*). The above-mentioned solid mesoblastic band, which exists for a very short time only, may perhaps be homologised with the chorda dorsalis of Vertebrates, and the chorda of the higher

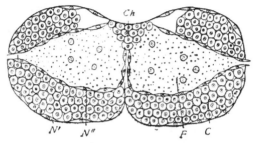

Fig. 112.—Transverse section of Nerve-cord of Embryo of *B. germanica* (Oc. 4, Obj. D.D. Zeiss). *C*, cellular layer; *F*, fibrillar substance (*punkt-substance* of Leydig); *Ch*, cellular band; *N¹ N¹¹* inner and outer neurilemma.

Worms, since in these types also the chorda forms a solid cellular band of meso-hypoblastic origin, lying between the nervous system and the hypoblast. The peripheral nerves arise as direct prolongations of the fibrillar substance of the nerve-cord.

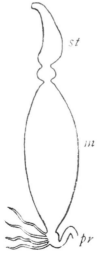

Fig. 113.—Alimentary Canal of Embryo of *B. germanica*. Copied from Rathke, loc. cit., but differently lettered. *st*, stomodæum, already divided into œsophagus, crop, and gizzard; *m*, mesenteron; *pr*, proctodæum, with Malpighian tubules (removed on the right side). × 12.

Alimentary Canal.—The epithelium of the mesenteron is formed out of the hypoblast, whose cells assume a cubical form and gradually absorb the yolk. The epithelium of the stomodæum and proctodæum is derived, however, from two epiblastic involutions at the fore and hind ends of the embryo. The muscular coat of the alimentary canal is contributed by the splanchnic layer of the mesoblast. The mesenteron in an early stage of development appears as an oval sac of greenish colour (fig. 113), faintly seen through the body-wall. The cæcal tubes are extensions of the mesenteron, the Malpighian tubules of the proctodæum. The epiblastic invaginations may be recognised in all stages of growth by their chitinous lining and layer of chitinogenous cells, continuous with the similar layers in the external integument.

Tracheal System.—Tubular infoldings of the epiblast, forming at regular intervals along the sides of the embryo and projecting into the somatic mesoblast, give rise to the paired tracheal tubes, which are at first simple and distinct from one another.*

Heart.—The wall of the heart in Insects is of mesoblastic origin, and develops from paired rudiments derived from that peripheral part of each mesoblastic band which unites the somatic to the splanchnic layer. In this layer two lateral semi-cylindrical rudiments appear, which, as the mesoblastic bands meet on the dorsal surface of the embryo, are brought into contact and unite to form the heart (fig. 111). The heart is therefore hollow from the first, its cavity not being constricted off from the permanent perivisceral space enclosed by the mesoblast, but being a vestige of the primitive embryonic blastocœl, which is bounded by the epiblast, as well as by the two other embryonic layers. Such a mode of the development of the heart was observed by Bütschli in the Bee, and by Korotneff in the Mole Cricket. I am convinced, from my own observations, that the heart of the Cockroach originates in this way, though it is to be observed that, in consequence of

---

* In *Gryllotalpa* (Dohrn), as in Spiders, some Myriopods and *Peripatus* (Moseley, Phil. Trans., 1874), each stigma, with its branches, constitutes throughout life a separate system. The salivary glands arise in the same way, not, like the salivary glands of Vertebrates, as extensions of the alimentary canal, but as independent pits opening behind the mouth. Both the tracheal and the salivary passages are believed to be special modifications of cutaneous glands (Moseley).

Patten's results,* the question requires further investigation. According to Patten the mesoblastic layers of the embryo pulsate rhythmically long before the formation of the heart. Patten also states that the blood-corpuscles are partially derived from the wall of the heart.

Reproductive Organs.—In *P. orientalis* the reproductive organs are developed as follows:—The reproductive glands have a mesoblastic origin. The immature ovaries and testes take the form of elongate oval bodies, which prolong themselves backwards into a long thin thread-like cord or ligament (figs. 114, 115). These lie in the perivisceral space, between the

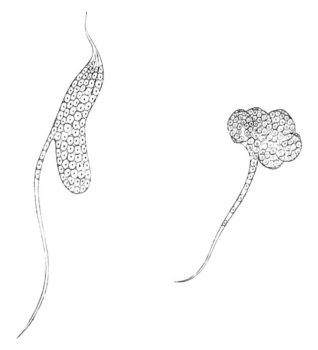

Fig. 114.—Young Ovary of *B. germanica.*   Fig. 115.—Young Testis of *B. germanica.*
(Oc. 2, Ob. DD, Zeiss.)   (Oc. 2, Ob. DD, Zeiss.)

somatic and splanchnic layers of the mesoblast, and on the sides of the abdomen. The glands divide tolerably early into chambers, which have, however, a communicating passage (figs.

* Loc. cit.

114, 115). From their backward-directed prolongations arises the epithelium of the vasa deferentia and oviducts. All other parts of the reproductive ducts are developed out of tegumentary thickenings of the ventral surface in the last abdominal segment, and the last but one. These thickenings are at first paired,* but afterwards blend to form single organs (fig. 118). Within the tegumentary thickenings just described, there

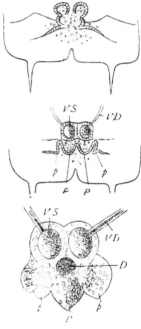

Figs. 116, 117, 118.—Three stages of development of tegumentary portion of Male Sexual Organs of *P. orientalis*. (Oc. 1, Ob. B B, Zeiss.) *V D*, vas deferens; *V S*, vesicula seminalis; *D*, ductus ejaculatorius; *P*, *p*, penis and its lateral appendages.

appear in the male Cockroach two anterior closed cavities which unite to form the single cavity of the permanent mushroom-shaped body (*vesicula seminalis*). A posterior cavity becomes specialised as the ductus ejaculatorius, while the hindmost part of the thickening, which is at first double, afterwards by coalescence single, forms the penis (figs. 117, 118). The

* This arrangement persists only in *Ephemeridæ* among Insects (Palmen, Ueb. paarigen Ausführungsgänge der Geschlechtsorgane bei Insekten, 1884).

accessory reproductive glands have also a tegumentary origin. In the female Cockroach the chitinogenous epithelium of the integument gives rise to the uterus, vagina,* and accessory glands, the muscular and connective tissue layers of the sexual apparatus being formed out of loose mesoblastic cells.†

JOSEPH NUSBAUM.

Post-embryonic Development.

At the time of hatching the Cockroach resembles its parent in all essentials, the wings being the only organs which are developed subsequently, not as entirely new parts, but as extensions of the lateral edges of the thoracic terga. The mode of life of the young Cockroach is like that of the adult, and development may be said to be direct, or with only a trifling amount of metamorphosis. In the Thysanura even this small post-embryonic change ceases to appear, and the Insect, when it leaves the egg, differs from its parent only in size. It is probable that development without metamorphosis was once the rule among Insects. At present such is by no means the case. Insects furnish the most familiar and striking, though, as will appear by-and-by, not the most typical examples of development with metamorphosis. In many text-books the quiescent pupa and the winged imago are not unnaturally described as normal stages, which are exceptionally wanting in Orthoptera, Hemiptera, Thysanura, and other "ametabolous" Insects. It is, however, really the "holometabolous" Insects undergoing what is called "complete metamorphosis," which are exceptional, deviating not only from such little-specialised orders as Thysanura and Orthoptera, but from nearly all animals which exhibit a marked degree of metamorphosis. We shall endeavour to make good this statement, and to show that the Cockroach is normal in its absence of conspicuous post-embryonic change, while the Butterfly, Bee, Beetle, and Gnat are peculiar even among metamorphic animals.

---

* Genital pouch of the preceding description.

† Indications, which we have not found time to work out, lead us to think that the development of the specially modified segments and appendages in the male and female Cockroach needs re-examination. We hope to treat this subject separately on a future occasion.—L. C. M. and A. D.

Animal Metamorphoses.

To investigate the causes of metamorphosis, let us select from the same sub-kingdom two animals as unlike as possible with respect to the amount of post-embryonic change to which they are subject. We can find no better examples than Amphioxus and the Chick.

The newly-hatched Amphioxus is a small, two-layered, hollow sac, which moves through the sea by the play of cilia which project everywhere from its outer surface. It is a Gastræa, a little simpler than the Hydra, and far simpler than a Jelly-fish. As yet it possesses no nervous system, heart, respiratory organs, or skeleton. The most expert zoologist, ignorant of its life-history, could not determine its zoological position. He would most likely guess that it would turn either into a polyp or a worm.

The Chick, on the other hand, at the tenth day of incubation, is already a Bird, with feathers, wings, and beak. When it chips the shell it is a young fowl. It has the skull, the skeleton, the toes, and the bill characteristic of its kind, and no child would hesitate to call it a young Bird.

Amphioxus is, therefore, a Vertebrate (if for shortness we may so name a creature without vertebræ, brain, or skull), which develops with metamorphosis, being at first altogether unlike its parent. The Chick is a Vertebrate which develops directly, without metamorphosis. Let us now ask what other peculiarities go with this difference in mode of development.

Amphioxus produces many small eggs ($\frac{1}{10}$ mm. in diameter) without distinct yolk, and consequently segmenting regularly. The adult is of small size (2 to 3 in. long), far beneath the Chick in zoological rank, and of marine habitat.

The Fowl lays one egg at once, which is of enormous size and provided with abundant yolk, hence undergoing partial segmentation. The Fowl is much bigger than Amphioxus, much higher in the animal scale, and of terrestrial habitat.

Which of the peculiarities thus associated governs the rest? Is it the number or size of the eggs? Or the size, zoological rank, or habitat of the adult? The question cannot be answered without a wider collection of examples. Let us run over the great divisions of the Animal Kingdom, and collect all the facts which seem to be significant. We may omit the Protozoa, which never develop multicellular tissues, and in which segmentation and all subsequent development are therefore absent.

PORIFERA (Sponges).—Nearly all marine and undergoing metamorphosis, the larva being wholly or partially ciliated.

CŒLENTERATES undergo metamorphosis, the immediate product of the ovum being nearly always a *planula*, or two-layered hollow sac, usually devoid of a mouth, and moving about by external cilia. In many Cœlenterates the complicated process of development known as Alternation of Generations occurs. The sedentary Anemones pass through a planula stage, but within the body of the parent. Among the few Cœlenterates which have no free planula stage is the one truly fluviatile genus—Hydra.

WORMS are remarkable for the difference between closely allied forms with respect to the presence or absence of metamorphosis. The non-parasitic freshwater and terrestrial Worms, however (*e.g.*, Earthworms, Leeches, all freshwater Dendrocœla, and Rhabdocœla), do not undergo metamorphosis. In the parasitic forms complicated metamorphosis is common, and may be explained by the extraordinary difficulties often encountered in gaining access to the body of a new host.

All POLYZOA are aquatic (fluviatile or marine), and all produce ciliated embryos, unlike the parent.

BRACHIOPODA are all marine, and produce ciliated embryos.

ECHINODERMS usually undergo striking metamorphosis, but certain viviparous or marsupial forms develop directly. There are no fluviatile or terrestrial Echinoderms.

LAMELLIBRANCHIATE MOLLUSCA have peculiar locomotive larvæ, provided with a ring of cilia, and usually with a long vibratile lash. These temporary organs are reduced or suppressed in the freshwater forms. There are no terrestrial Lamellibranchs.

SNAILS have also a temporary ciliated band, but in the freshwater species it is slightly developed (*Limnæus*), and it is totally wanting in the terrestrial *Helicidæ*.

CEPHALOPODA, which are all marine, have no ciliated band, and the post-embryonic changes do not amount to metamorphosis. There is usually a much larger yolk-sac than in other Mollusca.

CRUSTACEA usually pass through well-marked phases. *Peneus* presents five stages of growth (including the adult), the earlier being common to many lower Crustacea. The Crab passes through three, beginning with the third of *Peneus*; the Lobster through two; while the freshwater Crayfish, when hatched, is already in the fifth and last.

FISHES seldom undergo any post-embryonic change amounting to metamorphosis. *Amphioxus* (if *Amphioxus* be indeed a fish) is the only well-marked case.

AMPHIBIA develop without conspicuous metamorphosis, except in the case of the Frogs and Toads (Anura), which begin life as aquatic, tailed, gill-bearing, and footless tadpoles.

REPTILES, BIRDS, and MAMMALS do not undergo transformation.

This survey, hasty as it necessarily is, shows that habitat is a material circumstance. Larval stages are apt to be suppressed in fluviatile and terrestrial forms. Further, it would seem that zoological rank is not without influence. Metamorphosis is absent in Cephalopoda, the highest class of Mollusca, and in all but the lowest Vertebrates, while it is almost universal in Cœlenterates, Echinoderms, and Lamellibranchs.

It has often been remarked that the quantity of food-yolk indicates the course of development. If a large store of food has been laid up for the young animal, it can continue its growth without any effort of its own, and it leaves the egg well equipped for the battle of life. Where there is little or no yolk, the embryo is turned out in an ill-furnished condition to seek its own food. This early liberation implies metamorphosis, for the small and feeble larva must make use of temporary organs. Some very simple locomotive appendages are almost universally needed, to enable it to get away from the place of its birth, which is usually stocked with as much life as it can support.

Some animals, therefore, are like well-to-do people, who can provide their children with food, clothes, schooling, and pocket-money. Their fortunate offspring grow at ease, and are not driven to premature exercise of their limbs or wits. Others are like starving families, which are forced to send their children to sell matches or newspapers in the streets. It is a question of the amount of capital or accumulated food which is at command.

The connection between zoological rank and the absence of metamorphosis is also explained by what we see among men. High zoological position ordinarily implies strength or intelligence, and the strong and knowing can do better for their offspring than the puny and sluggish. It does not cost a Shark or a quadruped too much to hatch its young in its own body, while Spiders and Earwigs,* which are among the highest Invertebrates, defend their progeny, as do Mammals and Birds, the highest Vertebrates.

But what has all this to do with habitat? Are fluviatile and terrestrial animals, as a rule, better off than marine animals? Possibly they are. In the confined and isolated fresh waters at least, the struggle for existence is undoubtedly less severe than

---

* It may be useful to point out the following examples of parental care among animals in which, as a rule, the eggs are left to take care of themselves. It will be found that in general this instinct is associated with high zoological rank (best exemplified by Mammals and Birds), land or freshwater habitat, reduced number of eggs, and direct development.

AMPHIBIA.—The eggs are sometimes hatched by the male (*Alytes obstetricans, Rhinoderma Darwinii*), or placed by the male in pouches on the back of the female (*Pipa dorsigera, Notodelphis ovifera, Nototrema marsupiatum*), or carried during hatching by the female (*Polypedates reticulatus*).

FISHES.—The Stickleback and others build nests. Of eleven genera of nest-building Fishes, eight are freshwater. The number of eggs is unusually small. Many Siluroids have the eggs hatched in the mouth of the males, a few under the belly of the female. The species are both marine and freshwater, the eggs few and large. Lophobranchiate fishes usually have the eggs hatched by the male. They are marine; the eggs few and large. Many sharks hatch their eggs, which are very few, within the body. *Mustelus lævis* has a placenta formed out of the yolk-sac.

INSECTS.—De Geer has described the incubation of the Earwig, and the care of the brood by the female. The cases of the social Hymenoptera, &c., are universally known.

SPIDERS.—The care of the female spider for her eggs is well known.

CRUSTACEANS.—The Crayfish hatches and subsequently protects her young. *Mysis, Diastylis (Cuma)*, and some Isopods hatch their eggs. *Gammarus locusta* is followed about by her brood, which shelter beneath her when alarmed. *Podocerus capillatus* builds a nest among corallines. Several of the *Caprellidæ* hatch or otherwise protect their young. All these, except the Crayfish, are marine; the eggs commonly fewer than usual.

ECHINODERMS.—Many cases of "marsupial development" have been recorded in the species of the Southern seas. Here development, contrary to the rule in Echinodermata, is direct.

in the waters of the sea. This is shown by the slow rate of
change in freshwater types. Many of our genera of land and
freshwater shells date back at least as far as to Purbeck and
Wealden times, while our common pond-mussel is represented
in the Coal Measures. The comparative security of fresh
waters is probably the reason why so many marine fishes enter
rivers to spawn.

More important, and less open to question, is the direct action
of the sphere of life. The cheap method of turning the
embryo out to shift for itself can seldom be practised with
success on land. But in water floating is easy, and swimming
not difficult. A very slightly-built larva can move about by
means of cilia, and a whole brood can disperse far and wide in
search of food, while still in a mere planula condition—hollow
sacs, without mouth, nerves, or sense-organs. Afterwards the
little locomotive larva settles down, opens a mouth, and begins
to feed. Nearly the whole of its development is carried on at
its own charge.

The extra risks to which marine animals are exposed also
tell in favour of transformation, for they are met by an increase
in the number of ova. Marine species commonly lay more eggs
than freshwater animals of like habits. The Cod is said to
produce nine million eggs; the Salmon from twenty to thirty
thousand; the Stickleback only about one hundred, which are
guarded during hatching by the male. The Siluroid fish, *Arius*,
lays a very few eggs, as big as small cherries, which the male
carries about in his mouth.

Without laying stress upon such figures as these, which
cannot be impartially selected, we can safely affirm that marine
forms are commonly far more prolific than their freshwater
allies. But high numbers increase the difficulty of providing
yolk for each, and thus tend to early exclusion, and subsequent
transformation. We may rationally connect marine habitat
with small eggs, poorly supplied with yolk, segmenting regularly, and producing larva which develop with metamorphosis.

In fresh waters dispersal can seldom be very effective. The
area is usually small, and communicates with other freshwater
basins only through the sea. Migration to a considerable distance
is usually impossible, and migration to a trifling distance use-

less. Moreover, competition is not too severe to prevent some accumulation of food by the parent on behalf of the family.

On land the conditions are still less favourable to larval transformation. Very early migration is altogether impossible. Any kind of locomotion by land implies muscles of complicated arrangement, and, as a rule, there must be some sort of skeleton to support the weight of the body. The larva, if turned out in a Gastræa condition would simply perish without a struggle.* Nor is great precocity needful. The terrestrial animal is commonly of complicated structure, active, and well furnished with means of information. It can lay-by for its offspring, and nourish them within its own body, or at least by food stored up in the egg.

The influence of habitat upon development may be recapitulated as follows :—

MARINE HABITAT.—Eggs many. Yolk small. Segmentation often regular. Young hatched early. Development with metamorphosis. [The most conspicuous exceptions are Cephalopoda and marine Vertebrata.]

FLUVIATILE HABITAT.—Eggs fewer. Yolk larger. Segmentation often unequal. Young hatched later. Development direct, or with late metamorphosis only. [The most obvious exceptions are Frogs and Toads, which develop with metamorphosis.]

TERRESTRIAL HABITAT.—Eggs few. Yolk large [except where the young are supplied by maternal blood]. Segmentation often partial. Young hatched late. Development without metamorphosis. [An exception is found in Insects, which usually exhibit conspicuous metamorphosis, though the yolk is large, and the type of segmentation partial or unequal.]

Let us now take up the exceptions, and see whether these are capable of satisfactory explanation.

1.—Cephalopoda and marine Vertebrates, unlike other inhabitants of the sea, develop without metamorphosis. But these are large animals of relatively high intelligence, well able to feed and protect their young until development is completely accomplished.

* The minute and early larvæ of *Tænia* and *Distomum* may appear to contradict this statement. They really inhabit the film of water which spreads over wet grass, though they are capable of enduring dry conditions for a short time, like Rotifers and many Infusoria.

2.—Frogs and Toads, unlike other fluviatile animals, develop with metamorphosis. The last and most conspicuous change, however, from the gill-bearing and tailed tadpole to the air-breathing and tailless frog, hardly belongs to the ordinary period of embryonic development. When the tadpole has four limbs and a long tail it has already reached the point at which the more primitive Amphibia (*Menopoma, Proteus,* &c.) become sexually mature. The loss of the tail, the lengthening of the hind limbs, and the complete adaptation to pulmonary respiration, relate to the mode of dispersal of the adult. Cut off from early dispersal by the isolation of their breeding-places and the difficulty of land migration, Frogs migrate from pool to pool as full-grown animals. The eggs are thus laid in new sites, and very small basins—ditches and pools which dry up in summer—can be used for spawning. To this peculiar facility in finding new spawning grounds the Anura no doubt owe their success in life, of which the vast number of nearly-allied species furnishes an incontrovertible proof. But the adaptation to terrestrial locomotion necessarily comes late in life, after the normal and primitive adult Amphibian condition has been attained. It is by a *secondary adult metamorphosis* that the aquatic tadpole turns into the land-traversing frog. The change is not fairly comparable to any process of development by which other animals gain the adult structure characteristic of their class and order, but (in respect of the time of its occurrence) resembles the late assumption of secondary sexual characters, such as the antlers of the stag, or the train of the peacock.

3.—Lastly, we come to the exceptional case of Insects which, unlike other terrestrial animals, develop with metamorphosis. The Anurous Amphibia have prepared us to recognise this too as a case of secondary adult (post-embryonic) metamorphosis. Thysanuran or Orthopterous larvæ cannot differ very widely from the adult form of primitive Insects. From wingless, hexapod Insects, like Cockroach larvæ in all essentials of external form, have been derived, on the one hand, the winged imago, adapted in the more specialised orders to a brief pairing season exclusively spent in migration and propagation ; on the other hand, the footless maggot or quiescent pupa.

Insects, like Frogs, disperse as adults, because of the difficulty of the medium, aerial locomotion being even more difficult than locomotion by land, and implying the highest muscular and respiratory efficiency. The flying state is attained by a late metamorphosis, which has not yet become universal in the class, while it is not found in other Tracheates at all. *Peripatus*, Scorpions, and Myriopods become sexually mature when they reach the stage which corresponds to the ordinary less-modified Insect-nymph, with segmented body, walking legs, and mouth-parts resembling those of the parent.*

The Caterpillar is not, as Harvey† maintained, a kind of walking egg; it is rather the primitive adult Tracheate modified in accordance with its own special needs. It may be sexually immature, imperfect, destined to attain more elaborate development in a following stage, but it nevertheless marks the stage in which the remote Tracheate ancestor attained complete maturity. Where it differs from the primitive form, hatched with all the characters of the adult, the changes are adaptive and secondary.‡

The Genealogy of Insects.

To construct from embryological and other data a chart of the descent of Insects, and of the different orders within the

* It is possible that the curious cases of agamogenetic reproduction of the larvæ of *Aphis*, *Cecidomyia*, and *Chironomus* are vestiges of the original fertility of Insect larvæ.

† "Alia vero semen adhuc imperfectum et immaturatum recludunt, incrementum et perfectionem, sive maturitatem, soris acquisiturum ; ut plurima genera piscium, ranæ, item mollia, crustata, testacea, et cochleæ : quorum ova primum exposita sunt, veluti origines duntaxat, inceptiones et vitelli ; qui postea albumina sibi ipsis circum circa induunt ; tandemque alimentum sibi attrahentes, concoquentes et apponentes, in perfectum semen atque ovum evadunt. Talia sunt insectorum semina (vermes ab Aristotele dicta) quæ initio imperfecte edita sibi victum quærunt indeque nutriuntur et augentur, de eruca in aureliam ; de ovo imperfecto in perfectum ovum et semen."
—*De generatione*, Exc. II., p. 183 (1666). Viallanes justifies this view by applying it to the histolysis and regeneration of the tissues in Diptera. But these remarkable changes are surely secondary, adaptive, and peculiar, like the footless maggot itself, whose conversion into a swift-flying imago renders necessary so complete a reconstruction.

‡ The reader is recommended to refer to Fritz Müller's Facts and Arguments for Darwin, especially chap. xi. ; to Balfour's Embryology, Vol. II., chap. xiii., sect. ii. ; and to Lubbock's Origin and Metamorphoses of Insects.

class, is an attempt too hazardous for a student's text-book.[*]
A review of the facts of Arthropod development led Balfour[†]
to conclude that the whole of the Arthropoda cannot be united
in a common phylum. The Tracheata are probably "descended
from a terrestrial Annelidan type related to *Peripatus*. . . .
The Crustacea, on the other hand, are clearly descended from a
Phyllopod-like ancestor, which can be in no way related to
Peripatus." The resemblances between the Arthropoda appear
therefore to be traceable to no nearer common ancestors than
some unknown Annelid, probably marine, and furnished with a
chitinous cuticle, an œsophageal nervous ring, and perhaps with
jointed appendages. Zoological convenience must give place to
the results of embryological and historical research, and we
shall probably have to reassign the classes hitherto grouped
under the easily defined sub-kingdom of Arthropoda.

Sir John Lubbock has explained, in his very interesting
treatise on the Origin and Metamorphoses of Insects, the
reasons which lead him to conclude "that Insects generally
are descended from ancestors resembling the existing genus
Campodea [sub-order Collembola], and that these again have
arisen from others belonging to a type represented more or less
closely by the existing genus *Lindia*" [a non-ciliated Rotifer].

Present knowledge does not, therefore, justify a more definite
statement of the genealogy of Insects than this, that in common with Crustacea they had Annelid ancestors, and that
Lindia, *Peripatus*, and *Campodea* approximately represent three
successive stages of the descent. When we reflect that Cockroaches themselves reach back to the immeasurably distant
palæozoic epoch, we get some misty notion of the antiquity and
duration of those still remoter ages during which Tracheates,
and afterwards Insects, slowly established themselves as new
and distinct groups of animals.

---

[*] Those who care to see a bold experiment of this kind may refer to Haeckel's
Schöpfungsgeschichte.

[†] Comp. Embryology, Vol. I., p. 451.

CHAPTER XI.

THE COCKROACH OF THE PAST.

BY S. H. SCUDDER, OF THE U.S. GEOLOGICAL SURVEY.

SPECIAL REFERENCES.

BERENDT, G. C. Mémoire pour servir à l'histoire des Blattes antédiluviennes (Ann. Soc. Entom., France, V.). Paris, 1836. 8vo.

BRODIE, P. B. A History of the Fossil Insects in the Secondary Rocks of England. London, 1845. 8vo.

GEINITZ, F. E. Die Blattinen aus der unteren Dyas von Weissig (Nova Acta. Acad. Leop.-Carol., XLI.). Halle, 1880. 4to.

GERMAR, E. F., und BERENDT, G. C. Die im Bernstein befindlichen Hemipteren und Orthopteren der Vorwelt. Berlin, 1856. Fol.

GOLDENBERG, F. Zur Kenntniss der Fossilen Insekten in der Steinkohlen-formation (Neues Jahrb. Miner). Stuttgart, 1869. 8vo.

———— Fauna Saræpontana Fossilis. Heft 1–2, Saarbrücken, 1873, 1877. 4to.

HEER, O. Ueber die fossilen Kakerlaken (Viertelj. Naturf. Ges., Zürich, IX.). Zürich, 1864. 8vo.

KLIVER, M. Ueber einige Blattarien . . . aus der Saarbrücker Steinkohlen-formation (Palæontogr. XXIX.). Cassel, 1883. 4to.

KUSTA, J. Ueber enige neue Böhmische Blattinen (Sitzungsb. böhm. Ges. Wissensch, 1883). Prag. 8vo.

SCUDDER, S. H. Palæozoic Cockroaches (Mem. Bost. Soc. Nat. Hist., III.). Boston, 1879. 4to.

———— The Species of Mylacris (Ibid). Boston, 1884. 4to.

———— A Review of Mesozoic Cockroaches (Ibid). Boston, 1886. 4to.

———— Triassic Insects from the Rocky Mountains (Amer. Journ. Sc. Arts [3], XXVIII.). New Haven, 1884. 8vo.

———— Systematische Uebersicht der fossilen Myriopoden, Arachnoideen und Insekten (Zittel, Handb. Palæont. I. Abth., Bd. II.). München, 1885. 8vo.

WESTWOOD, J. O. Contributions to Fossil Entomology (Quart. Journ. Geol. Soc., Lond., X.). London, 1854. 8vo.

LIKE all useful scavengers, the Cockroach is looked upon nowadays as an unmitigated pest. It has, however, a certain right to our regard, for it comes of a venerable antiquity. Indeed, palæontologically considered, no Insect is so interesting as the Cockroach. Of no other type of Insects can it be said that it occurs at every horizon where Insects have been found in any numbers; in no group whatever can the changes

wrought by time be so carefully and completely studied as
here; none other has furnished more important evidence concerning the phylogeny of Insects. Even the oldest known air-
breathing animal has been claimed (though I think erroneously)
as a Cockroach; yet, however that may be, it is certain that in
the most ancient deposits which have yielded any abundance of
Insect remains, the Coal Measures, they so far outnumber all
other types of Insects, that this period, as far as its hexapodal
fauna is concerned, may fairly be called the *Age of Cockroaches.*
And though the subsequent periods show an ever-diminishing
percentage of this family when compared with the total syn-
chronous Insect fauna, yet the existing species are counted by
hundreds, and the fecundity of some, attested by every house-
wife, may be looked upon as a sufficient explanation of the
persistence of this antique type. The Cockroach is, therefore,
a very aristocrat among Insects.

Our knowledge of its past is derived almost entirely from its
wings; perhaps because these organs are the farthest removed
from the nourishing fluids of the body, which on death become
one of the agents, or at least the media, of putrefaction and
consequent obliteration. At all events, whatever the cause,
these chitinous membranes, with their network of supporting
rods, and even not infrequently with the minutest reticulation
of the membrane itself, are preserved with extraordinary fidelity,
and in such abundance that, by comparison with similar parts
in existing forms, we may reach some general conclusions
concerning the life of the past of no little interest.

The first thing that would strike an observer, looking at the
ancient Cockroaches, would be their *general* resemblance to the
living. Excepting for their usually larger size,* were we to
have the oldest known Cockroaches in our kitchens to-day, the
householder would take no special note of them—unless, indeed,
the transparency of their wings (shortly to be mentioned) were
to give them a somewhat peculiar aspect. There would be the
same rounded pronotal shield, the same overlapping wings,
coursed by branching veins, the same smooth curves and oval
flattened form of the whole creature, and doubtless also the

---

* Yet none were so large as our largest living forms; their average size was very
nearly that of *Periplaneta americana.*

same scurrying movements. Indeed, some accurate observers—so, I suppose, we must call them—have failed to take note of some important and very general distinctions between the living and the dead. Thus Gerstaecker, in a work begun twenty years ago, and not yet finished, said, near its beginning,[*] "Not a single species of Insect has yet been found in the Carboniferous rocks which does not fall, on closer examination (*mit voller Evidenz*), not only in an existing order, but even almost completely in the same family as some living form, and only presents striking distinctions when compared with the species themselves." He further specifies the Cockroaches described from the Coal Measures, by Germar and Goldenberg, as agreeing in every distinguishing family characteristic with those of the present day.

In one sense, indeed, this is true. We separate the living Cockroaches from other kinds of Orthoptera as a "family" group, and "Cockroaches" have existed since the Coal Measures at least; yet the structure of every one of the older types is really so peculiar that none of them can be brought within the limits of the family as it now exists. We recognise ours, indeed, as the direct descendants of the ancient forms, but so changed in structure as to form a distinct group. A parallel case is found in the Walking-sticks, and is even more obvious. The recent researches of M. Charles Brongniart have brought to view a whole series of forms in Carboniferous times, which are manifestly the progenitors of living Walking-sticks, with their remarkably long and slender stick-like body, attenuated legs, and peculiar appendages at the tip of the abdomen. Existing forms are either wingless or else have opaque elytron-like front wings, and very ample, gauzy, fan-like hind wings; while the Carboniferous species are furnished with four membranous wings, almost precisely alike, and so utterly different from those of existing types that, before the discovery of the bodies, these wings were universally classed as the wings of Neuropterous Insects (sensu Linneano). Thus Gerstaecker, in the very place already quoted, says of these same wings, known under the generic name *Dictyoneura*, that they show at least a very close relationship to the *Ephemeridæ* of to-day.

[*] Die Klassen und Ordnungen der Arthropoden. Leipzig, 8vo, p. 292.

One principal difference here alluded to—the exact resemblance, except in minor details, of the front and hind wings, and, as consequent therewith, *equal diaphaneity in both*—is found indeed in all palæozoic insects, with exceedingly few exceptions;[*] it is one of their most characteristic and pervading peculiarities. It marks one phase of the movement in all life from homogeneity to heterogeneity—from the uniform to the diverse. In the Cockroaches of to-day a few are found in which the tegmina are nearly as diaphanous as the hind wings; but in the great mass the texture of the tegmina, as in Orthoptera generally (excepting most Gryllides), is decidedly coriaceous; and in some, *e.g.*, *Phoraspis*, the veins are nearly obliterated in the thickness and opacity of the membrane, so as to resemble many Coleopterous elytra.

Three principal differences have been noticed between the ancient and modern forms of Cockroaches. Doubtless others could be found were we able to compare the structure of all parts of the body; and perhaps future research and more happy discovery may yet bring them to light; at present, however, we are compelled to restrict our comparisons to the wings alone.

First, we have to remark the similarity of the front and hind wings in the ancient types: a similarity which extends to their general form (the extended anal area of the hind wings in modern types being as yet only slightly differentiated); their nearly equal size (a corollary, to a certain extent, of the last); the general course of their neuration (true, in a limited sense only, of modern types); and the complete transparency of the front as well as of the hind wing.

Second, the same number of principal veins is developed in the front and hind wings of ancient Cockroaches; while in the front wings of modern types two or more of the veins are blended, so as to reduce the number of the principal stems below the normal, the hind wing at the same time retaining its original simplicity. These principal veins are six, counting the marginal vein, which here merely thickens the anterior border, as one; to use the terminology of Heer, and starting from the anterior margin, they are the *marginal, mediastinal, scapular,*

---

[*] A few elytra of Coleoptera are recently announced from the Silesian "culm."

externomedian, *internomedian*, and *anal.* The general disposition of these veins is as follows:—The mediastinal and scapular veins, with their branches, which are superior (*i.e.*, part from the main vein on the upper or anterior side), terminate upon the anterior margin. The internomedian and anal take the opposite course, and their branches are inferior, or, at least, directed toward the inner margin; while the externomedian, interposed between these two sets, terminates at the tip of the wing, and branches indifferently on either side.

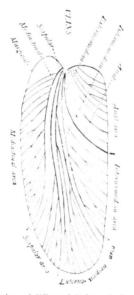

Fig. 119.—Schematic view of Wing of Palæozoic Cockroach, showing the veins and areas.

Now these veins are all present in both front and hind wings of palæozoic Cockroaches, and also in the hind wings of existing species; but in the front wings or tegmina of the latter the number is never complete, the externomedian vein being always amalgamated either with the scapular, or with the internomedian, and the mediastinal frequently blended with the scapular vein.

The hind wings are thus shown to be conservative elements of structure, since they have preserved from the highest antiquity both their transparency and their normal number of

veins. They have retained the use to which they were first put,
and the changes that have come about, such as the wider expansion of the anal area, have been in fuller development of the
same purpose; while the front wings, in virtue of their position
in repose, have become more and more protectors of the hind
wings, and have gradually lost, in part, if not entirely, their
original use. The hind wings of existing Insects, thus pro-
tected, have given less play to selective action, and have become
to some degree interpreters for us of the more complicated
structure, the more modernised anatomy, the more varied
organisation of the front wing.

A third distinction between palæozoic and modern Cockroaches
is found in the veinlets of the anal area. These, unlike the
branches of the other veins, do not part from the main anal
vein at various points along its course, but form a series of
semi-independent veinlets, and in palæozoic Cockroaches take
the same general course as the main anal vein, or "anal
furrow" (the curved, deeply sunken vein that marks off the
anal area from the rest of the front wing, both in ancient and
modern Cockroaches), and terminate at sub-equidistant intervals
upon the inner margin; while in modern Cockroaches these
veins either run sub-parallel to the inner margin and terminate
on the descending portion of the anal furrow, or they form a
fusiform bundle and terminate in proximity to one another and
to the tip of the anal furrow.

These differences, which were mentioned by Germar and
Goldenberg, and their universality pointed out in my memoir
on Palæozoic Cockroaches,* seem to warrant our separating the
older forms from the modern as a family group, under the name
of *Palæoblattariæ;* this family has been thus characterised:—

Fore wings diaphanous, generally reticulated, and nearly
symmetrical on either side of a median line. Externomedian
vein completely developed, forking in the outer half of the
wing, its branches generally occupying the apical margin;
internomedian area broad at base (beyond the anal area),
rapidly tapering apically, and filled with oblique mostly parallel
veins, having nearly the same direction as the anal veinlets,
which, like them, strike the inner margin.

* Memoirs Bost. Soc. Nat. Hist., III., 23 seq. (1880).

About eighty palæozoic species have been published up to the present time, and have been grouped in two sub-families and thirteen genera. Besides these, Brongniart has not yet given any hint of how many have been found at Commentry, a French locality which may be expected to increase the number largely, and about twenty undescribed species are known to me from the American Carboniferous rocks.

The two tribes or sub-families differ in the structure of the mediastinal vein; in one type (*Blattinariæ*) the branches part from the main stem as in the other veins, at varying distances

Fig. 120.—*Etoblattina mazona* Scudd. × 3. (The outline of natural size.)
Carboniferous, Illinois.

along its course (see the figure of *Etoblattina*); in the other (*Mylacridæ*) they spread like unequal rays of a fan from the very base of the wing (see the figure of *Mylacris*). What is

curious is that the latter type has been found only in the New
World, while the former is common to Europe and America.
The latter appears to be the more archaic type, since it is
probable that the primeval Insect wing was broad at the base,
as is the general rule in palæozoic wings, and had the veins
somewhat symmetrically disposed on either side of a middle
line; in this case the mediastinal and anal areas would be
somewhat similar and more or less triangular in form, and the

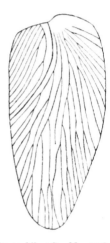

Fig. 121.—*Mylacris anthracophilum* Scudd.   × 2.   Carboniferous, Illinois.

space they occupied would be most readily filled by radiating
veins; such a condition of things, which we find in the
Mylacridæ, would naturally precede one in which the mediastinal
vein, to strengthen the part of the wing most liable to strain,
should, as in the *Blattinariæ*, follow the basal curve of the
costal margin, and throw its branches off at intervals toward
the border, much after the fashion of the mediastinal vein.

This view of the relative antiquity of the two tribes of
Palæoblattariæ is supported by the fact that while in both of
them the internomedian branches show a tendency to repeat
the general course of the anal nervules, as in the corresponding
veins of the costal region, this tendency is lost in modern types;
and among those ancient *Blattinariæ*, which are esteemed
highest in the series, there is a marked tendency toward a loss

of this repetition of the style of branching of the mediastinal and anal offshoots by the scapular and internomedian respectively.

A certain amount of geological evidence may also be claimed in support of this view. A survey of the species of the two groups found up to the present time in America, published and unpublished, shows that all the *Mylacridæ* are found below the Upper Carboniferous, while more than half the *Blattinariæ* are found in or above it. This results largely from a recent and as yet unpublished discovery of *Blattinariæ* in the Upper Coal Measures of Ohio and West Virginia, which in their general features are much nearer than previously discovered American Cockroaches to the European *Blattinariæ*, the latter of which come generally from Upper Carboniferous beds. The *Mylacridæ* have therefore been found in America in strata generally regarded as older than those which in Europe have yielded Cockroaches, and this gives a sufficient explanation why no *Mylacridæ* have yet been found in the Old World. In America one is mostly dealing with absolutely older forms, and they naturally give that continent a more old-fashioned look, when we regard the Carboniferous fauna as a whole. As already stated, a wing from the French Silurian (*Palæoblattina Douvillei* Brongn.) has been claimed as a Cockroach, but without good reason, and to see a real old Cockroach one must look to America.

Up to this point we have contrasted the palæozoic Cockroaches with the existing forms only, and finding such important distinctions between them, we naturally turn with some curiosity to the intermediate mesozoic and tertiary formations.

Now, not only are the mesozoic species as numerous (actually, but not relatively) as the palæozoic, but a recent discovery of a Triassic fauna of considerable extent, in the elevated parks of Colorado, presents us with a series of intermediate forms between those peculiar to the Coal Measures and those characteristic of the later mesozoic rocks. Excluding, however, for a moment this Triassic fauna, we may say of the later mesozoic species that they are *Neoblattariæ*, not *Palæoblattariæ*, though they still show some lingering characteristics of their ancestry. Thus the front wings are in general of a less dense texture than in modern times, but without the perfect diaphaneity of the palæozoic species; in some the anal veins fall in true palæoblattarian fashion on the inner margin, while in others which cannot be dissociated generically from them, the anal veins are disposed as in modern types. But in all there is a loss of one of the principal veins, or rather an amalgamation of two or more—a characteristic of more fundamental character. As a general rule, moreover, to which we shall again advert, the mass of the species are of small size, in very striking contrast to the older types.

To return now to the Triassic deposits of Colorado, we recognize here an assemblage of forms of a strictly intermediate character. Here are *Palæoblattariæ* and *Neoblattariæ*, side by side. The larger proportion are *Palæoblattariæ*, but all of them are specifically, and most of them generically, distinct from palæozoic species, and all rank high among *Blattinariæ*; still further, the species are all of moderate size, their general average being but little above that of mesozoic Cockroaches,

Fig. 122.—*Neorthroblattina Lakesii* Scudd. × 5. Trias, Colorado.

and only a little more than half that of palæozoic types. The *Neoblattariæ* of this Triassic deposit are still smaller, being actually smaller than the average mesozoic Cockroach, and one or two of them, of the genus *Neorthroblattina* (see figure of *N. Lakesii*), have marked affinity to one of the genera of *Palæoblattariæ* (*Poroblattina*) peculiar to the same beds, differing mainly in the union or separation of the mediastinal and scapular veins; while others, as *Scutinoblattina*, have a

Phoraspis-like aspect and density of membrane. This novel assemblage of species bridges over the distinctions between the *Palæoblattariæ* and *Neoblattariæ*. We find, first, forms in which the front wings are diaphanous, with distinct mediastinal and scapular veins, and the anal veinlets run to the border of the wing (*Spiloblattina, Poroblattina*); next, those having a little opacity of the front wings, with blended mediastinal and scapular, and the anal veins as before (some species of *Neorthroblattina*); then those with still greater opacity, with the same structural features (other species of *Neorthroblattina*); next, those having a coriaceous or leathery structure, blended mediastinal and scapular, and anal veins falling on the inner margin (some species of *Scutinoblattina*); and, finally, similarly thickened wings with blended mediastinal and scapular, and anal veins impinging on the anal furrow (other species of *Scutinoblattina*).

It is not alone, however, by the union of the mediastinal and scapular stems that the reduction of the veins in the wings of later Cockroaches has come about; for in many mesozoic types the externomedian vein is blended with one of its neighbours, while in others not only are the mediastinal and scapular united, but at the same time the externomedian and internomedian.

As regards the other structural distinction between the *Palæoblattariæ* and *Neoblattariæ*—the course of the anal nervules—there is much diversity, and very imperfect knowledge, since this very portion of the wing is not infrequently lost, a fracture most readily occurring at the anal furrow. In most of the mesozoic genera, the anal nervules, as far as known, strike the margin; but the larger portion of these show a decided tendency to trend toward the tip of the anal furrow, as in many modern forms. This feature can hardly be considered as firmly established in mesozoic times, and the same genus, as *Scutinoblattina*, may contain species which differ in this respect.

A further peculiarity of mesozoic Cockroaches, already alluded to, is their generally small size. The average length of the front wing of palæozoic Cockroaches has been estimated to be 26 mm., that of the Triassic *Palæoblattariæ* is about 16 mm., while that of the mesozoic *Neoblattariæ* is 12·5 mm. One exception to this small size must be noted in the species from the Jura of Solenhofen, all of which were large and some gigantic, one wing reaching the length of 60 mm., or about the size of our largest tropical *Blaberæ*. If we omit these exceptional forms, the average length of the wing of the mesozoic Cockroach would be scarcely more than 11 mm. Now an average of the 243 species of which the measurements are given in Brunner's Système des Blattaires (1865), gives the length of the front wing of living Cockroaches as a little over 18 mm.; so that the mesozoic Cockroaches were as a rule considerably smaller, the palæozoic Cockroaches much larger, than the living.

Nearly eighty species of mesozoic *Neoblattaræ* are known, and they are divided into thirteen genera,* one of which, *Mesoblattina* (see figure of *M. Brodiei*), contains upwards of twenty species, mainly from the Lias and Oolites of England. The Upper Oolite has proved the most prolific, considerably

Fig. 123.—*Mesoblattina Brodiei* Scudd. × 4. Purbecks, England.

more than half the species having been found in the English Purbecks, while nearly a fourth occur in the Lias of England, Switzerland, and Germany. Many of the English species have been figured in Brodie's Fossil Insects of the Secondary Rocks of England, in Westwood's paper on Fossil Insects in the tenth volume of the Quarterly Journal of the Geological Society, and in the memoir alluded to above. No species has yet been found in rocks of different geological horizons, and the

* See a paper on mesozoic Cockroaches now printing in the Memoirs Bost. Soc. Nat. Hist., Vol. III., p. 439 seq.

genera of the Trias are peculiar to it. So, too, are some of the genera of the Oolite, but all of the Liassic genera occur also in the Oolite.

Among these mesozoic Cockroaches are some of very peculiar aspect; one, *Blattidium* (see figure of *B. Simyrus*), found only in the lower Purbecks, has ribbon-shaped wings with parallel

Fig. 124.—*Blattidium Simyrus* Westw. × 3. Lower Purbecks, England.

sides, longitudinal neuration, and anal nervures with a course at right angles to their usual direction; another, *Pterinoblattina* (see figure of *P. intermixta*), geologically widespread, is very broad, more or less triangular, and has an exceedingly fine and delicate neuration, so arranged as to resemble the barbs of a feather.

A comparison of the neuration of the tegmina of mesozoic and recent Cockroaches, to determine as far as possible the immediate relations of the former to existing types, gives as yet little satisfaction. The prolific genera, *Mesoblattina* and *Rithma*, may be said to bear considerable resemblance to the *Phyllodromidæ*, and the peculiar neuration of *Elisama* is in part repeated in the *Panchloridæ*, as well as in some *Phyllodromidæ* and *Epilampridæ*. *Scutinoblattina* also reminds one in certain features of some *Epilampridæ*, like *Phoraspis*. The other genera appear to have no special relations to any existing type. As a whole, it would appear as if the *Blattariæ spinosæ* approached closer to the mesozoic forms than do the *Blattariæ muticæ*.

Fig. 125.—*Pterinoblattina intermixta* Scudd.   × 4.   Upper Lias, England.

As to the tertiary Cockroaches we know very little, exceedingly few having been preserved, even in amber—that wonderful treasury of fossil Insects. Here first we come across apterous forms, *Polyzosteria* having been recognised in Prussian amber,* together with winged species, which seem to be *Phyllodromidæ;* these are the only *Blattariæ spinosæ* known from the Tertiaries. Of the other group, we have *Zetobora*, one of the *Panchloridæ*, and *Paralatindia*, one of the *Corydidæ*, from American rocks, and *Heterogamia* and *Homœogamia*, one from Parschlug in Steiermark, the other from Florissant in Colorado, belonging to the sub-family *Heterogamidæ*. Others are mentioned, generally under the wide generic term *Blatta*, from Oeningen, Eisleben, Rott, and even from Spitzbergen and Greenland; but little more than their names are known to us. *Paralatindia*, from the Green River beds of Wyoming, U.S., is the only tertiary Cockroach yet referred to an extinct genus; but close attention has not yet been paid even to the few tertiary Cockroaches which we know. There is no reason to suppose that they will be found to differ more from the existing types than is generally the case with other

---

* The wingless creature from the Carboniferous deposits of Saarbrücken, described by Goldenberg as a Cockroach, under the name of *Polyzosterites granosus*, appears to be a Crustacean.

Insects. The more we learn of cænozoic Insects, the more truly do we find that the early Tertiary period was in truth the dawn of the present, the distinction between the faunas of these remotely separated times (though not to be compared in character) being scarcely greater than is found to-day between the Insects of the temperate and torrid zones.

We began this review with the statement that no Insect was so important palæontologically as the Cockroach. This would more clearly appear had we space to pass in review the geological history of all the Insect tribes; for then it could be shown that it was only in the passage from palæozoic to mesozoic times that the great ordinal groups of Insects were differentiated, and that the Triassic period therefore becomes the expectant ground of the student of fossil Insects. Up to the present time we do not know half a dozen Insects besides Cockroaches from these rocks. Yet, notwithstanding this advantage on the part of the Cockroaches, how meagre is the history, how striking the "imperfection of the geological record" concerning them, the following tabulation of the fossil species by their genera will show.

It here appears that there are about 80 species known from the palæozoic rocks, two or three more than that from the mesozoic, and only nine from the cænozoic! When we call to mind that half the palæozoic Insects were Cockroaches, and that seven or eight hundred species exist to-day, what shall we say of the paltry dozen* from the rich tertiaries? Shall we claim that these figures represent their true numerical proportion to their numbers in the more distant past? Then, indeed, must the palæozoic period have been the Age of Cockroaches; for all research into the past shows that a type once losing ground continues to lose it, and does not again regain its strength. The Cockroaches of to-day are no longer, as once, a dominant group; they are but a fragment of the world's Insect-hosts; yet even now the species are numbered by hundreds. If this be a waning type, what must its numbers have been in the far-off time, when the warm moisture which they still love was the prevailing climatic feature of the world; and how few of that vast horde have been preserved to us! The housekeeper will thank God and take courage.

* This includes all possible forms; our table shows but nine.

GEOLOGICAL DISTRIBUTION OF FOSSIL COCKROACHES.

Figures in *italics* represent the number of American species; in roman, of European.

	Carboniferous.									
	Lower.	Middle.	Upper.	Permian.	Trias.	Lias.	Upper Jura.	Oligocene.	Miocene.	TOTALS.
PALÆOBLATTARIÆ.										
Mylacridæ—Mylacris	*10*	..	..	..	..	..	..	..	..	10
Promylacris ..	*1*	..	..	..	..	..	..	..	..	1
Paromylacris ..	*1*	..	..	..	..	..	..	..	..	1
Lithomylacris ..	*2*	*2*	..	..	..	..	..	..	..	4
Necymylacris ..	*2*	..	..	..	..	..	..	..	..	2
Blattinariæ—Etoblattina ..	*1*	1	15+*6*	3+*1*	*1*	..	..	..	..	28
Spiloblattina ..	..	..	..	..	*4*	..	..	..	..	4
Archimylacris ..	*3*	..	..	..	..	..	..	..	..	3
Anthracoblattina	..	2	6	4	*1*	..	..	..	..	13
Gerablattina ..	*1*	1	10	..	..	..	..	..	..	12
Hermatoblattina	..	..	1	1	..	..	..	..	..	2
Progonoblattina	..	..	2	..	..	..	..	..	..	2
Oryctoblattina ..	*1*	..	1	1	..	..	..	..	..	3
Petrablattina ..	*1*	..	..	1	*2*	..	..	..	..	4
Poroblattina ..	..	..	..	..	*2*	..	..	..	..	2
	(23)	(6)	(41)	(11)	(10)					(91)
NEOBLATTARIÆ.										
Not yet referred to sub-families:										
Ctenoblattina	..	..	..	..	..	1	2	..	..	3
Neorthroblattina ..	..	..	..	..	*4*	..	..	..	..	4
Rithma	..	..	..	..	..	2	10	..	..	12
Mesoblattina	..	..	..	..	..	7	15	..	..	22
Elisama	..	..	..	..	..	1	5	..	..	6
Pterinoblattina ..	..	..	..	..	..	3	6	..	..	9
Blattidium	..	..	..	..	..	..	2	..	..	2
Nannoblattina ..	..	..	..	..	..	..	3	..	..	3
Dipluroblattina ..	..	..	..	..	..	..	1	..	..	1
Diechoblattina ..	..	..	..	..	..	..	2	..	..	2
Scutinoblattina ..	..	..	..	..	*3*	..	..	..	..	3
Legnophora	..	..	..	..	1	..	..	..	..	1
Aporoblattina	..	..	..	..	..	3	6	..	..	9
					(8)	(17)	(52)			(77)
Phyllodromidæ—"Blatta" ..	..	..	..	..	..	..	..	3	..	3
Periplanetidæ—Polyzosteria ..	..	..	..	..	..	..	..	2	..	2
Panchloridæ—Zetobora	..	..	..	..	..	..	..	*1*	..	1
Corydidæ—Paralatindia	..	..	..	..	..	..	..	*1*	..	1
Heterogamidæ—Homœogamia	..	..	..	..	..	..	..	*1*	..	1
Heterogamia	..	..	..	..	..	..	..	..	1	1
								(8)	(1)	(9)
GRAND TOTALS ..	23	6	41	11	18	17	52	8	1	177

SAMUEL H. SCUDDER.

APPENDIX.

PARASITES OF THE COCKROACH.

Spirillum, sp. [Vibrio].   SCHIZOMYCETES.
Rectum.
Ref.—Bütschli, Zeits. f. wiss. Zool., Bd. XXI., p. 254 (1871).

Hygrocrocis intestinalis, Val.   CYANOPHYCEÆ.

Filaments of a very minute Alga abound in the rectum of the Cockroach, where this species is said by Valentin to occur. The intestine of the Crayfish is given as another habitat. Leidy observes that the filaments which he found in the rectum of the Cockroach are inarticulate, and do not agree with Valentin's description of the species.

Ref.—Valentin, Repert. f. Anat. u. Phys., Bd. I., p. 110 (1836); Robin, Végét. qui croissent sur l'Homme, p. 82 (1847); Leidy, Smithsonian Contr., Vol. V., p. 41 (1853); Bütschli, Zeits. f. wiss. Zool., Bd. XXI., p. 254 (1871).

Endamœba (*Amœba*) *Blattæ,* Bütschli.   RHIZOPODA.
Rectum.
Ref.—Siebold, Naturg. wirbelloser Thiere (1839) *fide* Stein; Stein, Organismus d. Infusions-thiere, Bd. II., p. 345 (1867); Bütschli, Zeits. f. wiss. Zool., Bd. XXX., p. 273, pl. xv. (1878); Leidy, Proc. Acad. N. S. Phil., Oct. 7th, 1879, and Freshwater Rhizopods of N. America, p. 300 (1879).

Gregarina (*Clepsidrina*) *Blattarum,* Sieb.   GREGARINIDA.

Encysted in chylitic stomach and gizzard; free in large intestine.

Ref.—Siebold, Naturg. wirbelloser Thiere, pp. 56, 71 (1839); Stein, Müll. Arch., 1848, p. 182, pl. ix., figs. 38, 39; Leidy, Trans. Amer. Phil. Soc., Vol. X., p. 239 (1852); Bütchsli, Zeits. f. wiss. Zool., Bd. XXI., p. 254 (1871), and Bd. XXXV., p. 384 (1881); Schneider, Grégarines des Invertébrés, p. 92, pl. xvii., figs. 11, 12 (1876).

Nyctotherus ovalis, Leidy. INFUSORIA.

Small and large intestines.

Ref.—Leidy, Trans. Amer. Phil. Soc., Vol. X., p. 244, pl. xi. (1852).

Plagiotoma (Bursaria) blattarum, Stein. INFUSORIA.

Rectum.

Ref.—Stein, Sitzb. d. königl. Böhm. Ges., 1860, pp. 49, 50.

Lophomonas Blattarum, Stein. INFUSORIA.

Rectum.

Ref.—Stein (*loc. cit.*) ; Bütschli, Zeits. f. wiss. Zool., Bd. XXX., p. 258, plates xiii., xv. (1878).

L. striata, Bütschli. INFUSORIA.

Rectum.

Ref.—Bütschli, Zeits. f. wiss. Zool., Bd. XXX., p. 261, plates xiii., xv. (1878).

Gordius, sp. NEMATELMINTHA.

Specimens in the Museum at Hamburg, from Venezuela. Obtained from some species of Cockroach.

Oxyuris Diesingi, Ham. NEMATELMINTHA.

Rectum, frequent.

Ref.—Hammerschmidt, Isis, 1838; Bütschli, Zeits. f. wiss. Zool., Bd. XXI., p. 252, pl. xxi. (1871).

O. Blattæ orientalis, Ham. NEMATELMINTHA.

Rectum (much rarer than *O. Diesingi*).

Ref.—Hammerschmidt (*loc. cit.*) ; Bütschli, Zeits. f. wiss. Zool., Bd. XXI., p. 252, pl. xxii. (1871).

Other species of *Oxyuris* are said to occur in the same situation, *e.g.*, *O. gracilis* and *O. appendiculata* (Leidy, Proc. Acad. N. S. Phil., Oct. 7th, 1879), and *O. macronura* (Radkewisch, quoted by Van Beneden in Animal Parasites, Engl. trans., p. 248).

Filaria rhytipleurites. NEMATELMINTHA.

Encysted in the fat-body of the Cockroach ; sexual state in the alimentary canal of the Rat. *Spiroptera obtusa* is similarly shared by the Meal-worm (larva of *Tenebrio molitor*) and the Mouse.

Ref.—Galeb, Compt. Rend., July 8th, 1878.

Acarus, sp.   ARACHNIDA.

Found by Cornelius upon the sexual organs of a male
Cockroach.

Ref.—Cornelius, Beitr. zur nähern Kenntniss von *Periplaneta
orientalis*, p. 35, fig. 23 (1853).

Evania appendigaster, L.   INSECTA (*Hymenoptera*).

A genus of Ichneumons, parasitic upon *Periplaneta* and *Blatta*.

Ref.—Westwood, Trans. Ent. Soc., Vol. III., p. 237 ; Ib., Ser.
II., Vol. I., p. 213.

Symbius Blattarum, Sund.   INSECTA (*Coleoptera*).

The apterous female is parasitic upon *P. americana* and *B.
germanica*.

Ref.—Sundevall, Isis, 1831.

SENSE OF SMELL IN INSECTS.

SINCE the printing of the sheets which describe the organs of
special sense, we have become acquainted with two experimental
researches of recent date, instituted for the purpose of determining
whether other organs, besides the antennæ, may be specially concerned with the perception of odours by Insects.

Prof. Graber (Biol. Centralblatt, Bd. V., 1885) has described
extensive and elaborate experiments upon various Insects, tending
to the conclusion that the palps and the cerci may be sensitive to
odours, and that in special cases the palps may be even more
sensitive in this respect than the antennæ. Cockroaches, decapitated, but kept alive for some days, were found to perceive odours
by means of their cerci. His general conclusion is that Insects
have no special sense of smell, but that various parts of the surface
of the body are furnished with nerve-endings capable of perceiving
strong odours. Prof. Graber's results are known to us only through
the abstract given by Prof. Plateau in the paper next to be
mentioned.

Prof. Plateau (Compt. rend. de la Soc. Entom. de Belgique, 1886)
relates experiments upon the powers of scent resident in different
organs of the Cockroach. Two Cockroaches had their palps (maxillary and labial) removed ; two others had the antennæ removed.
An evaporating dish, 8 inches in diameter, was then partly filled with